THE
MARINES OF
MONTFORD
POINT

THE MARINES OF
MONTFORD POINT

AMERICA'S FIRST
BLACK MARINES

MELTON A. McLAURIN

The University of North Carolina Press

Chapel Hill

© 2007 The University of North Carolina Press

All rights reserved

Set in Charter, Franklin Gothic, and Campaign types
by Tseng Information Systems, Inc.
Manufactured in the United States of America

This book was published with the assistance of the
Z. Smith Reynolds Fund of the University of North Carolina
Press.

The paper in this book meets the guidelines for
permanence and durability of the Committee on
Production Guidelines for Book Longevity
of the Council on Library Resources.

Library of Congress Cataloging-in-Publication Data
McLaurin, Melton Alonza.
The Marines of Montford Point : America's first Black
Marines / Melton A. McLaurin.
p. cm.
Includes bibliographical references and index.
ISBN-13: 978-0-8078-3097-0 (cloth : alk. paper)
1. Montford Point Camp (Camp Lejeune, N.C.)   2. United
States. Marine Corps—African Americans—History—20th
century.   3. Camp Lejeune (N.C.)—History—20th century.
4. United States—Race relations—History—20th century.
I. Title.
VE23.M35   2007
359.9′608996073—dc22
2006028179

11 10 09 08 07   5 4 3 2 1

Contents

Maps and Illustrations

Maps

Illustrations

Illustrations appear in three topical groups:

Preface

This project began with a chance conversation in the spring of 1999 with Dr. Clarence Willie, Lieutenant Colonel, Retired, United States Marine Corps. After his career in the Marine Corps, Willie obtained a doctorate in education and, in 1999, was serving as assistant superintendent of schools in Brunswick County in southeastern North Carolina. A member of the history faculty at the University of North Carolina Wilmington who specialized in the American South and race relations, I was at the time associate vice chancellor for academic affairs. Willie asked me if I knew about the Montford Point Marines, and I responded that I was vaguely aware of them. Telling me that he had known several legendary Montford Point drill sergeants, Willie began to talk of his dream of bringing the Montford Point story to a larger audience.

As we talked, we realized that a number of circumstances might make a video documentary project possible. Willie had access to the Montford Point Marines Association, originally established as an organization for Marines who trained at Montford Point from 1942 until 1949, but now open to all active-duty military personnel and all honorably discharged veterans. The Montford Point Marines Museum, an arm of the association, is located at the site of the original Camp Montford Point on Camp Lejeune, forty miles up the road from Wilmington at Jacksonville. Both Jacksonville and Wilmington have active Montford Point Marines Association chapters, which meant that we could quickly identify interview subjects. The UNC Wilmington history department had established contact with Finney Greggs, First Sergeant, Retired, a Vietnam era career Marine who served as the extraordinarily cooperative volunteer director of the museum. The university had a professionally staffed television studio that had produced several documentaries. I knew the history of the segregated South, knew the resources of the university, and could speak to university administrators about at least beginning to record the story of the men who trained at Montford Point. All we had to do was coordinate the effort among the various institutions and obtain funding.

Throughout the project, the UNC Wilmington team worked closely with Greggs and the Montford Point Marines Museum. Greggs developed a list of Montford Point veterans in North Carolina and arranged to transport them to the UNC Wilmington Television studio for taping. He also arranged for a

UNC Wilmington Television team to interview Montford Point veterans from across the country at the association's annual July national meeting in St. Louis in 2001 and Arlington, Virginia, in 2004. In 2005 the team traveled to Charleston, South Carolina; Charlotte, North Carolina; Washington, D.C.; and Montford Point to tape interviews arranged through Greggs. Working with Greggs, the team selected interviewees who had entered the Marine Corps in each of the years during which Camp Montford Point operated as a segregated training facility.

Funding for the interviews came primarily from various units within UNC Wilmington, especially the Office of the Chancellor; the Division of Public Service and Continuing Studies, in which UNC Wilmington Television is housed; and the Division of Academic Affairs. Additional interviews and transcription services were supported by the Department of the Navy, Office of Naval Research, through a grant to South Carolina State University.

Before the interview process began, I developed a list of fifteen basic questions used for each interview. The basic questions focused on the interviewee's background, reasons for joining the Corps, boot camp and other training experiences, experiences with racism within the Corps and in the civilian world, assignments after boot camp, combat experience, and thoughts about having been a Montford Point Marine. The list contained suggested follow-up questions for several of the fifteen basic items, which could be used at the discretion of the interviewer. In addition, each interview was concluded by asking the subject to speak about whatever he wished. When possible, Willie conducted the interviews; otherwise, I did. Interview subjects did not see the list of questions prior to their interview session to ensure that we received candid responses. The entire UNC Wilmington Television team, especially Dustin Miller, Director, and Heidi Messina, Producer/Director I, devoted countless hours to the project, making every effort to help the Montford Point veterans feel at ease during the interview sessions.

At the end of the project we had interviewed sixty-one individuals, for a total of more than 2,800 minutes. This volume contains some of the best interview excerpts, arranged according to the topics addressed by the basic questions. It is difficult to say that the material included is the very best, because so much of the material is superb. Many of the interviewees had waited literally their entire lives to be able to tell their stories to someone, and the interview process proved to be both exhilarating and sobering for members of the team. In interview after interview, we heard powerful stories told with eloquence and dignity, with passion and pride. The stories that poured forth were the more poignant because we were acutely aware the interviewees understood that we were in a race against time to record their stories, and frequently told us so. Sadly, several of the men we were fortunate enough to meet and tape, and whose words are included in this volume, are no longer with us.

Each of the interview segments is taken from a transcript created by a professional transcription service. The words on the page are the words of the interviewee exactly as they appear in the transcript, with only minor exceptions. For the sole reason of making the work more readable, I have removed such obvious vocal distractions as "um" and "ah," stammers, and words used to begin responses, such as "okay" and "well," that are without significance to the meaning of the text. On a very few occasions, I have corrected spellings of place names that clearly resulted from the transcription process and that the reader might find confusing—for example, replacing "Kenston" with "Kinston," the name of a town in eastern North Carolina. When an understanding of the text required the insertion of additional material, I inserted such material, never more than a few words, in square brackets. Most such occasions resulted from the lack of inflection, gestures, or facial expressions that make clear the meaning of the spoken word on the interview tape but do not translate to print. Otherwise, the words the reader reads are the words the Montford Point veterans spoke. The Montford Point veterans brought a wide range of social and educational backgrounds, experiences, and accomplishments to the interview sessions. To convey this diversity and to ensure that the individuality of each interviewee was respected, in no case was grammar or syntax altered, although I have, as helpful for reading, regularized punctuation and capitalization from the transcript to conform to customary usage. In making these minor editorial changes I hope I have made the volume more readable while preserving the authenticity and meaning of specific interview texts.

Unlike the Buffalo Soldiers or the Tuskegee Airmen, whose stories have received considerable scholarly attention and exposure in the popular media, the men of Montford Point remain virtually unknown. I personally have spoken with young black Marines on the grounds of the original Camp Montford Point who knew nothing of its history. Conversations with numerous white career veterans of the Corps revealed that they were equally unaware of the historical significance of Montford Point and the men who trained there. This work is intended primarily to acquaint the public with the experience of a remarkable group of men, to give those men the opportunity to present their experiences and accomplishments to the public in their own words.

The words in this volume are powerful words, spoken by men who have endured much. They are words spoken with flashes of anger and humor, sometimes with sorrow, sometimes with great wisdom, always with a pride fostered by incredible accomplishment in the face of adversity. They are words to be heard, words to be pondered, words that hold deep meaning and significance for American society in the twenty-first century.

THE
MARINES OF
MONTFORD
POINT

Introduction

The men who reported for duty at Camp Montford Point in August 1942 were the first African Americans to serve their nation as Marines since the American Revolution. Theirs is a story of honor, duty, and patriotism, characteristic of what has come to be known as the Greatest Generation. It is also the story of achievement and ultimate triumph in the face of unrelenting racial prejudice, of an unyielding determination to prove their mettle as fighting men to a nation that endorsed a policy of segregation based upon the doctrine of white supremacy. Even the Marine Corps they joined did not welcome them. Theirs is a significant American story, a major episode in the country's military and civil rights history, a story that reveals much about the price individual African Americans paid to gain acceptance into one of the nation's most hallowed institutions. It is also a story that remains largely unknown, except to those who lived it.

African Americans fought to be accepted into military service throughout the history of the nation, although they have always served their country. During the American Revolution the British promised male slaves freedom in exchange for their support, a position the United States never adopted. Despite the obvious gap between America's rhetoric of freedom and equality and its practice of legitimizing a form of chattel slavery based upon race, some African Americans, both free and slave, joined the armed forces of the United States. Many joined in the hope that their loyalty would earn them their freedom. While some states outlawed slavery during the Revolution, the new nation did not. Slavery, and the racial ideology upon which it rested, were integral to both the economic and social systems of the fledgling United States.

With independence, the racial ideology and economic realities of slavery prevented the new nation from fully redeeming its promises of equality and freedom. The Constitution of the United States, ratified in 1789, protected the institution of slavery, and prejudice against blacks was widespread even within states that had rejected slavery. This prejudice was written into federal military policy when, in 1792, Congress limited service in state militias to "free able bodied white male citizens." Six years later, the secretary of war declared that "no Negro, Mulatto or Indian" could enlist in the United States Navy or Marines. The Army and the Marines retained their ban on black enlistments. Desperate for men who would serve under the appalling conditions of life at sea, the Navy began to accept limited numbers of free black sailors, especially after 1798, as the United States attempted to protect its shipping from both the French and the British, who were embroiled in a worldwide battle for naval supremacy.

With the outbreak of the War of 1812, once again British military might threatened the young nation's survival, and the nation altered its racial policies to enlist the aid of black Americans to avoid defeat. Finding sailors for the young American fleet again proved a difficult task, and the Navy again responded by enlisting free blacks; more than a hundred of them served in Commodore Oliver Hazard Perry's fleet of nine ships that repelled a potential invasion by defeating the British fleet in the Battle of Lake Erie on September 10, 1813. Free black sailors also served under Lieutenant Thomas McDonough in his victory over the British on Lake Champlain on September 11, 1814.

Free blacks fought as well under General Andrew Jackson at the Battle of New Orleans in the first week of January 1815. They did so, however, not as members of the American army, which continued to bar African Americans from enlistment. Instead, Jackson employed a Louisiana militia unit from New Orleans, the Battalion of the Free Men of Color. Louisiana had banned blacks from militia service after it became an American possession with the Louisiana Purchase of 1803, but the new British threat dictated a change in policy. Organized as a segregated unit, the Battalion of Free Men of Color boasted three black officers and drew many of its members from black refugees who had supported the French during the Haitian Revolution. It also contained crewmen from the fleet of the notorious pirate captain Jean Lafitte. The 500 blacks in Jackson's 6,000-man army fought gallantly, engaging in hand-to-hand combat with the British and sustaining heavy casualties. When the war ended in a virtual stalemate and a peace agreement removed the British threat, the United States returned to its policy of excluding blacks from military service. The black veterans of the New Orleans campaign soon saw their hopes for more equitable treatment dashed in a society increasingly committed to slavery and a racist ideology.

Even with the outbreak of the Civil War, the United States continued to refuse to enlist African Americans. For the entire first year of that conflict the War Department maintained its resistance to black troops, even though commanders in the field called for a reversal of the policy. Eventually, military necessity and the Emancipation Proclamation forced a nation caught up in a brutal, prolonged conflict to utilize a much-needed source of manpower. In the fall of 1862, as President Abraham Lincoln prepared to issue the Emancipation Proclamation, the United States began enrolling black troops in an organization separate from the regular army, the United States Colored Troops. Some 186,000 African Americans served in the Union army in segregated units, such as the famed 54th Massachusetts Regiment. Another 30,000 African Americans served in the Union navy, many as able-bodied sailors. When the Emancipation Proclamation became effective on January 1, 1863, these black soldiers and sailors understood fully that the victory for which they fought would destroy slavery, and, they hoped, bring them the liberties of citizenship.

After the Civil War, Congress retained the United States Colored Troops, composed of two infantry regiments, the 24th and 25th, and two cavalry regiments, the 9th and 10th. This decision reflected the policies of the Reconstruction Congress, which granted citizenship to African American males with the Fourteenth Amendment to the Constitution and extended the franchise to them with the Fifteenth Amendment. During the late nineteenth century the units of the U.S. Colored Troops fought in the Indian Wars on the western frontier, primarily in the Southwest, where the cavalry regiments gained fame as the "Buffalo Soldiers." Black troops also fought in Cuba during the Spanish-American War of 1898, some with Theodore Roosevelt's Rough Riders. Both the 9th and 10th Cavalry participated in the famous charge up San Juan Hill, their heroics in that battle briefly receiving press attention equaling that given to Roosevelt's Rough Riders. All four black regiments saw combat duty in the Philippine Insurrection, a nasty and little-known war fought from 1899 to 1901 between American forces and Philippine nationalists seeking independence under the leadership of Emilio Aquinaldo. When President Woodrow Wilson sent American troops under General John J. Pershing into Mexico in 1916 to chase down the Mexican revolutionary Pancho Villa, whose troops had conducted raids into the American Southwest, units from the U.S. Colored Troops joined the expedition.

Ironically, by their service in the Spanish-American War and the Philippine Insurrection, black troops helped the United States conquer territories populated by darker-skinned peoples. The nation partially justified both wars with racial theories that proclaimed it the duty of the "white race" to tutor darker, and thus supposedly inferior, peoples in the concepts of democracy and "civilization." Conquest abroad only fanned the flames of white supremacy at home. In the late nineteenth century and the early twentieth, southern states and the federal government adopted increasingly harsh segregationist laws and practices. In the infamous *Plessy vs.*

Ferguson case of 1896, the Supreme Court established the "separate but equal" doctrine, essentially making segregation a federal policy. Emboldened by this decision and the federal government's repeated failure to protect the civil liberties African Americans had gained during Reconstruction, state legislatures in the American South passed legislation segregating African Americans in almost every aspect of life. Southern states also simultaneously removed blacks from the political process by stripping them of the right to vote through a variety of legislative acts that civil rights organizations would spend the next half century challenging in federal courts. By the early twentieth century, the doctrine of white supremacy had become the official policy of the United States. The federal military and civil service were segregated, "separate but equal" had been proclaimed the law of the land, and the federal government had acquiesced in, if not encouraged, the segregation and disenfranchisement of African Americans by the states of the South. Even outside the South, although blacks continued to be politically active, courts enforced restrictive covenants that created segregated neighborhoods while rampant and blatant discrimination in employment denied African Americans equal economic opportunities.

This dramatic shift in racial policy was readily apparent in the American military when the United States entered World War I in 1917. The draft established in that year to provide the millions of servicemen necessary to prosecute the war made African Americans eligible to serve, and by the war's end, over 367,000 had done so. The manner in which the military employed African Americans during World War I, however, signaled disappointment for those who hoped their service would result in more equitable treatment when hostilities ended. Rather than employing African Americans in their traditional combat roll, the Army placed almost 90 percent of its black troops in segregated service units, such as stevedore and labor battalions, and created only two black combat units, the 92nd and 93rd Divisions. Only the 92nd fought under American command; the 93rd was assigned to the French forces. Another 10,000 African Americans served in the Navy, not as able-bodied seamen but in the mess and stewards branches.

Throughout World War I, the Marine Corps refused, as it had since the Revolution, to enlist blacks. With the war's end, both the Army and the Navy continued their policy of racial segregation and the use of black personnel primarily in service units, not as combat troops. As America prepared to enter the Second World War, the Marine Corps remained a white enclave. Whether this policy of racial exclusion reflected the high percentage of white southerners in the Corps's ranks, the highest of any of the services,

4   INTRODUCTION

or the ideal of a small, close-knit brotherhood of warriors, it was endorsed and defended by the Corps's leadership.

When the war clouds gathering over Europe unleashed their fury with the German invasion of Poland in 1939, America began military and economic preparations for war. The nation inaugurated its first peacetime draft in that year and vastly expanded defense-related expenditures. The scope of the economic preparation was enormous, and African Americans were determined to employ every possible legitimate tactic to prevent their exclusion from what promised to be an economic banquet. Blacks in the South, under the repression of legal segregation and the threat of lynch mob violence, could do little to ensure that they would benefit from the nation's preparations for war. But in the urban centers of the North, where African Americans enjoyed the franchise, millions of them who had fled the South during and after World War I had created strong civil rights organizations capable of demanding more equitable treatment from the federal government.

As it became increasingly obvious that without pressure the federal government would not ensure that African Americans be included in the war effort's economic opportunities, northern civil rights organizations took action. A. Philip Randolph, president of the Brotherhood of Sleeping Car Porters, in collaboration with other leaders of the nation's most powerful civil rights organizations, including the National Association for the Advancement of Colored People and the Urban League, threatened to send 100,000 marchers into the streets of Washington on July 1, 1941, unless the federal government guaranteed more equitable treatment for African Americans. Worried about the power of southern Democrats in Congress, President Franklin D. Roosevelt resisted the demands rather than risk the southerners' opposition to his foreign and domestic agendas. After a flurry of negotiations convinced Roosevelt that the march would indeed be held unless the federal government made it possible for African Americans to enjoy both the rewards and risks of the war effort, on June 25 he signed Executive Order 8802. In an effort to appease southern congressional leaders, the order allowed continued racial segregation, both by private firms contracting with the government and within government agencies. However, it expressly forbade governmental agencies or firms receiving government contracts from discriminating "in the employment of workers in defense industries or Government because of race, creed, color, or national origin" and created the Fair Employment Practices Commission to enforce the order.

Executive Order 8802 directly and immediately affected the Marine

Corps, the only branch of the American military that still excluded blacks. The Corps made no secret of its unhappiness with the order. Major General Thomas Holcomb, Commandant of the Corps, observed that "the Negro race has every opportunity now to satisfy its aspirations for combat in the Army" and declared, "If it were a question of having a Marine Corps of 5,000 whites or 250,000 Negroes, I would rather have the whites."

Faced with a directive from the commander in chief to accept African Americans, the Corps had no choice but to abandon its policy of racial exclusion. The Corps's reluctant enlistment of African Americans was indicative of the manner in which World War II would transform race relations in the United States, creating the conditions that would eventually lead to the demise of legal segregation. For the moment, however, like the Army and Navy, the Corps could, and did, insist on a policy of rigid racial segregation within its ranks. Rather than send black enlistees to the East Coast training facility at Parris Island, South Carolina, the Corps elected to send them to a separate facility. In 1941 the Corps had acquired the Marine Barracks, New River, North Carolina. The sprawling new base, renamed Camp Lejeune a year later, was located in coastal southeastern North Carolina, near the tiny town of Jacksonville in Onslow County. The Corps opened its segregated training facility in August 1942, on an area of Camp Lejeune called Montford Point, ironically at the initial location of the Camp Lejeune command post.

The Corps chose Colonel Samuel A. Woods, a career officer from South Carolina, as the first commander at Montford Point. He selected an experienced staff of officers, noncommissioned officers, and especially drill instructors from men who had served in locations such as the Philippines, Nicaragua, and the Caribbean. Such service, the Corps's leadership reasoned, indicated their experience with "colored" troops. While Woods expected the new enlistees to receive training equal to that received by white recruits at Parris Island, some of his all-white staff greeted the black recruits with undisguised racial prejudice and open hostility.

The Corps charged Woods and his staff with quickly identifying those African American recruits with leadership potential to replace the original white drill instructors, a task that was accomplished by late 1943. The rigor of the training only increased under the newly minted black drill instructors, who were determined to see their charges emerge from boot camp every bit the equals of the Marines trained at Parris Island. Operating until 1949, this bifurcated command structure of black drill instructors and white officers churned out more than 20,000 Marines. While African Americans gradually worked their way into the ranks of the drill instructors and noncommissioned officers, the officer corps remained all white, and the basic rule of racial etiquette at Montford Point never varied: at no time was a black man to be in a position to give orders to white Marines.

The career aspiration of camp commanders, who worked to send well-trained Marines into the Corps's ranks, and the presence of black drill instructors tempered the racism black Marines faced at Montford Point. In the civilian world off base, deep in the segregated South, there was no such restraint on the blatant racism Montford Pointers encountered. The Marine Corps decided to construct the training camp for black enlistees at Camp Lejeune for reasons of cost and efficiency, without any consideration of the difficulties African American recruits inevitably would encounter in that location. Still the nation's most impoverished region in the 1940s, the American South clung to its policies of rigid segregation and near-total disenfranchisement of African Americans, and to the racist ideology that undergirded them. Even as recruits came south to Montford Point, millions of blacks were fleeing the region to escape the daily humiliations of life in a segregated society. They fled northward to enjoy greater social freedom, to exercise their right to vote, and especially to embrace the economic opportunities of a nation at war that promised a better life for them and their families. Those African Americans who remained in the segregated South, the vast majority, faced the constant challenge of living in a legally segregated, staunchly racist society that ultimately depended upon the threat of violence to keep them in a subservient position.

While in the uniform of their country, the men of Montford Point endured every form of racial discrimination. On trains they were forced to occupy segregated cars, and on buses they were obliged to sit in the rear and to yield their seats to whites. Restaurants denied them service, and theaters, if they admitted them at all, required that they be seated in segregated areas. Whites insulted them on sidewalks and berated them with racial epithets. The police, both military and civilian, made sure they did not stray into the "white" areas of Jacksonville or other communities. Resistance was dangerous and usually futile. Black Marines stationed at Montford Point and elsewhere in the South endured this flagrant discrimination for more than two decades.

While coping with segregation and racial discrimination in the civilian world and within the Corps, the men of Montford Point served the nation in three wars and in brief periods of peace between conflicts. Almost all of their service occurred during a time in which racial segregation remained legal throughout the American South and racial discrimination permeated practically every aspect of life in the rest of the nation. Their record of service under such circumstances stands as a remarkable testament of their devotion to and faith in their country.

Of the 19,168 African Americans who served in the Corps during World War II, 12,738, or two-thirds, served overseas. Montford Point Marines who remained stateside included members of units assigned to naval supply depots at Norfolk, Philadelphia, and McAlester, Oklahoma, as well as members of the five Marine depot companies that remained in training at the war's end. Overseas assignments, however, did not necessarily place Montford Point Marines in combat. Most young African American men who joined the Marine Corps during World War II hoping to engage the enemy saw their hopes disappointed. The majority were assigned to duty stations in the Pacific outside the combat zone. The two combat units created at Montford Point, the 51st and 52nd Defense Battalions, despite rumors of assignments in forward areas of the Pacific theater, essentially drew guard duty on islands secured by other units. To the frustration of the men in their ranks, who felt that their skin color determined their lack of combat assignments, the 51st saw duty in the Ellice and Mariana Islands and the 52nd served in the Marshall Islands and Guam only after these islands were fully under the control of American forces. Both battalions served as replacements for white units employed in the support of the American invasions.

Ironically, the Montford Point recruits who saw combat in the Pacific were those with the least combat training: they were members of ammunition and depot companies who supported amphibious landings on some of the war's bloodiest beaches, including those on the islands of Saipan, Pelelui, Iwo Jima, and Okinawa. In the confusion of the battlefield, ammunition carriers and depot company personnel became riflemen who engaged the enemy, at times in hand-to-hand combat. They acted as stretcher bearers, removing both the wounded and the dead from the front lines, and served on picket lines protecting secured beachheads and airfields, in addition to fulfilling their primary mission of seeing that frontline troops received the ammunition and supplies required to support their advances. Their courage and performance under fire earned the admiration of the white combat units they supported and unequivocally demonstrated what the men of Montford Point already knew—that they possessed the ability to perform as the equals of Marines who had trained at Parris Island or Camp Pendleton, California.

The performance of African American Marines in the Pacific during World War II did not, as many had hoped, lead to their full acceptance in the Corps. Instead, faced with the necessity of retaining black Marines, the Corps continued its old segregationist policies while reducing the percentage of blacks in its ranks. Rather than the 10 percent envisioned by the Navy, the Corps planned for its postwar force of 100,000 men to contain no more that 2,800 black marines, a figure reduced to 1,500 in 1947. Rumors swept through the ranks of the black Marines who remained in service that both they and all future black recruits would be forced into the Stewards Branch, causing some to refuse to reenlist. In fact, black Marines were assigned either to the Stewards Branch or to a new Training Company created at Montford Point in June of 1946, whose graduates were to be assigned as general duty Marines organized in segregated units.

The Corps developed, and revised, several plans for stationing units composed of black Marines during the immediate postwar period. The Corps planned to station black Marine depot units at Port Chicago, California, in the San Francisco Bay area; the Marine Corps Barracks in McAlester, Oklahoma; the Marine Barracks at the Naval Ammunition Depots in Hingham, Massachusetts, and Fort Mifflin, Pennsylvania; the Marine Barracks at the Naval Supply Depot in Scotia, New York; and naval facilities in Bayonne, New Jersey. The Corps canceled these plans when they came under fire from base commanders concerned about the possibility of racial conflicts with local townspeople and laborers. After what seemed like endless agonizing over where to station the black Marines, the Corps finally adopted a solution in late 1947. The plan adopted envisioned only 1,388 African Americans in the Corps, of which almost a third, 420, would serve in the Stewards Branch. The plan retained Montford Point as a segregated training facility and called for segregated black service units to be stationed at Montford Point and the Marine Corps Barracks at Naval Ammunition Depots in Earle, New Jersey; Fort Mifflin, Pennsylvania; and Lualualei, Hawaii.

After World War II, support for segregation was crumbling in much of America, in large measure because of conditions and circumstances created by the war. Approximately a million African Americans served their country in the military during World War II, with nearly half serving overseas, where many encountered race relations superior to those in the United States. After entering into harm's way to defend a nation that regarded them as second-class citizens, they returned home determined to defeat segregation and racism. Millions of northern white troops who had passed through bases in the American South had observed the harsh realities of segregation firsthand and were now more prepared to support African American calls for its demise. The large black populations in the major urban centers of the

North and Midwest, created as blacks fled the segregated South for personal freedom and war industry employment, were strategically placed politically. Their votes could deliver victory in elections in major industrial states, and thus in national presidential elections. An American public shocked and appalled by the horrors of the Holocaust was receptive to demands by African Americans that the nation put an end to systematic discrimination and redeem its promise of liberty and equality for all.

In an uphill fight for reelection and under pressure from northern civil rights organizations, despite staunch opposition from the segregated South, in July 1948 President Harry Truman signed Executive Order 9981, which finally abandoned racial segregation as a federal policy and required the desegregation of the military. The Corps was slow to carry out President Truman's executive order to integrate. It deactivated Montford Point as a training facility in September 1949, more than a year after Executive Order 9981 was issued, sending new black recruits to its training camps previously reserved for whites at Parris Island and Camp Pendleton. It did not seek to expand the number of blacks within its ranks, and most of the men trained at Montford Point who remained on active duty continued to serve in segregated units.

In June 1950, the Korean War began when North Korean Communist forces invaded South Korea. It was the first major armed conflict of a prolonged Cold War in which the United States and its allies sought to prevent the spread of Communism from the Soviet Union and China into countries allied with the Western democracies. The Korean War finally persuaded the Marine Corps to integrate its ranks fully. Once begun, integration occurred quickly and without major incidents, as Marines on the battlefield concentrated on staying alive, not worrying about the skin color of others in their outfit. Because so few African Americans had entered the Corps since the closure of Montford Point the previous September, it was primarily men trained at Montford Point who initially integrated the Corps at unit level. Montford Point Marines served in all the major campaigns of the Korean conflict, this time as frontline troops as well as in service and supply units.

While racism continued to exist within the Marines' ranks, by the end of the Korean Conflict the Corps was fully integrated. The nation, too, was experiencing a fundamental change in race relations, in large measure because African American veterans of both World War II and the Korean War refused to accept second-class citizenship in the country they had fought to defend. Throughout the nation, even in the Deep South, black veterans occupied leadership positions in a variety of civil rights organizations and were determined to end legal segregation in the United States. In 1954 the Supreme Court ruled that segregation of public schools was unconstitutional, a ruling rapidly expanded to all public institutions. A year later in Montgomery, Alabama, African Americans began a decade-long struggle for equality that played out in the streets of the South's major cities, in federal courts, and in the halls of Congress. The 1963 march on Washington and the eloquence of a young Martin Luther King Jr. moved the conscience of a nation. Violence perpetuated against civil rights activists in Birmingham, Alabama; Neshoba County, Mississippi; and elsewhere in the South appeared on television screens across the country, convincing the nation that the time to end segregation had come. In June 1964 Congress passed the Civil Rights Act, finally outlawing segregation in the United States. While racism continued to haunt both the Corps and the nation, segregation as a legal system was dead, and the Marines of Montford Point had played an important role in its demise by first joining, then integrating, a revered fighting service.

As the nation struggled to confront the injustices of racism and segregation, it was becoming increasingly enmeshed in a nasty conflict in southeast Asia, itself part of a larger global struggle by colonized peoples for liberation from Western occupiers. Less than a decade after the end of the Korean War, Montford Point veterans answered the call to duty in Vietnam to participate in what was seen as a continuation of America's effort to prevent the spread of Communism. Some served in the secret phase of the war, before the Tonkin Gulf Resolution of August 1964 officially brought the United States into the conflict. By the time the United States committed to a military strategy in Vietnam, the vast majority of Montford Point Marines had left the Corps, including those who retired with twenty years of service. The Montford Pointers who remained were seasoned veterans, many of whom had served in Korea. In Vietnam, as in Korea, they fought on the front lines, or "in country," in a war without clearly delineated enemy lines, as well as serving in support units. Montford Point veterans engaged in some of the most memorable campaigns of that long, bloody, and politically divisive war. They served when American involvement was at its height, especially at the sprawling American base at Da Nang, in the siege of Khe Sahn, and during the audacious Tet Offensive launched by the North Vietnamese in January 1968.

The Corps in which African Americans served in Vietnam was fundamentally changed from the Corps they had entered at Montford Point. The Corps's ranks were fully integrated, with black officers in command of integrated units. The overwhelming majority of black Marines who served in

Vietnam had never experienced segregation within the Corps's ranks and knew nothing of a segregated boot camp or all-black units. Many had never heard of Montford Point, although they owed their ability to join and serve in an integrated Corps to the men who had trained there and who had chosen to make the Corps their career.

The ranks of those who trained at Montford Point are rapidly thinning. In little more than a decade from now, they will be gone. Their accomplishments are little known, but not because they are insignificant. Throughout World War II, when the vast majority of Montford Pointers served, racial prejudice denied them both officer status and combat duty. When battlefield conditions demanded that they act as combat troops, they displayed bravery and initiative in the face of enemy fire. The duties assigned to Montford Point troops, moving supplies and munitions to the front lines, lacked the glamour of the role of the Tuskegee Airmen, or even the black Army combat units who served in Europe. The tasks they performed, often under withering enemy fire, were, however, essential to victory in the Pacific. Even in the integrated Corps that fought in Korea and Vietnam, few Montford Pointers obtained commissions and the higher profile that command opportunities afforded. In both conflicts, most career Montford Point veterans served as part of the unheralded ranks, most as noncommissioned officers, whether in combat or service assignments. They were among those who carried out the daily tasks of pursuing campaign strategies on the ground. In both Korea and Vietnam they faced the grim and brutal realities of war with courage and tenacity.

While serving their country, the men of Montford Point helped undermine and ultimately eliminate segregation as a policy of the United States and as a legal system of discrimination in the American South. They gained entry into the nation's most celebrated elite fighting service, a branch of service that to this day carries enormous symbolic, indeed mythic, significance in American culture. They endured training at a segregated base and served in segregated units to prove to their fellow Americans that African Americans could be good Marines. They not only gained entry into the Corps; they also integrated the ranks of the Marine Corps at unit level, conclusively demonstrating their ability to fight alongside fellow Marines of every ethnic and racial background. Their determination and perseverance made possible a career in the Corps for thousands of younger African Americans who followed them. Montford Point veterans who themselves made the Corps their career created the opportunity for young black Marines to obtain commissions, rise in the ranks, and eventually obtain the rank of general and become base commanders. Their story is a quintessentially American story, a story they can tell with unequaled authenticity, a story that still speaks to the nation about race relations in its past, and a story that holds deep significance for both the present and the future. Theirs is, quite simply, a story that deserves to be told.

n May 1942 Major General Thomas Holcomb, Commandant of the Marine Corps, ordered the Corps's Southern, Eastern, and Central Recruiting Divisions to begin recruiting African Americans on June 1. The Southern Division was to supply approximately half of the initial 900 recruits envisioned, the other two divisions about 200 men each. Given the opportunity, young men, and some no longer young, responded. The Corps instructed recruiters to enlist only those with the skills needed to prepare Montford Point, still very much under construction, for the training of future recruits. As a result, the initial recruits who trained at Montford Point were, on average, better educated and slightly older than their counterparts at the white boot camp at Parris Island. Many had some college education, although others had lacked an opportunity to continue their education beyond elementary school. A number of professionals, especially teachers, joined, as did some skilled tradesmen and laborers. Other recruits had participated in ROTC, the Boy Scouts, or high school drill teams. They came from a variety of backgrounds, from the rural South and the big cities of the North, from small towns and country hamlets, from tenant farms and urban factories. Like their white counterparts, they were representative of the nation. Unlike their white counterparts, however—or at least to a different degree—they were, whether or not they sought to be, representatives of their race.

Fred Ash I was born in Mississippi, a little town called Delisle. It's a French town. I [lived] with mother, naturally, and a father, and my whole family lived mostly with my grandmother, my mother's mother. We were very, very poor actually, but we were sort of wealthy, because we had livestock they call oxen. And at the age of twelve or thirteen, I think I was what I would say a professional ox driver. My parents had two yokes of oxen. Oxens was powerful animals, more so than mules and horses. And we'd use them for plowing. We'd use them for cleaning up new ground and whatever else that was necessary that they needed heavy equipment, like they didn't have during that time, but they do have today. We use our oxens to do that. And salaries was very low. For a yoke of oxens and a driver, the salary was only about $2.00, $2.50 a day.

My education was a little bit slim. During the time I was going to school, we only had the little rural school, one-room school. We only had about three months of schooling. And then they kept on raising it, raising it. They raised it up to six months, and I ended up, before I came in the Marine Corps, I dropped out in about the eighth grade; but after I got in the Marine Corps, I finished my education. I went on to complete the twelfth grade.

Adner Batts I was born at Edgecombe, North Carolina, seventy-five years ago, this day [said in 2004]. I was born in a family of two boys, two girls. I lost my dad when I was a year old, I don't remember him, and my mother, when I was seventeen. Where we lived was just on the inside of the Pender County line, on Highway 17, south, seventy-five yards south, just on the inside of the line. I was raised in a home with the five of us, and I was a seventh grade dropout. Lost my mother when I was seventeen years old. I attended school at a little place you call Edgecombe, well, of course, that was where the [train] station was, the trains was running, in those days. And the school room carried about six grades. And then when you got to seventh grade, you had to go to Rocky Point. And we had to get a bus to go to Rocky Point. Of course, all the communities, about five communities, which namely, Woodside, Topsail, Edgecombe, Brown Town, and others, had to purchase a bus. The state wouldn't provide a bus because black people in that area wasn't making enough money to purchase a bus, so the churches got together, purchased a bus. And then we started going to school at Rocky Point, so that's where I dropped out of seventh grade at Rocky Point, in North Carolina.

Herman Darden Jr. Well, I'm from Washington, D.C. I did my high school training there, graduated from Dunbar High School, in Washington, D.C., went to the Junior ROTC; at that time, they were just called the Cadet Corps. And I rose to the rank of commander of my battalion, and I happened to be in the company that won first prize. We used to have a drill competition at the old Griffith Stadium, in Washington, D.C. Well, this was just between the black schools, because there were two school districts. We were in District 13, which was all black, so our competition sportswise, and otherwise, was just between the black schools. And when the war started in 1941, actually, I was still in school at that time, and the war started in 1941, I applied and was accepted as a apprentice machinist at the Navy yard, Washington Navy Yard, working on five-inch guns, torpedo tubes, and things of that nature.

Charles Davenport I am from a town south of Pittsburgh, called Monongahela, Pennsylvania; it's named after the Monongahela River. I was born on July the 28th, 1923, in that town. I went to school there, graduated from Notting Hill High School in 1941. I majored [in] a commercial course at that time. After graduating form high school, and prior to that, my dad was a master electrician, and he taught my brother and I the electric trade. And following graduation, I went to work at a local hospital.

David Dinkins I was born July 10th, 1927. I was born in Trenton, New Jersey. And when I was six or seven years old, my mother and father separated. My mother came to New York City, where she lived with her mother, my grandmother. And they were domestics; they cooked and cleaned for folks for a dollar a day. For these were the Depression years. So we lived in Harlem. As I love to tell people, we moved a lot. We moved when the rent was due. It seemed like a good time to move. But I was a happy child. I never, never went to bed hungry, and my clothes were clean, because my mother and grandmother scrubbed them, and didn't have holes 'cause they sewed them up. I had toys. When the little white children got through with their toys, they [my mother and grandmother] brought their toys home. So I did all right. And then I went to Trenton about junior high school, lived with my father. And I was there in Trenton up through high school, entered the service, and college. Then I came back to New York, where I've been ever since. And I got involved in government and politics and eventually became the mayor of New York City, elected in '89, served for one term, four years, commencing January 1st, 1990.

Gene Doughty I was born in the city of Stamford, often confused with Stamford in California, but this is Stamford, Connecticut. I was born there in 1924, and at the age of six moved with my family to New York City, where I remained until the time I was selected to go into the Marine Corps. That would include all of my preliminary education, my primary education. I had one year in college at City College, majored in physical and health education. I elected to go into the Marine Corps once I had found out that the doors were open in recruitment for Afro-Americans.

Frederick Drake   I was born in south Alabama, Marengo County. And I was from a long line of long livers. My mother, I buried her about two years ago [said in 2003]. She was 102. Her mother didn't live quite as long. She lived to be 99. But her two grandmothers lived to be, one 116 and one 127. They lived a long time, and it was a strong family of skilled slaves in Marengo County.

But anyway, that's where I was born, and my mother was a schoolteacher and my father was a businessman of a sort in that day. We moved from Marengo County into Jefferson County, which is Birmingham [and] Bessemer, Alabama. And my uncles all were coal miners. Well, my dad said, none of my boys, he had four boys, he said, none of my boys will be down there digging no coal.

And I went on. I finished high school and enrolled in college, a [African Methodist Episcopal] church school there in Birmingham, Payne University [Daniel Payne College]. Dad, his business was hauling coal. We lived in a coal mining community there. And he wasn't able to send [me to] a major college. But I went on and enrolled in any way at Payne. And, 'cause he [my father] had made a vow, said none of my boys will ever work in the coal mine. All my uncles did. But his [my father's] oldest son went on and got a job in the coal mine. This was in, I think I went to work in the coal mine about '48 [1938]. I went to work in there. And I was going to get enough money where I could go to college. I worked down there. But the war came along. And after Pearl Harbor, we had to serve.

James Ferguson   I was born Washington, D.C., on April the 27th, 1924. I'm an only child, son of Lucy and Henry Ferguson. I attended school in Washington, D.C. I graduated from one of the top high schools in the United States, and that was Dunbar High School. And it was segregated. And Dunbar High School was such a good high school because so many of the teachers at Dunbar High, due the segregation, they had to teach high school when they normally would have been teaching at a school such as Harvard, Notre Dame, and places like that. So we were beneficiaries of all of these great teachers, and I took four years of Latin. When I left, graduated from Dunbar, I could read Latin as fluently as I can read English. The whole time that I was overseas in the Marine Corps, I took my Latin book, Virgil's *Aeneid*, and I read Virgil's *Aeneid* like people read the Bible, and I still have that book at home now. But I'm not that good in Latin because you have to stay in practice and I'm not, I haven't practiced reading Latin now in years.

Overall, I had a very good education in D.C. I liked D.C. and I still live in D.C., and things have improved a lot.

I was an only child, son of Henry and Lucy Ferguson. And my mother was born in Danville, Virginia; my father was born in Charlottesville, Virginia. And I'd like to tell you a story about my father's grandfather, who was a slave. And he [my father] used to tell me many stories about his grandfather and his stories that he told him. So, before my father died, I got him on tape, and one story that he would tell me about his grandfather is that he would constantly be trying to escape. He had whip marks all over him for being caught after trying to escape. And then one escape attempt, my father says, he got all the way to the Potomac River before the paddy roll caught him. Now, they used to call the [slave] patrol the paddy roll. Their job was to capture escaped slaves. So they caught him, but they never would kill him because he was a good worker. But the sign of being a good worker and escapee were all the strike marks on his back. And I did get that on tape, so that's an old history of my father's father, great-grandfather and his experiences as a slave.

Paul Hagan Before I went in the Marine Corps, my mother and father died when I was a little baby. So, I don't remember anything about my mother and my father. But I had a brother and a sister, two brothers and a sister. We was from Alabama but we come to Georgia, and that's where we were living. So when they [my parents] died, we had a home and everything, and we lost everything we had because we was so young, we didn't know what tax was about. And I went from place to place and the people that raised me, they raised me on a farm in a place they called Roopville, Georgia, until I was old enough to join the Marine Corps. They wasn't no kin to me. And, of course, like I said, I didn't have no kin people in Georgia. The ones that was in Alabama, I didn't know nothing about them. So we had no kin, I just knew that the people that took me in was a friend of my mother and father. When I went in the Marine Corps, my education level was the seventh grade back in that day. But I still, after [I] become Marine Corps, I finish high school. We worked on that farm sunup to sundown, six days a week. And I really enjoyed myself because I didn't have no home or anything. And they treated me just like I was one of their children.

F. M. Hooper I was raised in Brooklyn, New York. My mother and father migrated from the state of North Carolina and four children, myself, I am the oldest, and I have one brother and two sisters. I'm a graduate of Boys'

High School, Brooklyn, New York. I played; I liked to play in the streets of Brooklyn. We played soldier, cowboys and Indians. I attended movies, and I loved to watch Marine Corps movies, especially during World War II. And during the war I observed the battleship USS *North Carolina* being constructed, as well as U.S. Marines guarding the ship at the Brooklyn Navy Yard. My mother was a former schoolteacher, but she, at the time raising four children, she was just a housewife. My father was a laborer. He did work at the Brooklyn Navy Yard also during World War II. While I was in school I worked part-time jobs and also summer jobs in the garment section of Manhattan. As well as stores, downtown in Brooklyn, grocery stores, and I did a lot of work on my own. I worked in local candy stores and selling newspapers, did a lot of odd jobs, you know, so, just went around the city and tried to [get jobs in] like people's homes. I used to go in and the lady would ask me to do some windows for her, which I did.

Leroy Mack I was born and raised in Brooklyn, New York. My mother, Margaret Mack, or Margaret Jenkins first, is from West Virginia. My father, Leroy John Mack, is from Charleston, South Carolina. He is, or he was at that time of meeting my mother, he was a reserve sailor. He had sailed in the United States Navy as a cook. My brother was bitten on the ear in Brooklyn and my father said, it's time for us to move, so we moved to Amityville, Long Island. I had gone to school in Brooklyn, and attended PS 14. And when we moved to Amityville, then I attended Amityville Junior High and High School. But high school wasn't for me. Sports was the thing for me, and finally my father looked at me and he said, it's time for you to realize that schooling is not for you. So I suggest you join the Marine Corps.

Archibald Mosley I was born in Carbondale, Illinois, which is southern Illinois. And they called it Little Egypt because that it's on the borderline of the South. You have southern weather, as well as northern weather. It's so many miles away from Chicago, and so you don't get the winds off of the lake. But you do get the breezes from the south. It's only fifty miles north of where the Ohio and the Mississippi River meets. That's where I was born. And the reason I mentioned about Cairo, Illinois, where the Ohio and Mississippi meets is fifty miles north is that you are coming from the South on the Illinois Central from New Orleans and going to Chicago or vice versa.

If you leave Chicago going to New Orleans to visit a relative, you can sit anywhere you want on the Illinois Central until you get to Cairo, Illinois. You're going across the Mason-Dixon Line and you have to sit in the front, first coach of the steam engine train. And the reason I emphasize steam engine is in those days, the steam engines were done by coal. And that is what my father's occupation was. My father's occupation was known as a boilermaker. And he cleaned out those trains, steam engine trains, and kept them running and functioning.

He insisted that education was important in our family. And there were seven kids, four girls and three boys. And out of the bunch, all of us but one out of seven ended up being a professional person in life, during those days of the '20s and the '30s.

Herman Nathaniel Before I joined the Marines, I lived in Sumter, South Carolina. I was born in Sumter, South Carolina. Went to Lincoln High School. Graduated from Lincoln High School. And went a little while at Morris College, which is also in Sumter. And also, a short stint at South Carolina State [University]. And afterwards I took a welding course and went to take a job in Chester, Pennsylvania, at Sun Ship Building.

Carrol Reavis I'm the fifth child of seventeen children in the family. I was born on May 11th, 1923, in Virginia, a place off Western Road, about twelve miles from the North Carolina line. And my father worked for my grandfather, who ran a mill that ground corn and wheat owned by a white family, [a member of which] was the chief of police in the town of Lawrenceville, Virginia. This was in 1923. In 1925, the dam broke, and we had to move back to my grandmother's house about ten miles away into a slave house. Most people have forgot about slavery, but my grandmother's father had inherited part of a plantation, including the main house, and they still maintained a couple of the slave houses.

We moved into the slave house. My father at that time had six kids, six of them, and I grew up there, and then in 1926, this must [have been] '26 or '27, [we had] the big snow. That was the year that Lindbergh flew across; we used to hear that Lindbergh crossing Atlantic. I was a little kid at that time, but I can remember. I must've been four or five years old. So I grew up there, and my mother kept having children. By the time I was seven years old, the Depression came along. You've probably heard of that, and my grandfather had left, and we went into almost slavery again, because everything was tight, no money.

My grandmother got sick and she died. So my father, with being the oldest son of that family, wound up with three of his sisters and one brother, plus his own family and no money, 'cause all the money they had in the bank had been gone. So he sold, he hocked the house and just hocked everything, and we went back into slavery again with nothing. We had to go back into sharecropping, and that's where I grew up, and I've been working ever since. I finished the third grade in school. By the time I was twelve, I was working full time. Fifteen, I was a grown man. Sixteen, I was in the Civilian Conservation Corps, where my family received $25.00 a month. I stayed there until it broke up in 1942. I was in there when the war broke out, and then I went to work for the Navy, the Yorktown Navy Yard depot at the TNT plant there. And then I became a third-class fireman, worked in the fire, boiler room. I was drafted from there into the Marine Corps in 1943.

Steven Robinson I attended public schools in [the] city of Pittsburgh. I graduated from Schilling High School in May of 1942 at the age of seventeen, at which time I was interested in enlisting in the 99th Pursuit Squadron, which was at that time training down at Tuskegee. I was a student pilot. I was flying at Jay Creek Trainer at the Greensburg Airport just out, about fifty miles southeast of Pittsburgh. And I logged about forty hours flying time.

And I had a foster brother who was older than I who was graduated Penn State, who was at that time down at Tuskegee. As a matter of fact he graduated from Tuskegee and was a fighter pilot in Italy and, as a matter of fact, was killed in Italy while in combat. But upon graduating from high school in 1942, I attempted to enlist, as I said, in the Air Corps. It was the Air Corps then, not the Air Force.

And they told me that I didn't have the qualifications because at that time, they only asked Americans to take over the list for people who has at least a Bachelor's Degree. Of course, I was just out of high school. And while my attempting to [enlist], of course, I was told that the requirements were dropping from the War Department almost monthly. They said keep trying back, that maybe I would be accepted later on, but not then. However, on my way after about maybe a month or so, I was noticed by [a] recruiting sergeant, the gunny sergeant at the post office area of Pittsburgh. He saw me down just about every other day and he wanted to know why I was coming down and I told him I was coming down to enlist in the Air Corps. He asked me if I was interested in the Marine Corps. And I told him not at that particular time.

George Taylor Well, I was born in Indianapolis, Indiana. My mother, we moved to Chicago when I was four years of age. My grandmother raised me. And my grandfather. My dad was a barber in Chicago. But my mother and father separated when I was a young boy. And then, my grandmother and grandfather raised me until I was grown. And my grandfather was a plaster contractor. And he learned me how to plaster. And my [grandfather was a] very religious person, Church of God in Christ, so, you know, no smoking, no gambling, no, none of that dancing, and all that stuff. And I didn't go no further than the eighth grade. Plus there in Chicago, at the time I came up, it was rough, out there in that street.

Joseph Walker I was born in Richmond, Virginia, April 20, 1924. My family moved back to Durham [North Carolina] in 1925. And of course at that time there was only three of us [children] in our family who were living. An older sister, two brothers who had passed, and of course myself and a younger brother, were the ones who actually moved back to Durham. My mother was a homemaker; my dad worked at Liggett and Meyers Tobacco Company in downtown Durham, N.C. I finished high school in 1942, and from there I went on to New Jersey. My brother-in-law had a job waiting for me, so naturally everything was supposed to been five girls in my family and two boys, all eight of us living, so somebody had to get out and do some work. Even though we knew there was a war going on.

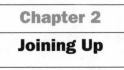
he men of Montford Point joined the Corps for reasons as varied as their backgrounds and, for the most part, for reasons similar to those of white recruits. Some responded to the Marines' reputation as a fighting service, hoping to become one of a band of fierce warriors, a modern gladiator. Some succumbed to the allure of adventure, to the opportunity to travel to exotic places. For others, the romance of serving in the Corps was symbolized by the appeal of the famous dress blue uniform and the impact they hoped it would have upon members of the opposite sex. With the nation just beginning to pull out of the Depression and conditions still difficult, especially in the South, economic considerations inevitably were an underlying factor for many enlistees. Some joined specifically to obtain employment, or to escape the poverty of the tenant farm or the mill town, although employment was among the least frequently mentioned reasons for joining. Facing the draft, which had been instituted in 1939, some joined to avoid being drafted into a branch of the service in which they did not wish to serve, and some were drafted into the Corps. Many knew that African Americans had not previously been admitted to the Corps, and some joined specifically to ensure an end to the Corps's practice of racial exclusion. Others were completely unaware of the Corps's racist history; a few joined with no idea they would be sent to a segregated training camp. To a man, however, they shared a fierce determination not just to complete their training successfully, but to excel, to prove to the world they could be exemplary Marines.

Al Banker I joined the Marine Corps because I felt it was the proper thing to do. To be patriotic to my country. I felt that this is history in the making. And I felt that I wanted to be a part of it. That's the reason I decided to volunteer for the Marine Corps. I was frightened, and I said to myself, what did I do? And then I realized that this is it. I'm in this Marine Corps, and I'm going to stick it out to the end. Because, at that time there were never any colored troops in the Marine Corps. It was an all-white unit. And we were reminded of that fact. And this was the first time that we were allowed to join the Marine Corps.

Ellis Cunningham Knew nothing about the Marine Corps. As far as I was concerned, there was the Army. And the one branch of the Army that I was particularly interested in was the cavalry, and that's because I knew this guy in the horse cavalry. They [the horse cavalry], they rode horses and wore the large campaign hats. . . . I was on liberty, because I didn't see them at work, I just saw them going on liberty. Well, that's what I wanted. Campaign hat, riding boots, and a horse.

That's the way, that's what I thought, and that's the way I felt when I went to register for the military. I went on the 10th of November, 1943, and how I know it was the 10th, because I put it down as my birthday. And that was not my birthday, incidentally, but I didn't know this was the Marine Corps's birthday at the time. And why I put it down as my birthday was, people at the draft board there, when the question came up, when's your birthday, that's the first time I realized that gee whiz, you might be in trouble here. Your birthday passed a few weeks ago, and you didn't register. So now if you say what your real birthday is, you're going to jail. . . . So I said, today is my birthday. And that's the birthday I kept throughout the Marine Corps.

So anyhow, they pack us up after a couple of weeks, and took us to Camp Jackson, at [Columbia, South Carolina], you know, it's Fort Jackson, but then it was Camp Jackson. That's where they conduct the examination, and assigned you to where you were going. And this was in December of '43. So, you had a long line of examination stations there. Doctors and psychologists and what have you. And hundreds of us there, being processed. And each person you go to, they ask you some questions, and you answered the question, and they would write the results out on a piece of paper, and they'd give it to you, and send you to the next station. So, by the time . . . the day was over, you had a handful of papers, and, of course, the paper meant nothing to me, but I carried them to the next person.

But at each one of those stations [they] asked which branch of the service you'd prefer. And I answered Army, every time. And the person would stamp Navy, every time. So when the day was over, all the papers I had read Navy. Although I wanted Army. And so they packed me up, and, after spending a day or two there, got me in a group going to Great Lake, Illinois, for the Navy.

But they made a mistake and asked, would anybody like to go back home for Christmas? You can come back afterwards. Yes, I would, very much. So that's how I got back home for '43 Christmas. Went back home, and, of course, comes back after Christmas, and started the same process over again, preparing us to go to Great Lake, Illinois, because we were already assigned to the Navy.

Again, the petty officer at Georgia was moving us around the street, and I guess, going to take us to Illinois. Then [a Marine appeared, and] I figured he was a Marine recruiter, and had the petty officer halt the group of us, and all he said to him [the petty officer] was, I need thirty-two of these people here to go to the Marine Corps. The petty officer says, shrugged and said, take them, take what you need.

And that's when he [the Marine recruiter] said, you, you, and you, I was one of those yous. Get over there. I got over there. And, they load us on a truck, and head us up to Montford Point. I had never heard of Montford Point before this, but that's how I got to Montford Point.

Turner Blount Well, I'm eighteen. So I got a Social Security Card. They said once you get a Social Security Card, you're gonna have to join the draft, if you're eighteen. So I signed up for the draft, of course. I had no knowledge of being drafted into the military service. And within thirty days or more, about thirty days afterward, I was Class IA, of course. And shortly after that, I was ordered for examination into the military service. I had no knowledge of the Marine Corps at all. I was thinking of the Army and the Air Force or those. But at the examination center, a friend of mine, from my town, Keysville, [Georgia], we was examined the same time. And as we was leaving the building, we had a choice of going into the Army or the Marine Corps or whatnot. So he said to me, he says, let's join the Marines. That's the toughest thing going up. I said, okay. And we joined the Marine Corps. That's how I got in the Marine Corps.

Herman Darden Jr. Well, of course the reputation of the Marines was known to be rough and ready. And my mother asked me why [I joined]. I said, well, they're supposed to be first in battle, and first back home, so I don't want to stay out too long. And the day I went and reported to the Marine draft station, I walked in, and the recruiting sergeant was sitting there reading a book, or a paper. I walked up to the desk. I stood there, nothing. So I cleared my throat. He said, I know you're there. Well, thank you. And he looked at me. At that time, I was very small. I was weighing about 121 pounds. Five foot five. And he looked at me. You're going into the Marines, as small as you are? He was a big dude. I told him, you made it; I know damn well I can. So, that was my entrance, more or less.

And then when I became eighteen, actually, it was, the draft was in vogue, but even though it was the draft, you had a choice between the branches of service. And the day that I went in, I chose the Marines. Only four would be selected out of the whole group were Marines, four for the Navy, and the rest went in the Army. And I was chosen. I had chose to go into the Marines. And when I got home and told my mother, she looked at me, and looked at my daddy, and she said, this boy is in the Marines. He said, I told you he was crazy.

Charles Davenport To tell the truth, I had a dispute on a job site, and out of the dispute, I'm a little hot tempered, and I told the boss I didn't have to work for him. The United States government had a job for me, and I walked off the job that day, and into Pittsburgh, and enlisted in the Marine Corps. However, prior to that, around May, about 1942, I read in the paper, and then I later heard from the radio, that President Roosevelt was signing a law that was going to provide for black people to enlist in the Marine Corps.

I had a good friend there, who was like a brother to me, and he and I both decided to enlist in the Marines. And we later found out that the enlistments were going to commence in August. However, the 7th of August, my friend got married, and in getting married, he wasn't interested in the Marines Corps at that time, and so I didn't want to go by myself, and I waited and worked, too, and continued to speak with my boss where I worked.

This is when I was pushed too far, on my desire to go into the Marines. And I guess you could say that I had [the reputation of] kind of a toughie, and I liked to fight. I was very good at wrestling, and I was moderate as far as fistfighting was concerned, and being small of stature, and things like that, I got pushed around quite a bit, and it was in me to show that even though I was small in stature, I was big enough and strong enough, and willing to be in the best fighting force they had, and I joined the Marine Corps.

David Dinkins Everybody, with the rare exceptions of those persons who were 4F, [or] had some disability, or perhaps were in some essential occupation, everybody else went [into military service]. So you never gave a thought to not going. . . . And people were dying that you knew. So-and-so's big brother who lived across the street or around the corner.

And I figured a way to stay alive is to be well trained. Well, and the way to be well trained is to be a Marine. And so I tried to enlist in the Marine Corps. Well, the idea is you have to enlist before you get drafted, because once you're drafted, they tell you where you're going. You say you want Navy, they give you Army. You say you want Army, they give you Navy. Nobody gets what they wish. So, I set out to enlist. In 1945 there were no recruitment offices in Trenton, New Jersey, where I then lived. So, in succession, not necessarily in this order, but I went to Camden, to Philadelphia, to Jersey City, to Newark, to New York.

I went, actually went to all those places attempting to enlist. I was either told that we have our quota of Negro Marines, or you have to go to the state of your residence. So I pestered them in Philadelphia so long and so much that they finally let me fill out the papers. And I took the physical and they said you have high blood pressure. Now, at that time I weighed about 128 pounds soaking wet. And so I didn't believe it. And so I stopped at a doctor's office in Philadelphia, blood pressure normal. I went home to the family physician who had been an Army surgeon, blood pressure normal. So I go back to Philadelphia, they take my pressure on my left arm, right arm, lying down, standing up, always high. But I was so persistent that they wrote a letter to my draft board and gave me a copy. It said if this man passes the physical and requests the Marine Corps, put him in the Marine Corps. And so, on the 10th of July, 1945, I turned eighteen, I registered for the draft, and requested immediate induction. And I think it was the 18th, pretty sure it was the 18th of July, I was called.

Roland Durden I graduated 1943, but I was one year ahead of my class, because in junior high school we had what you call a rapid advance class. And you took two terms in one term. And when I turned eighteen I became the voluntary inductee into the service, and I volunteered for the U.S. Marine Corps.

My mother and father were separated, although I saw my father on a regular basis. It was during the Depression, so he didn't have good jobs, put it that way. Neither did my mother. I know about the relief, the home relief. I worked part time at the YMCA on 63rd Street, serving tea twice a week. And, though I finished high school, then I worked at the Y on a full-time basis, in the cloakroom. And as soon as I turned eighteen and then I wanted to join the Marine Corp to become a man.

I went in March of 1944. And I was hoping to get training, the experience. During that time we had a lot of movies that promoted loyalty and camaraderie and heroes at that time. So, I think maybe I was influenced that way. Plus I couldn't get a decent job at that time, even in the war.

I was not sure at this time I knew anything about the history of blacks, Negroes, as we were called at that time, not being able to join the Marine Corps. But I do know that, in the Navy, we generally served as mess men.

Hulon Edwards I joined the Marine Corps August of 1946, but let me add this. I was a draftee in the U.S. Army, for three years, during World War II. I was drafted at the age of seventeen. My next birthday, I would have been eighteen years of age, and I was, had my calling card, that's what we call it then, I got my card, to go to war, the calling card. And so I went to the county seat, and went and reported on Monday, 16th day of December, in 1942. Then I left there, and went to Camp Shelby, Mississippi, where they had an Army National Guard unit, a Army hospital station there, which is about sixty miles from Mendenhall. We called, we got a bus, and they told us that we'll be away for about, overnight at least. So, my brother, by the way, my brother and I went as a team. He had a calling card as well, and so, we went and had our examination at about 13:00. [That is,] 1:00. 13:00 is the way, you know, in the Marine Corps. Now, I didn't know that at that time, what it meant, but 1:00, 13:00 that evening, we all went for the examination, and I was the smallest one. That was my nickname, Little One, and they passed me. And my brother didn't pass. He got poor health. I was called in, [but he had] poor health. I guess, a number four, failed number four, and so he didn't never get to go.

In the Army, I joined the Army, and I went to Fort Jackson, South Carolina, after leaving Camp Shelby, Mississippi. I went to Fort Jackson, South Carolina, and went through basic training there, we called it at that time, in the Army. Went through basic training, for thirteen weeks, and from there, I went to Fort Dix, New Jersey, and about right after Christmas, then I caught a ship.

For the first time in my life, I was seeing anything over a sailboat, and I went to North Africa, and Casablanca. We landed there after thirty-one days at sea. And I landed at Casablanca, North Africa. And I went on up with the Fifth Army, the Army Air Corps, 15th Air Corps, I was attached to. And I went down into Barbados, off Africa, stayed there for about twelve months or so. Then we left and went up into Italy, and we went to France, and we went to Germany, then back to Italy. Then I was discharged to come back to, and come back to be in [civilian] life. Tried to be in [civilian] life, that didn't work, and then I went, that's when I joined the Marine Corps.

Paul Holtsclaw I'm from Statesville, North Carolina, and my family is the Holtsclaw family. And when I came into the Marines, I was working out of Sedalia, North Carolina. That is the school where I taught. And I just thought it would be nice to come into the Marines, so I went to Salisbury, North Carolina, and joined the Marines. And when I joined the Marines, they sent us back to our home place in December. And then I went into the service in January of '43. Well, the family Holtsclaw, my father was a Spanish-American War veteran. He fought with Teddy Roosevelt. And his name was William Green Holtsclaw. And mother's name was Emma Bessie Holtsclaw. Her original name was Allison and was from a family of Indians. And we were always taught to do the right thing and to obey God and keep his Commandments, and I just thought it would be nice that I go into the service because I've always had a feeling of loyalty to my country and duty to God, duty to country and duty to self.

Oliver Lumpkin I didn't join the Marines. The Marines selected me. I was in line, being examined, and they had our records following us. And when I was going down the line, fellow reached over and says, you come with me. And he pulled me out, and I stood there. And the rest of the fellows that we came together with, they went on. And I didn't see them anymore until I got back home. I went to Macon [Georgia] the next day and was inducted in the Marine Corps.

Reuben McNair I really didn't really have a background of how many black Marines was there [in the Corps], but I did know that, apparently, there wasn't too many in the Marine Corps. Even at that rate, I still selected Marines over the Navy. And knowing that this was the beginning, which they led me to think, the beginning, and it should have been a great opportunity for me to start out as a youngster right out of high school. And I thought this would be a thing to do.

I'd taken a look around at what was going on. And I looked at the Navy uniform. I looked at the Marine uniform. I watched the marching and the things was going on. And I just selected the Marines. They just looked like a group of people that I wanted to be with.

The first black Marine out of the state had returned back and was in dress blues and I had an opportunity to meet this young fellow. And it was very impressive to me. And, for a memory now, I didn't enter the Marine Corps until February the 17th, 1944. So, there was a couple [of black] people there before me. So, the opportunity to have some idea that there were someone else there of African American descent was [important], I had an opportunity to know about that.

Walter Maddox I volunteered for the Corps in December of 1942. Which is quite a story, as far as I'm concerned. I'm a native of St Louis. I grew up with a bunch of guys, we used to call ourselves. We grew up in the American Legion Complex [in a] drum and bugle corps, [from] 1937 until I went into the Marine Corps. Incidentally, after I got out the Marine Corps, I went back into drum and bugle corps on the national level. We used to call ourselves the Big Five. We played, but we were not musicians, I think. And we were recruited by the Navy for the Navy band. However, Lafayette Demarco Travis Jackson III tried to enlist into the Tuskegee Airmen, and he was accepted. But they were moving at a slow pace, because they were building the facilities down in Tuskegee. So he got mad at the Tuskegee Airmen, and was gonna take it out on them and join the Marine Corps.

That's what started. So he naturally, the rest of us followed him into Marine Corps. I was seventeen years old in '42. In '43 I would have been eighteen and been eligible for the selective service draft. Fortunately, they had the draftees down here at Jefferson Barracks. What do you call it, the national cemetery, which is a well-known place, an historical place, it was created during the Civil War and so forth.

Anyway, those guys were coming into St. Louis on leave, recruiting, looking like, what's this Army character? Uh, something like Beetle Bailey. [Their] Dress wasn't fitted, and so forth, because they would outfit them as fast as they could. And I just didn't want to look like that. So that's when I went on and joined, volunteered for the Marine Corps in December '42. However, I was fortunate, since I had joined the Marine Corps in '42, I went in there, see, I was sworn in as a Marine Corps reserve, USMCR. I still have my dog tag. The recruiting sergeant said that they're still making a place for us down at Camp Lejeune, and therefore, go on back to high school, and they'd let me know. They'll call me when they have a place reserved. Well, this lasted until May of 1943 before I reported down to Camp Lejeune.

My father was in the last two months of World War [I]. My mother, she was dead set against me going in the military, and she wouldn't sign for me to join the Marine Corps. Well, we became aware of the Tuskegee Airmen, and I think just about every kid, since we were, I guess you'd say pro-military, 'cause we grew up in the American Legion, in drum and bugle corps, we were well aware of marching maneuvers, as we know it now. Musicianship, and so forth. And we were just military orientated, not knowing that really military orientated from the American Legion. We joined then what they called the SAL, the Sons of the American Legion.

This is from World War I, and we, it was just something that we grew up knowing. And so when the time came for us to be threatened by being drafted, you know, when the draft took, we didn't wanna go into the Army, on account of the draftees to come down in the city, you know, on liberty. And that was just second nature for us. Wasn't no doubt about it, and we knew that. I'll tell you, when world war, we entered the World War II, I was in Boy Scouts, I was in Scout camp. And it was just something that [we] knew was gonna happen to us. I don't believe in predestination, but. It was a matter of choice. But our first choice by our so-called leader was the Tuskegee Airmen. He was accepted, but he was delayed and he got mad at the Tuskegee Airmen. Gonna take it out on them and join the Marine Corps, which he did.

Archibald Mosley That was back in those days when Tom Mix and Buck Jones and Hopalong Cassidy was one of my favorite cowboys. And they had what's known as serials, every Saturday. And you'd wanna go back and see what happened in that serial. Because where it would end the previous Saturday, he [the cowboy] was in the stagecoach and it went off a cliff. And you wanted to know did he die, or what happened in that cliff. You'd still pay that dime to go back to see what happened the next Saturday. You would go back and find out that he wasn't in the stagecoach when it went off the cliff. He fell out of the stagecoach just before it went over the cliff. Now this was a double feature; you got to see two pictures for that dime, up until twelve years of age. And when you got over twelve, you had to pay 25¢. That was no problem, getting the dime or the quarter to go back.

And the double feature, the first part of the feature, you had to sit through a war picture, where you saw Marines. And I was a fanatic about cowboys. I had to sit through these war pictures to see my cowboy show. And I saw these uniforms. And I fell in love with those uniforms. And I told my two buddies, I said, look, man, don't you think that a black man would look good in those Marine Corps uniforms? Just look how it looks. It's got some red in it, it's got some blue. It, it's just beautiful. And so, actually, three of us from Carbondale, Illinois, ended up in the Marine Corps.

Joseph Myers My brother got a call. My brother William went to see this movie *The Fighting Devil Dogs* with John Wayne. And that's when we decided that we want to go in the Marines, we wanted to be Marines. See, I had applied for Officer Candidate School. And I also applied for admission into the 92nd, you know, the Tuskegee Airmen, in other words.

See, I'd applied for admission there. And they were so long in granting me that. And grabbed the guy in behind us. So, me and Steve, we went to see this picture *The Fighting Devil Dogs*. And we decided then that we were going in the Marine Corps. Not knowing that they didn't have no Negroes in the Marine Corps. But when we went down there, and the guy, the gunnery sergeant said, You are going in the Marine Corps?

I said, yeah. [He said,] You know what, you don't want to go there. That's the first to fight, first to fight and first to die. And I said, I don't mind dying. I said, people dying in the streets. I would rather die, I said, but I am going to take a whole lot of them with me. See? So, we were inducted into the Marine Corps in Chicago. And I was shipped to Jacksonville, North Carolina, to do my basic training.

Norman Payne And at that time I was in high school, and shortly after that, my father died. My thinking always has been, you know, if someone asks me about my life, and my lifestyle, and my education, and things like that, I think I always say this. Do you understand the time and period in which I lived? Normally when I talk to someone that's younger than I am, and I'm talking to them, they can't totally grasp what it was. Because they're living in a different time zone than I was in. When I say time zone, I mean this: lifestyle was different; society was different. So what may have affected me and the way I think, and the way I thought at that time is totally different, perhaps of someone, same age, in a different period of time.

So the war came and all. And I think my first thing was that, where do I fit in, okay? Didn't bother me, up until the time that my father died. My father died in 1941. So that put me more or less on my own, totally on my own. And when you're on your own, at least for me, at that time, being fifteen years old, it was kind of scary, you know? I wasn't so much concerned with how I was going to live, but I think what [it] was I had broken up in my life was a family tie, you know?

And I think that's what was frightening to me. I think the next thing I did, in the next two years, was march down and say, well, I think I'll enlist in the service, okay? And I'm often asked, why did I want to be a Marine? I didn't want to be a Marine. I never even knew anything about the Marine Corps. I had been in the ROTC. I liked it very much. And I wanted to join the Army.

I accidentally got into the Marine Corps. And up until the day I got out,

I didn't like the Marine Corps. I didn't like the Marine Corps. I didn't like the experience I had in the Marine Corps. But there were two sides to it. Number one, I think having grown up without the benefit of and discipline of parents, anything I learned in the Marine Corps, I already knew, and it was repetition, as far as I was concerned. And I think at that time, I think I was one of the worst you ever wanted to see, you know?

George Taylor I was drafted. I didn't volunteer. I was drafted. And when I got drafted, they was gonna put me in the Army. And I asked them, I wanna get in the cavalry. And they say, you couldn't get in the cavalry because the cavalry's being cut out. And so, I says, well, the Army. He says, yes. So I go down the line. The guys says, no, Navy for you. I says, no, I'm not going in no Navy. He said, let's get out of here, in Navy.

I says, no. I'm not going in the Navy. Where you wanna go? I said, the cavalry. He said, the cavalry's being cut out. I said, get me in the Army. He said, no, no. Navy. I said, no. Send me to jail. Call the police, 'cause I'm not going in the Navy. Then a guy came out of the office and he looked my papers over. What did he tell you?, [he asked me.] I said, change your voice on me, I said, 'cause I'm not going in the Navy.

Then this lieutenant came out, with the bars on. Had a cigarette in his hand; he takes it out of his mouth. And he picks up the paper, and put one hand in his pocket. And looks at me; he looks at the paper. I said, you don't have to give me the double look. I'm the same guy you looked at when you came out of that back room there.

I says, and I'm not going in the Navy. And then he said, what about the Marines? I said, Marines, what's that? He showed me a picture up on the wall. He said, you got a choice between the Navy and the Marines. So I taken the Marines. And then they put me in charge of eight guys. And every one of them was bigger than I.

Johnnie Thompkins It was quite an accident that I got into the Marine Corps. I had usually, from '44 to '46, I usually went to Detroit to work during the summer months. And for some reason in '46 I decided I wasn't gonna do anything but party. And, I didn't have any money to go back [to college] my second year, but I always, I thought about it that I was gonna join the Coast Guard. That's where I wanted to go, and it ended up that I went up to the post office, I talked with the guy, I guess in May, about joining. [Later] went up there and the guy was standing at the door, I say, where is the Coast

Guard, [to] the Marine standing there, you know? He said, oh, they moved to Norfolk, their headquarters in Norfolk now, say if you want to join, you have to go all the way to Norfolk.

I didn't have any money to go to Norfolk. But he said, let me talk with you, and he took me in this room and he showed me, he had all the uniforms up there, and he says, this is a great outfit, you know? And I say, yeah, I know. I said, but I've talked with a few Marines around here, and these guys are 6'3" and weighing about 180 pounds and nothing but solid muscles. Look at me; I'm a 115 pounds, you know, five foot five.

But, anyway, the recruiter asked me, say, now, how old are you? and I said, I'm eighteen. He said, oh, no, no, now, come on now, you can't waste my time. I cannot send you down there, you know, and say you [haven't] got any proof; how about a birth certificate? I don't have no birth certificate. So, he says, can I talk with your mother? Yeah. He put me in the car and took me over to talk with my mother.

My mother said yeah, that's his birthday, December the 12th, 1927. He said, yeah, but he look like he's about thirteen or fourteen years old. [He] said, I'm not gonna take that [to the Marine Corps.] Do you have any, do you have a birth certificate? She said, no sir; he was born in South Carolina, and I've never gotten one. So, he said, well, what about college, the records in the public schools? [Mother] Said yeah.

So, he went down to public school and checked, and sure, when I first went into first grade and all that in it, my birthday was still December the 12th, 1927. He still didn't believe me, and he took me over to the college, and he checked my records over there, same date. So, he said, well, I don't know, he said, but I'm gonna have to take a chance. [He] said, but, you know you'll get in trouble if you're not eighteen. So it ended up that my mother was crying and all and didn't want to sign them [the papers].

And every time I talked about it, my mother passed and I just, I don't know, I've just been upset every since, you know. As it all ended up, though, she signed the papers and they took me off that day to Charlotte, North Carolina. But, I found out after I came back home that my father came home and said, where is June? She said, well, he joined the Marine Corps today. He joined who? The Marine Corps, and so he says, you know that boy, you know, he's not gonna do anything, he's not gonna make out like that. Well, she said, I signed it; he wanted to go.

And it all ended up, I went down to Charlotte, and lo and behold, I took a physical there, and then they took me over into South Carolina, and got another physical there, and I think he [the recruiter] went down to someplace there that you can go and check on births. So he must have found out that I was born in McCormick [South Carolina] and on 12 December '27. So, they brought me back and I stayed at the Y in Charlotte, they had a black Y there. So, that night, I don't know, there was a rough street there, people were yelling and screaming, ambulance running. I said, my God, what have I gotten into here?

And then, they put me on a bus the next morning from Charlotte and sent me to, and the guy had told, he kept telling me I was going to Jacksonville. I was under the impression I was going to Jacksonville, Florida. And I said, boy, it's good and warm down there, and all the beaches and all that, you know. So, it ends up that I get to Jacksonville, North Carolina.

James Wilson Well, I was born in Mississippi, a place called Utica, about thirty miles south of Jackson. And it was the posters that I saw, a Marine on the poster, and it said join the Marine Corps and see the world. And I thought, that's what I wanted to do. And I asked my father about it, talked with him about it and, of course, he sent me to my mother.

She said no, so I went on to school, and the following year I slipped away from school and went down to the recruiter and filled out the papers and took the physical and passed everything. And then I went back home and talked with them about it. And, I told them I had joined the Marine Corps. The Marine Corps gave me two weeks, and they told me I'd have to bring my father or mother, one of them had to sign, so I convinced the old man to do that.

And he did. And that was on November the 14th [1946], and I signed up but I didn't go back home after that. They sent us to Montford Point. And on the 16th, we got to Montford Point in Jacksonville late that evening, and Marines was there to meet us and put us on a little truck. Took us around to Montford Point. We called it Boonies back in the woods.

Most of the young men who came to Montford Point boarded a train to begin the journey that would take them into the service of their country. The rail lines funneled them to the East Coast, deep into the segregated South, to railway stations in such small eastern North Carolina towns as Wilmington and Rocky Mount. There they detrained to await a bus to carry them the final few miles to Jacksonville and Montford Point.

For those who lived in the South it was merely a journey through a segregated society they understood all too well. From childhood they had been taught the rules of segregation, written and unwritten, that governed every aspect of life in their native region. They understood, almost instinctively, the all-too-real perils of disobeying those rules. Some had dared to hope that becoming a Marine might earn them a measure of respect, some easing of segregation's restraints. They quickly saw their hopes disappointed as their train sped toward its destination. Rather than receiving increased respect for their patriotism, they were occasionally derided by whites for joining the Corps. Even in the service of their country, at every turn they encountered all the usual demeaning social requirements and expectations of the segregated society in which they lived.

For those raised north of the Mason-Dixon Line, the train ride into the segregated South seemed a surreal nightmare, delivering an abrupt, harsh introduction to the world of Jim Crow. Ironically, their journey proceeded normally until their trains reached Washington, D.C., the capitol of the nation they had pledged their lives to defend. At the Washington railway station they were forced to move to segregated coaches for their journey southward. They had heard stories from family members and friends about the degradation, violence, and fear that permeated the life of African Americans living in the South, but most had never experienced segregation. Some hoped that the stories they had heard about the brutal reality of the segregated South had been exaggerated. Whatever their secondhand understanding of segregation, their firsthand experiences with the system and the blatant racism upon which it rested soon extinguished their hopes. Instead, they saw their worst fears realized. It was a journey they would never forget.

Reuben McNair Well, there was quite a few things going on. Knowing that there was a war going and there was certain expectations. And growing up in the South, it was nothing unusual. You know, to travel, that I wasn't accustomed to. So, this was a thing that, you know, so far, it's riding, and being at certain areas of the bus or the train or whatsoever.

This was a thing that I was somewhat accustomed to. So, it wasn't something that come to me as a great surprise. The ride from Jackson [Mississippi] to Jacksonville to Fayetteville, North Carolina. It wasn't. I'm sure that this could've been a shocking thing for some of the fellows coming from the North to the South. Perhaps if I had grew up in Boston, Massachusetts, that area, and was used to an integrated neighborhood. Then you were coming from one area to another, then you would most certainly would have expected to remain in to that particular setting as you move south.

Herman Darden Jr. My parents were from Carolina, and I had traveled the southern route a number of times by train, or by auto, so actually, it was nothing strange, you know. I knew how the situation [was], I knew what to expect, and whatnot, and we knew what the situation was and so, we'd govern ourselves accordingly. In fact, if we were traveling, you had your little greasy bag there, or whatnot, and that was it.

Melvin Borden Anyway we, me and that guy, they put us on a train that night [in Birmingham, Alabama], the Dixieland Hummingbird. The other guy was a black guy, too. So, they said we need you in their quota or something, and I didn't know what they were talking about. And the black guy said, well I don't know why that white guy, why he got to pick on them but there was a quota, I think what they were looking for. And we got to Florence, South Carolina, we were messing around, there were some, you know, like, kids messing around, you know, train left us. Had all our ticket, our clothes, and everything on there. It said to be there [in] two hours. Before you knew it, we had messed around about three hours and the train was gone. So, we tried everywhere to try to, Red Cross, and the Navy Relief and everything, you know, that night we couldn't get anywhere. So, the guy told us at the recruiting station down there that the best thing you ought to do is, you ever heard of [Sergeant Edgar] Huff? [Huff was one of the first, most respected, and most feared black drill instructors at Montford Point.]

No, I ain't ever heard of no thing as Huff; who is Huff? Some buffalo or something? He said no. He said, you'll find out when you get there, if you get there.

So, we went down the road and started hitchhiking. So this guy was parked; he was tired. He said, well I'm going to Morehead City; he said, if y'all, you know if, if anyone of you can drive, and no one will have no license, well when I wake up you can go onto Morehead City if you want to go. We said, no sir, that's the wrong way. We didn't know where we was. You see, he had come right through there. So, the next day, the Red Cross put us on the train, give us a ticket. When we got to one [train station] with our clothes and everything in there. And then we caught the bus and come to Montford Point.

They had a separate place for the blacks on the train. And when we got to Wilmington, he put a separate place on the bus for blacks. Now he had another thing, they had a big sign up there said, do not get in front of white line. See, in other words, you couldn't get on the bus until all the whites got on the bus, see. And once all of them got on the bus, some of them were nice, and some of them when you walked by, some of them said, nigger don't you touch me. And that would kind of scare you but you had to go all the way back to the bus, go back.

Joseph Myers Well, we left, me and one other guy, there was two of us that were accepted. We left Chicago on a regular coach train. We had to sit in front of the train in the coach section right behind the diesel. And we went to Washington, D.C., getting transferred to another coach section. From there down to, not Jacksonville, not Raleigh. There is a little town up in Raleigh there that runs into Jacksonville. Jacksonville, the main connection between Jacksonville and the Atlantic Coast Line. See, we went down on Atlantic Coast Line. And a little Rocky Mount. What is the next one down there? Oh, there was no Wilson. Going, going, going south now.

We traveled in segregated cars. We are in front coach, right behind the diesel. But I was just used to that, because I worked on the railroad as a dining car waiter. Going down on the Ohio Railroad from Chicago, Illinois, to Birmingham, Alabama. And I was used to all the conditions as far as that's concerned, you see. As far as all the prejudice and stuff like that. So, when I went down to North Carolina, they put us in a coach car behind the diesel. I was used to that too. I remember one car of blacks. And the rest of the train was white. And we got to Wilson, [we] all cut out of the switches of the buses.

Joseph Carpenter I was put in charge with a group that went to Montford Point, designated to escort them to Montford Point. We were given meal tickets and, of course, a transportation request. And of course, this was my first time going south. I had gone to the northern part of Virginia, but I always went by car.

And this time I had to go on the train and of course it, and when you hit Washington, D.C., all of the blacks or African Americans were forced to get in the car right behind the coal car. If it had a base car, it'd be behind the base car. If it didn't have a base car, it's behind the coal car. So we were all in one car and we were going south and I had these meal tickets for the five [of] us to eat.

We wanted to eat up while we were traveling on the train, so I asked the conductor, you know, where could we eat? And he says, well, I'm sorry we don't have nothing for you. So [I] said, well don't you have a meal car around here? And he says, yes, but you all can't go there because that's back in the white section. So we decided to accept that and continue and we were going to Rocky Mount, was where we were to depart the train and catch a bus to go from Rocky Mount, North Carolina, into Jacksonville, North Carolina. Well, we decided that when we hit Rocky Mount we would stop and see if we could find something to eat.

And then, when the train pulled into Rocky Mount, the engine along with our car pulled way down the track. So we got off and all, and behind us were the coaches that all of the white passengers, and they in turn started into the train station and, not paying any attention to what we were doing, we were kind of following the crowd, until this big cop comes up to us and says, where the hell do you people think you're going? But he didn't say you people, he referred to us as niggers. He said, where are you going? And so we said, well, we're going in here to get something to eat. He says, well, you can't go in here, go around the side. So we weren't about to argue with him and I was a long ways from home, so it was too far to run back, so I decided I would do what he said do. So we did.

And when we got into the station there was a little narrow, for our part of the station where it said colored, there was a little narrow cart and, I don't know, maybe about eight feet wide, it could be ten feet wide and about twenty feet long. And at the end of the cart there was the sliding glass window.

So since I had all the meal tickets, I was kind of leading the group. So, we stood at the window waiting for the waitress to come over and, you know, to assist us. But she was talking to someone, some white fellow at the counter and looked over at us and ignored us and continued to talk. So, I thought maybe she just didn't recognize we were standing over there or that we wanted something. So naturally, I tapped on the window, not very hard 'cause I didn't want to upset anybody 'cause like I said, I was too far from home. So, she looked when I, after I tapped, she looked and then she turned away again.

So this time I knocked a little harder. So then she came over and said, what do you niggers want? So I said, well, you know, we wanted to get something to eat. And then after she put it that way, I decided, well, best that we don't bother to eat here. So I said, well, could you tell us where the bus station is 'cause we had to catch a Trailway Bus to go from Rocky Mount to Jacksonville, North Carolina.

So she told us where to go, so we went there and we thought we would get something to eat at the bus terminal. 'Cause we left D.C. about 7:00 in the morning and this could've been around, oh, around 3:00 or 4:00 in the afternoon. So, she told us where to go; we went to the bus station, and then we ran into the same problem.

So we weren't gonna go through the exercise again, so we decided, well, we'll forget this, we won't eat here and we'll wait 'til we get to Jacksonville and I'm sure we can find something to eat. So, at that time, Jacksonville was about four square blocks, and now, the bus pulled into the bus station, which is an old bus station, it's still there. And there's an apron, concrete apron, but when you stepped off the apron, you stepped off into sand. So, we wondered, where in the world are we going? So anyway, we looked at the bus station, we said, well, we won't bother to eat here either because we don't want to go through this. So we said when we got to the base, we'll get something to eat.

Charles Davenport First prejudice or discrimination that I suffered was at Rocky Mount, North Carolina. From Washington, D.C., to Rocky Mount, we were all over the train, and seated any place. And was in the diner, and things like that. But when we got to Rocky Mount, went in to see the station manager, and there were about eighty-six of us, coming down to the Marine Corps from the East Coast.

And we burst into the station. Well, it was about 2:00 in the morning, there was only one stationmaster there. I went to the window, and I called him buddy, and I said, I have to get my ticket straightened out, and, he asked me, who are you talking to, calling me buddy? And I told him, you. And he acted a little out of character; we got into quite a discussion and an argument, and the next thing we know, the police were there. And this man was wanting me to be arrested. He said I was rude to him, and so forth, and, when you're angry, a lot of words come out, we got into quite a discussion, and he refused to amend my ticket, and so forth, and the city police came into the station, and at that time I told him, I said you have no jurisdiction over me, because I'm a United States Marine.

So they followed that up with an Army MPs. They saw our orders, and the sergeant of the MPs ordered the stationmaster to correct my tickets. When we left the station and went out to the train, the train that had come into take us to Wilmington, North Carolina, was like a silver streak, all of the cars were made out of stainless steel. And they kept telling us, go up forward, go up forward.

And when we got up forward, the car we went into had wooden seats, it was one coach, and there was one small fan on each end of the coach. It was hot, it was dirty in there, and it was eighty-six of us men coming on the train at that time. Weren't seats enough for everybody. The conductor was very nasty over the train.

We had another argument at that location; they sent for MPs, and the MPs put the conductor in his place. This is bad enough that these people have to ride in this segregated car, and they're jammed in here like sardines, he said; you can at least be civil with them. So we rode on into Wilmington, North Carolina, then, when we segregated the car. And we realized then that we were in a different environment than what we were used to.

We had no problems going from Wilmington, North Carolina, to Jacksonville. Our bus driver was quite friendly, telling us about the base, and asking us where we were from, and we had a good time with the bus driver.

Gene Doughty Going down to North Carolina was another ballgame. When I saw signs showing, barring blacks entering certain stores, certain sectors of the town there, then I realized, hey, this does exist in the South. Especially when it comes to bathrooms, things of that nature. And certain cafes, where one could eat and couldn't eat, and had to resort to other places.

Some places, you didn't have at all. There were no openings, or no board-[ing houses], no restaurants or eateries. And just by good faith, we were able to meet people in the town, black people in town who accepted us and provided us with a good meal. And that's how I existed until I got into Montford Point camp.

As a nineteen-year-old, the sensitivity really was not instilled. That is to say, you know, I'd heard about it, you know? I guess maybe this is what I have to cope with. And a nineteen-year-[old] coping with something, well, that's a little far fetched there, because you really, you know, you would expect more anger than anything else there. But I sort of resorted to a calm view, a calm rapport. Um, accepting life as it is, understand? Whether I'm in North Carolina or whether in New York. Yes, and then the bitterness followed. The bitterness followed. But I learned to cope with that, also.

Roland Durden When you travel from New York to Washington, you travel on the Pennsylvania Railroad, and you could sit anywhere on the train. When you traveled south of the Mason-Dixon Line, which was south of Washington, you had to sit in the car behind the tender, and though there's, the windows were open, there was no air-condition[ing], so if you were in a khaki outfit or any kind of clothing, you were dirty by the time you got to, let's say Raleigh, North Carolina. As far as I know they were no different, they were all coaches at that time that I knew of. So, you sat in the regular seats, regular coach train. It was a passenger train when you travel on your own, it was a passenger train. Well, I'd been on a train as a kid going to Savannah, Georgia, but that was a segregated train, but I was a child so I wasn't well aware of the discrimination or the laws that we had at that time. But you learn when you're eighteen what law, segregation laws were like. Well, as far as being a black Marine, well, we were called Negroes at that time, you watched your step when you came out of the camp. You watched your step because of the MPs and also the regular police, policemen down there.

Leroy Mack Oh, that was something. We went across on a ferryboat to Jersey and we caught the train there. Well, there was a bunch, there were only four Afro-Americans going in the Marine Corps that day. There was myself, Oscar LeFlore Jr., and I can't think of the rest of them. I still got my original orders, I still have those.

Anyway, we got on the train and all the way down to Washington, oh, it was mixed up, we were having fun talking, what we're going to do and all the other people were talking about, they're going to Parris Island. And we said, no, we're going to Montford Point. Where the hell is that? Well, nobody knew and the furthest south I had ever been was Jersey City.

So when we got to Washington, the Pullman porter came back and he says, I'm sorry, but you're going to have to move. And they moved us to the back and everybody got all upset and, no, you can't, we're all going to the

Marine Corps. No, this is Washington, D.C., and you're crossing the Mason-Dixon Line, and so, everything is different here.

So that's when I really knew what segregation was about, because in, in New York, there was segregation all right, but it was hidden. So you didn't know anything about it. Then when the train stopped at Lumberton, North Carolina, and they put us off in the middle of the night and the four of us were sitting there at this bus station and the sheriff came. And he said, what are you boys doing? And we said, we're just waiting on the bus to take to Camp Lejeune. And he said, oh, you're gonna join the Serenes, huh? He said, I'll tell you what. Stay right here, don't wander around, just stay right here and the bus will come.

Well, sure enough, the bus did come, and there was nobody on the bus but the four of us, so we sat up front. We were talking to the bus driver and he was very amenable. But as you went down the highway, people would be standing on the highway with lamps and they'd flag the bus down. And the bus would stop and they got on. Well, when the white people started getting on, they sat on this side, on the right side of the bus; we sat on the left side, up front.

And then some people came and they said, you got to go to the back. And Joe Cruise, he was one of the others with us, he said, I'm not going to the back. You can't put me in the back, I'm on a public transportation. The man said, you see that sign back there, and they had a sign that says, blacks will occupy the seats from back to the front. And then some more people got on and a lady started whispering and she said, you better get back here. So, we finally got the message and we moved on back. Well, that was the first time I really saw racial prejudice at its peak. That stayed with us because when we got to Camp Lejeune, there was no transportation for us, we had to walk from the bus station downtown to Montford Point.

Norman Payne I was coming in as a civilian. So anyway, when we got to D.C., I think I was blowing up the nation's capital, you know? I think, when I say I was blowing up, you know, if you look at a youngster now, compared to my time, they may perhaps have been all over the world, okay? When I was born, we were three years into the Great Depression, okay?

That meant at that time, there's three-quarters of a million people out of work. And when you say out of work, that meant that there was no activity as you know it now, you know? Vacations and things like that, okay? So when you say nothing like that, you had a different tempo, a different way of thinking and travel was out of the question. So when I had the opportunity to, I had been on a train.

I had been to Springfield, Illinois, I'd been to Kansas City, and a couple more stops, but that was the total of everything they'd done. So the travel was not a premium like it is now, okay? So when we got to D.C., everything was segregated. That knocked me off my block, you know? You're in the nation's capital, you know, you can't go here, you can't go there, okay? So after we left, after the two-hour layover we left D.C. That's when they brought in what they called the Mason-Dixon Line, you know? We went down first class to Washington, D.C., and then when we got to Washington, D.C., you had to go into one coach. Okay, we had one total coach there, all right? I don't care how many people you had, that's all you had. So when we got into North Carolina, I think the hardest thing I ever had to adjust to was listening to Southern drawls, you know? The whole makeup of the South. I had come from a major city, you might say. I came up in a black community.

We were detrained in Washington, D.C.; you could see all the monuments, and you walk around, and we had a two-hour layover between trains. And I thought this was a wonderful sight, you know, very historic. And then we would go here, go there, and they would say, you couldn't come in. I think the older ones that I was with understood it far better than I did.

It wasn't that I didn't understand it; I couldn't relate to it. And when I said, I couldn't relate to it, I could not understand that here I am, part of the, soon to become part of the military, okay? And the federal government will not say, respect that uniform, and the person that's wearing it, okay? That, I had a hard time with. I had a hard time [with] that.

Steven Robinson   When I came in there were thirty Marines at the time I enlisted in Pittsburgh. I found out later that I was the second African American Marine to enlist from the city of Pittsburgh. There was one other fellow who enlisted from [Pittsburgh]. I was from what they call the Schilling Height District. And there was a man who enlisted from East Liberty; I believe his name was Charles Wilson. He enlisted before I did. He was the first.

I was the second from Pittsburgh. There may have been others from out surrounding areas such as Johnstown, but I was the second from Pittsburgh. Now the thirty that went in, there were twenty-nine whites and myself. My buddy was a white, young white Marine from Mount Levin, which was sort of a suburb of Pittsburgh, or rather, an upscale type of community. And he remembered me, and I didn't know him, but he remembered me from my,

I played football in high school. He remembered me from playing football at Schilling. We played there, a high school team and that was one of our tournaments in our city conference. He remembered me from there, and he asked me, he says, can I be your buddy? We'll be buddies, we'll hook up and connect up and we'll go to boot together. Well, I had no idea that I'd be separated from him in Rocky Mount, North Carolina. And I was sent to, we called it New River then and it later became Montford Point and, of course, now Camp Johnson. But he went to Parris Island [South Carolina] and I never saw him again.

Well, I'd have to say that it was the forerunner of the type of treatment that I received as an African American coming into the South. It was my first time. I'd never been south before in my life. My parents were southerners, but I, they never discussed it. They were born and raised in Atlanta, from middle-class background and stock, and I never knew anything. They never discussed the South around us kids. As a matter of fact, I don't know whether it was purposefully avoided or whether it just never came up. I recall that I'd never gone south before that, my sojourn down to Lejeune. And we got down and we were on a troop train. Troop train must have been about at least two miles long. And as far as I know, I never saw anybody on there that looked like me but me. The rest were white. We got to Rocky Mount, North Carolina, and I knew about Rocky Mount, North Carolina, because they had a rather outstanding bandleader by the name of Kay Kaiser, who was on the radio from Rocky Mount, North Carolina.

I detrained and they wouldn't let me walk from the coach up to the station. I had to walk, detrain out in the yard someplace, about a mile away from the station and walk, I think it was about 2:00 in the morning, walk along the tracks to the station. When I got to the station and the lights were on and I went in and sat down and put my duffel bag down. I knew that I had to catch a bus there.

I took my magazine out, I was reading a magazine when an African American man swept over; he was sweeping, and he swept over where I was and looked at me and said, you have to move to the other side. And I looked behind him and there was a police officer, who was looking at me in kind of a menacing sort of way. His attitude was sort of menacing when I think back in retrospect. And he didn't say anything. Just let the porter do the talking.

So I moved to the other side of the station. I thought he meant over because he wanted to sweep or mop so I moved over to another bench about ten or fifteen feet away. And maybe two or three minutes, he moved, swept over to me and says, I said you have to move, you have to go to the other side of the station out that door and around the side. So I went out the door and as I went out the door, something [said], look, look back and I looked back, I looked over at the station, at the entrance to the station, and I saw a sign. It had to be about three feet in width and maybe five feet in length and it says For White Only. Now, I heard about things like that. I don't know where. I couldn't point to the exact person that told me, that they had signs like that. This was the South, but I never experienced it. And that was the first time that the realization hit me that this was a different world. That these were different people. I had never seen anything like them. I went around to the side of the station and sure enough, they had a little room about, maybe, twelve by fourteen [feet] that African Americans were in. They were stacked in on top of one another. Had a little fourteen-, maybe twenty-watt bulb that you could barely see yourself around in the station there. Smell of urine. There were suitcases everywhere. Your eyes had to become accustomed to the dark. And then finally somebody said to me, I heard a voice say, hey, are you going into the Corps and I said, yes. He said, so am I. And I introduced myself and found that he was a fellow from New Jersey. There was another from Chicago. And I think the third was from Detroit. So we went in together and we stayed I think about the same platoon. We stayed in fairly close contact because of our meeting at the bus station there in Rocky Mount, North Carolina. But it was, it was sort of a devastating experience. It was, it was unreal. Absolutely unreal.

George Taylor I had all the guys' paper[s]; we was going to the camp. And I passed them all out to each one of them. I said, now, you go in if you want, that's your business. You gonna stay home or go wherever you wanna go. I got mine. And I'm going. I'm going and getting on the train.

Going down was sweet. Going down to, we got to Washington, D.C. Got to Washington, D.C., we had where we slept, and everything. The dining, where we ate. Got to Washington, D.C., they put us in a little straw coach. Little straw backs. Wasn't nothing in there. And I got to fussing about it. Because of what our papers said. And this old lady said, son, you're across the Mason-Dixon Line now. I said, that don't mean nothing. I'm with the government. She said, that don't mean a thing down here. I found out when I got down there, that didn't mean a thing, the government. See, the government taken us in, but the government didn't straighten out a lot of things that should have been straightened out. And so, I, being a northern boy, it was hard for me to accept a lot of that down South.

hile the construction of Camp Lejeune began in 1941, it was not until April 1942 that construction began at Montford Point, which was located on a small peninsula jutting out into the New River. Separated from Montford Point by a branch of the New River, the much larger Camp Lejeune extended southeastward to the Atlantic, providing miles of beach for amphibious landing training exercises.

The segregated camps shared the coastal environment of southeastern North Carolina. The land stretched inland from the Atlantic coast in an unrelentingly flat plain interlaced by brackish creeks flowing into the New River, which drained the region and emptied into the Atlantic south of Camp Lejeune. The region's porous, sandy soils supported forests of pine and scrub oak, beneath which spread a variety of rapidly growing indigenous shrubs such as wax myrtle, wild privet, and yaupon. An impressive array of clinging vines, including smilax, Virginia creeper, honeysuckle, red and yellow jessamine, and poison ivy made the forest almost impenetrable. The Carolina low country possessed every type of poisonous snake found in North America, including several varieties of both rattlesnakes and moccasins and the deadly coral snake. For much of the year, the air swarmed with insects, including mosquitoes, a tiny biting gnat called "no seeums" by the locals, and deer flies, whose bite could raise a welt the size of a quarter on exposed flesh.

The climate, too, could present formidable challenges. Summer, which often lasted, in effect, from early May until well into September, was oppressively hot and humid. Temperatures frequently hovered above 90° for weeks, and sometimes topped 100°. For the recruits unfortunate enough to arrive at Montford Point from June through August, boot camp proved an exceptionally harsh test of their physical endurance. Fall brought relief from the heat and humidity, but winter could see the thermometer drop to well below freezing, occasionally falling below 10°. After the winter cold, a brief

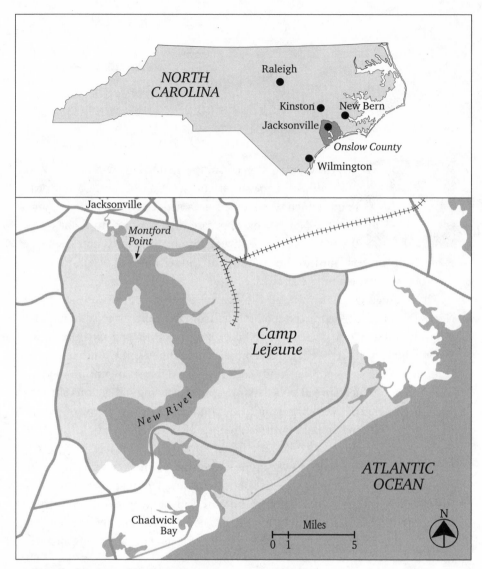

Montford Point and Surrounding Area

spring returned pleasant weather until the onset of the first summer heat
wave.

The first recruits to arrive at Montford Point in August 1942 marched into
a facility very much under construction. While some permanent, framed
wooden structures housed the officer corps and administrative offices, the
new recruits were assigned to "temporary" tentlike structures, which would
soon be replaced by barracks built of concrete blocks. Gradually the new

post began to take shape, with a complex of administrative buildings, mess halls, a chapel and theater, and buildings housing other services centered about the parade grounds and drill field.

Initially, all of Montford Point's officers, noncommissioned officers, and drill instructors were white, chosen for their service in the Philippines, Nicaragua, and the Caribbean, which was deemed to constitute experience with "colored" troops. Although the Corps remained committed to a segregationist policy, Colonel Samuel A. Woods, the first commander at Montford Point, demanded that the black recruits receive the same rigorous training as their white counterparts. The Corps also recognized the need to have African American drill instructors work directly with the recruits. By late 1943 the white staff had identified and trained recruits with leadership potential to replace the original drill instructors.

Boot camp demanded constant activity, and practically all movement, even going to the mess hall, was done on the double. Recruits performed a numbing variety of seemingly mindless activities designed to strip them of their individuality and mold them into a unit created to perform a specific task. Once recruits mastered the basics of Marine Corps discipline, they received instruction in hand-to-hand combat and the use of a bayonet, training on the rifle range, and plenty of close order drill. After recruits completed boot camp they were assigned to a unit that remained at Montford Point until it shipped out for duty overseas.

The Corps assembled the initial recruits trained at Montford Point into the 51st Defense Battalion. Designed to defend overseas bases, the Marine Defense Battalion consisted of units deploying 155 mm guns, 75 mm howitzers, and 90 mm antiaircraft guns; a special weapons group using 40 mm and 20 mm cannon and .50 caliber machine guns; a .30 caliber machine gun battery; a rifle company; and support batteries such as a searchlight battery. In December 1943, the Corps formed the 52nd Defense Battalion from 400 men taken from the ranks of the 51st.

Beginning in March 1943, however, the Corps increasingly began to organize troops trained at Montford Point into service units, either depot companies or ammunition companies. Fifty-one depot companies were organized between March 1943 and September 1947, the overwhelming majority during the World War II years. The Corps created twelve ammo companies, all between October 1943 and September 1944. While depot companies received minimal special training, ammo companies spent at least two months training with various types of ammunition, fuses, and detonators, in addition to practicing unloading ammunition during amphibious assaults on the nearby Atlantic beaches. The larger ammo companies, comprised of approximately 250 men, unlike the depot companies, were assigned and maintained their own fleet of jeeps, trucks, and trailers.

A close camaraderie developed among Montford Pointers, offsetting the constant segregation, rigorous training, and frequently harsh environment they endured. Even in boot camp, the men found time for a game of cards, conversation and cigarettes, or occasionally sharing mail from home. After graduating from boot camp, while awaiting permanent assignments Montford Pointers participated in pickup and organized sports contests, especially baseball, football, and basketball; performed in various musical groups; attended movies; and enjoyed considerably more personal leisure time for reading mail or writing letters back home. Always, the esprit de corps remained high, as the men understood that failure was not an option. They knew they had to prove themselves the equals of white Marines, both for their own sake and to ensure that African Americans after them would retain the opportunity to join the Corps. The men of Montford Point supported one another in their determination to become Marines and to be rewarded for their accomplishment.

Joseph Carpenter They put us in these huts and the next morning, incidentally, we had black DIs [drill instructors] at that time. There were still a few whites around, but basically, the black DIs were now taking over. We thought that would be good, but we found that worse than having the white DIs, 'cause they, the blacks, were determined to make us succeed and to be real Marines. And that was their main goal, was to be sure that we were gonna be better than everybody else.

Well, the next morning, you know, they get us out and they take us to one of the huts there. And, of course, we had to change, take our clothes off and package everything we wanted to send back home 'cause we had to give up everything we had. Even our watches, we had to send them home. Then they issued us a uniform, and they marched us to the Quarter Master barracks, and, of course, they fit us real quick. They slapped something on you, slapped a cap on your head and if it didn't fall off, it fit. And they threw jackets at us, and they kind of just size you up and they throw jackets at us. And later on they took us to chow and we got something, that's the first something to eat in a day and a half. Then we came back to the barracks and started recruit training with the DI, you know, called us out. He would call us. Well, the first morning, after we got our uniforms, I guess it was [the] second day, after we got our uniforms, he would call us out.

When he'd come out first off, he'd tell us, fall out, go back in. And then he'd call us out again. Soon as, we got to the point where we were just started taking the whole wall with us. Because all of us couldn't [get out of the door at once]. There was sixteen in the hut, and it's a small Quonset hut. They had four bunks on the ground level and then the upper bunks, four upper bunks on each side of it. And it had a narrow door; I guess the door was about wide enough for one person to get through, and he kept calling us and we weren't coming fast enough so we just started just tearing the wall out. I guess that's why they had those particular huts, 'cause they were easy to repair and they would just throw the wall up again.

Well, as far as the spirit is concerned, going through boot camp, I think most of the guys had a lot of high spirit. However, we had some problems with some of our DIS. We thought that they were, they worked us too hard, that they weren't fair with us. They were just fishing [harassing] us, and we thought that we weren't being treated properly. And it was unfortunate to a point because we [African Americans] didn't have any officers at all. We were all just enlisted, and the good thing about what we were doing is that we were fortunate, because if you were an African American and you enlisted in the Marine Corps, regardless of what your education, your training, your occupation was, you ended up there. So we had professors, we had lawyers, and people that had studied medicine, we had there. We had excellent leadership and that was a good thing, and those were the people that really kept us together because they were old enough and wise enough to guide us.

Ellis Cunningham And when we got to Montford Point, of course, I went into Building 100. That building is still standing there. Pull up in front of Building 100 and unload us again, and we fall in there, and that's about 3:30 in the morning. So they start processing. Everywhere you go, someone have to write up a three-by-five card on you and put certain information on there. The duty clerk, typewriter there, and it took us the better part of two hours to get these cards ready. All of [us] lined up in the hallway there, outside of the building, 3:30 in the morning, fix up a card on each one of us. And then we go over to what used to be called the receiving area. Or the new incoming, what you would call a receiving group.

And this was, you see pictures of the old recruit training area, was green huts, pressed cardboard huts, and I think those huts was equipped to hold about eight men each. You took off your clothing that you wore then, right then. They didn't wait 'til the morning at all. No, you took off your clothing right then. And . . . [we] put on a suit of utility, that had receiving group stenciled across the back. And these are the uniform outfits we used over and over and over, the incoming group would put them on, and wear them until we got ready to be elevated to another category.

And when you finished, you took them off, washed them, they had wash racks there, no washing machines, just a wash rack, with a scrub brush, and you washed those clothing that you took off, hang them on a line there. And when the evening came, someone took those clothes again and put them in the storage shed there. Whether they were dry or not, it didn't make any difference. And that's what we got. The people left the area the day before, just when we got there, they took off their clothing, and they were in the storage room there. They were washed and put on the line, and they didn't, of course, then they're not dry. But that didn't make any difference, that wasn't a concern either. You put [on] that uniform, wet or dry, fit or not, got into bed. And it was too late to get linen and blankets and stuff like that. You just step up on the bunk bed, we're gonna call you in a couple hours, anyhow.

So by 5:00, soon after, [they] pre-warned us that when you hear the calls for all extra men outside, that's you. You're the extra men now. So sure enough, we couldn't go to sleep anyhow, because it was miserable in there. All extra men outside. And that's when we got out there. And they start . . . [we had to] pick up any cigarette butt that may have got thrown out there. But you just raked there, and there wasn't a track left, anywhere, never a track, because you raked them out. It raked out everybody's track, and, then they line you up to go to chow.

Most places, I guess, they have a schedule to eat by. But we didn't have a schedule. At first, the mess hall be ready at 5:00, or 5:30, and each platoon would send a chow runner to the chow hall. They, the order to eat in, would be determined by these runners, so each one would run to get to the mess hall. And they didn't go inside the mess hall, you just lined up outside the door. And when the mess sergeant was ready, he came out and got the first guy in line, the first two guys in line, said, go back and get your platoon. And they would double time back to their platoon and be ready, and run the platoon to chow. That's where everybody would eat, the whole camp would eat that way, those people in training, not the permanent [personnel].

And we didn't stay in this category of this receiving [but] for a couple days. And they took us over, first they assigned us to a platoon or permanent platoon that you'd be training in, for boot camp. My platoon at this time was 364. That's the number of the platoon. And you'd be moved to another area. And the same day, just before you get to that new area, you're

Basic Training

Roger Smith, an African American photographer working for the Office of War Information, photographed members of the 51st Defense Battalion, the first combat unit formed at Montford Point, in training in March 1943. His images provide the best visual record of the training the men of Montford Point received. (Library of Congress)

Colonel Samuel Woods, the initial camp commander, inspects a platoon.

Practice on the drill field

Learning hand-to-hand combat skills

Instructors oversee a bayonet drill.

Running an obstacle course, rifles at the ready

Instructors grading Marines on the rifle range

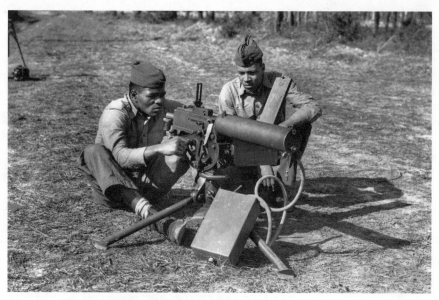

Learning to fire a .30 caliber machine gun

An antiaircraft gun crew

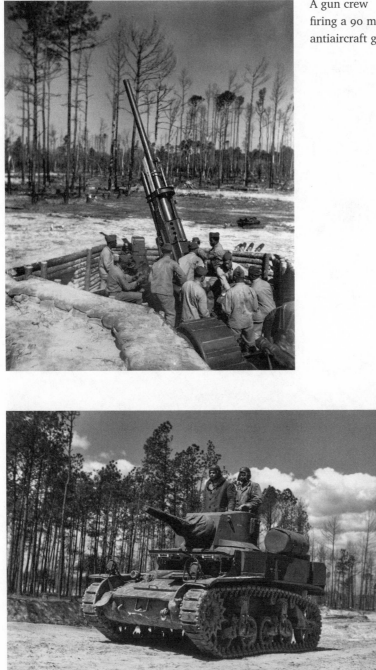

A gun crew
firing a 90 mm
antiaircraft gun

Operating a Stuart light tank, with a 37 mm gun.

A crew with the largest gun in the battalion arsenal, a 155 mm howitzer

The battalion's motor transport unit

issued all of the clothing that you'd need. The buckets that you need. Every-body got a bucket. I still have mine. You're issued, well the toilet articles first, then the gear. Including a rifle. And, then you're going to be assigned [a] hut, barracks where you're going to stay, we called the barracks. . . . And started to commence your training from there.

Melvin Borden Well, the first two weeks when I got there, I only feel sorry for the guy who was there 'cause I had come through enough of hard time, and trials and tribulations, it didn't bother me. And I thought, I was telling him, I said this will make a man out of you. I said, I think this is going to be very good for you 'cause I remember the first week we went on a hike. I carried a little kid for a while for a bar of candy. I like to eat. And I carried him. And he was behind the lines, so when the drill instructor find that out, that guy caught a punch for that. I just put him on my back, he just give out. We were going on a hike. And I just put him where I had packed, I just told him to climb on my back, I just put him on back. 'Cause I was used to hard work, I had, that's all I ever did in my life, see. So, there nothing they could do to bother me or hurt me or anything like that because I was used to running. I didn't have nothing, all I did was ran all the time. And you know, when you go to church in the country, your sister and them get a ride back in the car. I would run my way all the way behind the car. The car light, the taillight never got out of my sight. And I was used to that. So, it didn't bother me, training, anything didn't bother me.

What bothered me, I think the most important thing, what hurt me so bad, was this. We had some food or something, looked like, with [some-thing that caused] diarrhea or something, I don't know what it was. A guy, he messed on himself in the bathroom, and he washed his shorts out. But when he washed his shorts, you know, like they have Clorox to put in your shorts to get them clean. They didn't get them clean. So when, [Sergeant Edgar] Huff got his shorts that next morning. Sergeant Huff [a revered and feared DI], he got his shorts. He called all the two drill team and they told us all to fill up a bucket full of sand. And that's what made me fall out with him [Huff] from then on. I never didn't care too much because I figured [it] didn't have to be done. If the guy had ever did that on purpose, but we couldn't help what we ate. They tied him up against a tree and had us give him a sand bath. With that sand, do the wash, clean him up. So that's both-ered me and that sort of took a little bit from him [Huff] to me. I always feel that they [drill instructors] were great and I feel about the good instructor have to be hard. You can't be easy. You've got to be hard 'cause I say if I go into the battlefield I'm going to need some good training. But anyway, I was put in 9th Platoon and I got put back to the 11th Platoon. But I graduated with the 9th. Training wasn't nothing to me, I was used to just training, it didn't even bother me.

But anyway, the guy was crying that day. Got hot out there, we had been marching for about four hours, no water, no anything, nothing like that. So, I told him, I said look here, I'll tell you what I'll do. I say, I'm going to fall out and y'all came over to the dispenser, you could get some water. So I fell out and Huff say, take that boy that's at the dispenser, you know, see we won't let him die if you were wondering. So when we got behind the barrier, they put me down, you know, we talking.

So, I walked onto the dispenser, knowing that the dispenser, there was a private sitting on the step. I mistake a chief [officer] for a private, you know, the only way you can ever know, on one side [of the shirt sleeve], so the side facing upwards is bare, with nothing on it. So, he said, where you looking at going? I said, none of your damn business, what's it to you? And ever since then I caught hell. Running all the time. The other side [of the uniform] he was a chief. . . .

The most trouble was I wouldn't let them give me no shot [vaccination] 'cause wasn't nothing wrong with me. And I fought the shot, they give me one anyway. But I fought the shot. Wasn't nothing wrong with me. And they put me back to the 11th Platoon, came from the 9th to the 11th. But I just worked with recruiting thing, like that, see that they run and different things like that. But I graduated with my platoon and they graduated me with them.

A lot of them when I went through didn't make it. They hadn't had the experience of going through hard time, I don't think. And what you call, mama baby, they suffered a lot. And they worried a lot. When you in training like that, you can't complain how them people treat you because that go, you don't know how you going to be treated [if you complain]. So, I would tell them, I said the worser they treat you here the better off you will be. 'Cause I had been treated like that, and I had remembered, so it didn't bother me. But it bothered men, it bothered me too, you know. To see them, try to talk to them, try to encourage them and all.

Averitte Corley The training was very intensive. They gave you all phases of Marine Corps training. The same as all Marines got. The training and equipment and everything was equal, as far as I could see, with all Marines. They didn't spare anything on equipment and training. As I said, boot camp was very hard. Very harsh, at that time. But having prior military service, I was able to deal with it. Military is military.

Six by is a big truck, heavy duty truck. And with a Marine waiting in there [in the truck]. They used that as transportation to carry, there was five of us, to carry all five of us to Montford Point. When we got there, it was a hut, called Hut Number One. Where you got the word. You got the word, and here sits the big sergeant and two or three other Marines. And they gave you the word, what you would do and have you run everywhere you went. Everything, yes sir, no sir.

Actually, they were going to erase all civilian traits and things and make you a Marine. You're going to forget everything that you had learned in civilian life, and you're going to relearn; they retaught you about the Marine Corps. It was harsh because they, back then, the Marine Corps, if you forgot something they would impress you and impress you, there'd be some vicissitude. It'd be maybe a slap upside of the head or stamp on the toe or have you doing, maybe holding your hand out with an MI [rifle] on your hand for two hours. And things of this sort.

It wasn't to really be cruel; it was just to impress you on, make you not forget what they told you. And during that time, as I said, it was wartime, and they could only tell you once and if you didn't learn it then, they would make you learn it. We had excellent DIs. They weren't cruel. I'm not saying that. They just wanted you to learn and they only had a short time to teach you. And, because a lot of the units, they were sending units from Montford Point overseas every week. And we had to go through boot camp for twelve weeks. We had to qualify on the rifle range. This was, as I said, it was very intensive training.

Charles Davenport We realized we were in the South. We had heard from others that all of the white officers and the white noncommissioned officers that were training us, we heard that they signed a letter of intent, that they were desirous of being stationed and training black troops. And they treated us very fairly; they were tough as they could be, but they were fair, and we knew that something about the training that all Marines were getting.

Roland Durden Well, we had drill instructors who were, kept us on our toes. We marched a lot and we, of course, practiced all the other things, on the rifle range. We practiced how to fight judo style, how to use our bayonets, and all the duck-walking you could think of. As a youngster, I remember as a young man, it didn't bother me as much as it did the older men, thirty years old and thirty-four, whose muscles were sort of out of shape, I would say. I was in pretty decent shape since I did a lot of skating as a youngster.

Paul Hagan DI told me for at least a week, every night he would send me out to look for his shoes out in the woods. And, I go out, I couldn't find them, come back. I go out, I couldn't find them, come back. And so, finally, he stopped picking at me. It was rough. Oh, now, training, we had, I was trained real hard. Because we had what you called dungarees on. With a big pocket to put your poncho in when it was raining. And take it out. And they would fill that with sand and they would run us off into the pier, was a little pier there, and they run us off and get sand all wet and then run us around and around the parade field. And as for the infantry training, the only infantry training we had was hand-to-hand combat like that. Rest of the time we was drilling and thinking all the time. And that's the only training we had, combat, and all the rest of the time was, we were handling supplies and stuff.

They [the drill instructors] was all black, and I mean they were rough on us. I don't know, I guess the white must have told them how to do it, but they were really rough on us. And they was all black. We just had a hard time. I mean, they was really rough on us. But I thank God that we made it through boot camp. Well, in boot camp, being, like I said, it was hard on us. Any time our parents would send us boxes of food and stuff, they'd take it, open up, eat it right in front of us and wouldn't give us anything. They were so rough until, I don't know, they was real rough on us. And I mean, as far as I'm concerned, they treat us like dogs. Because back in that day, they allowed to hit on you, kick you, and everything. And that was happening right there in boot camp.

Archibald Mosley I said, well, I thought [I] was supposed to go to Camp Lejeune. And they explained, Camp Lejeune was for those other Marines. I said, what other Marines? Well, you aren't the right complexion to be a part of those other Marines. And here comes some people fussing and cussing with me and some of those other fellows. And I didn't like that. You know, you don't supposed to talk to me that way. But, you're in the Marine Corps now. And I didn't like it.

I made it through the day. And then that night, you put me in this hut. . . . I'm stuttering because I wanted to call it a barrack. It wasn't a barrack.

It was a hut. And time to go to bed, they blew the trumpet, lights go out and you're supposed to get in the bed. And the boys laughed at me. Because I got down on my knees and said, now I lay me down to sleep, I pray the Lord my soul to keep. Got into bed and start sniffing. And they laughed at me. Oh, we got a mama's boy. We got a mama's boy. I'll never forget that first night in Montford Point. Because here is a young boy who's being transformed in from a Sunday school boy and like they say, a mama's boy. Because I had trouble the first day I got there. Somebody cursing at me. 'Cause see if you said shoot in my day, Mama'd slap you in the mouth. And if you used anything stronger than shoot, she'd say, I gotta wash your mouth out, boy, with P[rocter] & G[amble] soap.

It's a great difference in a transformation from home to military life and military camp. But we made it through there. And that was another transformation from boot camp. Because what happened, after boot camp, you had to be placed in some place in the United States Marine Corps. Now, as I stated, when getting off that school-like bus, all of the people in charge were Caucasians. And, the transformation they wanted is that they wanted Afro-Americans to train Afro-Americans. And in picking them, I was glad and felt very fortunate to be picked as one of them. And one of the things that caused me to be picked, and I have to laugh about this, is because I didn't straighten them out. But when they pointed out here is one, here's a college boy. Now I hadn't matriculated too long in college. But I did, there in Carbondale is Southern Illinois University, did file for entry. But before I could finish one year of school, Uncle Sam called for my duties to get a degree in United States Marine Corps and major in fighting a World War II. As weapons instructor. Because out of 340 shots [during rifle practice], I hit the bull's-eye 330 times. So they said, well, this fellow ought to be able to be a good weapons instructor. And I was. I became a weapons instructor in the United States Marine Corps.

The majority of those in charge were white and Caucasian. But even when, as I stated a moment ago, [I was] chosen as a weapons instructor. I would say that when whites were in control of training and instruction and when we took over as weapons instructors and so forth, we [blacks] were worse on our own than the whites were on us when they were in charge. I think the whites realized that, well, now we don't want to act like we don't like blacks or that we are bigots or so forth.

Johnnie Thompkins Everything was on the double. You ran everywhere. I didn't have no leisure time in boot camp. Every time I look up, they were doing something new every day of the week. Seven days a week we were out there doing something, and then on Sundays, we would march us over to church and then bring us back. And I remember one day to break the monotony because we were cleaning up our rifles and all we had to be doing, so I'm shining shoes, and sometimes they fall us [out] and drill us on Sunday.

And the DI came in one day and said, hey, one Sunday say, I'll never forget, he said, we're going hunting today. I said, boy, good, that sound like a winner, you know, get a rifle, go out there, shoot some squirrels and rabbits and all like that. He said, yeah, I think I want rabbit today, and we went out there. And I think it had half of the camp. And what we would do, he'd say, break you off a good strong stick, and we broke off these sticks. He marched us out there, and we just took and surrounded the area, the platoon that's around there. And then beat on it, like they hunt in Africa for wild animals, you know? And these rabbits would come out, and we had to hit them with a stick, and guys were scared.

And we had one guy, the DI decided, I want squirrel. I got a taste for squirrel. And we went to the [tree], and we saw the squirrel up there. He told the boy, he said, go up there and get it. He said, now if you don't, if, when you come down if you don't have it I'm gonna kick your ass. And you know, that squirrel leaped to another limb, this boy leaped at the same time and had the squirrel and brought him down. And says, I got him, I got him. Then I said to myself, that DI didn't think that boy was gonna get that squirrel, but he got him up there. But that was the only leisure that we had.

[The spirit] was great among the boot camp because all, everybody in my platoon, we all helped each other. And there was some, you're gonna meet some people that are slow, you know, to catch on, and we would try to get them in the barracks there. And some guys, we had one guy, he definitely when he said, right face, he would go to the left. And they'd say, your other right, you know, your other left, and it end up like that. But it was great. We had about three guys in our platoon that flunked out, didn't make it. And I think some of them did it intentionally, even wetting the bed. This one boy would wet in the bed every night, and I think he knew that he, they probably was gonna let him go.

I think most of them was scared. After we come out they swore that they would, when they got boot camp, that when they went on liberty they was gonna kill the DI. Ends up that when we broke boot camp and went down on liberty, our first night of liberty, there I found the boys sitting around a table with the DI in the middle, and he had, we had beer all over the place.

They were all feeding him beer and buying him sandwiches. I said, you all supposed to kill that man there.

Walter Thompson Jr. Oh, it was a bad scene. Because when you got to the gate it was nothing there. [The gate] was handmade and rocks and bricks. And the bus turned around. And the flagpole was a skinned pine tree with the flags upon it. And, we didn't see nothing when we got off the bus. And the guy came got us. He was rough. He roughed us up a little bit there.

The first he'd say, I want all the whiskey. I want all the dice. I want all the knives and everything. And the guy [a recruit] went to open the little overnight bags and he [the drill instructor] went to kicking them. They weren't opening them fast enough. I said, this cat went out of his mind. Well, I had dressed in my zoot suit. I was suited down, baby. And when I got there I was suited out for the big pretty white hats, tall feather, and everything. And, like, he cocked his eye at me couple times. So, we marched on in. But marching wasn't nothing to me. Because I belonged to a drum corps. I know how to drill and all that stuff. So, that didn't bother me. And the way he did. And so, I walked on in. When we passed through the gate, he slapped me on the back of the head. That hat went all up and down when I put that case on. I carried a case all the time. The kids had made it big enough. He dusted it off and set it back upon my head. And we went on in. And, man, the world come to end. And then, after we got inside, that was the end of it, you know what I mean? I scrubbed the deck and every little cracks all night long with a toothbrush. And the rest of the guys, I guess they went to bed early.

I stayed. Right then, he changed guards on me, you know. I just took and scrubbed [with] that toothbrush. Well, that was the first real taste of the Marine Corps that I had, you know. That one broke in. Man, I had no bread, no nothing that night. And from then on it was run, run, run, run, run. And the suit that I wore, you know what I mean, the clothes. But they couldn't take that sand coming and running. The seams busted in the seat. Had to be on double all the time. And they let us run like that for about a week. The clothes were tore up. And they told us, [the] first uniform we got was wet. Dipped it in water. Come and put that on. And they issued you rest of the stuff, you know. The shoes and all that stuff. So, it was pretty rough.

Joseph Walker It was new to you; physically you had to run. They would not let us walk around the camp. If you wanted chow, you had to run. You'd come back from chow; you had to run. If you were going to the bathroom, you had to run. And of course you had some tricky guys who went in about two days before you did, and of course they try to throw the same thing on you the DIS threw on them. Such as hey boy go down there and get me a handful of sand out that ditch. You'd run down there and get it; now mind you they weren't instructors, but once you found out you tried it on them, too.

I was assigned to the 51st Defense Battalion. Now the 51st Battalion had an area of their own where they had their training. And that was Camp Knox, which was basically the artillery training area, and that's where I was assigned to the special weapons group. Camp Knox was adjacent [to Montford Point] across the little inland waterway, a footbridge, I don't know whether it was south or east, but it was back of Montford Point. In other words if you, if anybody's familiar with where the swimming pool was, or where it is in present time, it was in back of the swimming pool. Not into the water but back of the swimming pool, that particular area. Or out of the back gate; there wasn't a back gate there when we were there. A road leaving out, we had a footbridge, oh man that footbridge could tell you something, too. Some good things and bad things. . . .

Let me tell you exactly what happened to me. After I finished boot camp and got back from my furlough, they sent me over to 51st Defense Battalion. And then down into the bottom was where the special weapons group was. When I say special weapons group I mean we actually had training in all the small arms. The .45 [pistol], the Thompson's sub [machine gun]; when I say training on those small arms, we didn't fire them, but they had something for us to do during the time that we were waiting for the 52nd [Defense Battalion] to be formed. And we were over at the Montford Point area at that time, in the barracks.

We only had training with the MI rifle, which was boot camp. . . . And then of course the 30 mm antiaircraft gun, the .50 caliber, the 20 mm, all these are antiaircraft guns, were taught to us in the 51st Defense Battalion. Coast artillery we went on maneuvers in November of 1943, with the 51st, and that's where we got our training. We tried to observe everything that those guys did, all of the training they had to learn from them. Not knowing that we were gonna be left back in the one of the 400 [men] to help form the 52nd Defense Battalion, and that's basically what happened.

But we went on maneuvers; in fact, we were out in the Atlantic Ocean swimming in November. That was crazy, but we did it. The firing, you had to pay attention to something like that, especially 155 mm Coast Artillery, those guys had them, they fired them. And they put the target about ten

Camp Life

While at Montford Point in March 1943, photographer Roger Smith recorded scenes of camp life when the men of the 51st Defense Battalion were not involved in training. They reveal the close camaraderie that developed among the men. (Library of Congress)

Raw recruits arriving at Montford Point

New recruits trading civilian clothes for Marine Corps uniforms

Members of the 51st supplied office personnel while stationed at Montford Point.

The Montford Point library was used for both study and recreational reading.

Mess hall dining allowed little time for conversation.

The 51st had its own band, performing here as the flag is raised.

Organized musical groups included the battalion choir, shown here in practice.

The base chapel held services for Protestants, Catholics, and Jews.
In this photo, men are leaving a Sunday service.

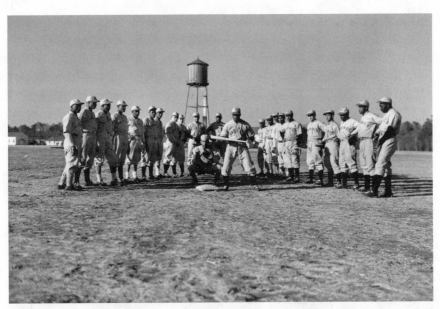

Baseball, basketball, and boxing helped fill the time until units shipped out to the Pacific. The 51st baseball team is pictured here.

Preparing to watch a movie at the base theater

Men of the 51st enjoying beers and music from a juke box

miles, nice white pretty sheet, triangular in shape. And you should see it dancing around.

In December of 1943 we found out that the 51st was gonna move out. They had a little trouble down in our particular area; there was a little firing going on and so forth, so they moved us up on the hill. They shelled until eventually the 51st left. And of course they moved us out from over there altogether, and this is where we held this special weapons training over at Montford Point itself.

Then when they formed the 52nd Defense Battalion, I was one of the 400 that helped form the 52nd. And I'm right back down that same hole [to the bottom in which the 51st had trained] with the special weapons group. And from there we took off for training, here comes some new guys. We train those guys. Here comes some more of them. We trained those guys. We would get to headquarters, motor transfer headquarters, with those guys and train them, basically, on motor transports.

Johnny Washington We got in cattle cars and went down in through the jungles to Montford Point. Where the hell start. Got in there one Sunday, about, I'd say about 3:00. And we got in there, they pulled off the cattle cars, and then put us in the barracks. And we stayed there for about half an hour, and they run us about three miles over to chow. We had strung out, it was about thirty of us strung out for about a mile. Double-time over at the chow. They [had] cold cuts. That's what they feeded us that Sunday evening. And we came back to the barracks, run all the way back to the barracks, which is taking about two hours before we got back and that together, and so forth. And we was issued linen, went down to the property room, they issued linens, so forth. The only time they issue you linen, they issue you MI rifles. So you had stood outside with your hands out, and you better not drop that rifle. You go to your knees, but you better not drop that rifle. And so you got your linen, learned how to make your rack up, whatever, all thing, this, that. This is something that I never did in my life. I used to make a bed at home, you know, but this is altogether different. They showed you how to make your rack and so forth, and military fold, and all of this. And that night, I couldn't sleep. Scared, and, I says, what the hecks am I in now? What did I do now?

Next day, which is Monday morning, we got up at 5:00, run to the chow. We got thirty-seven young civilians, didn't know how to march, didn't know your left from your right. You got to go in formation and run for chow, for the chow hall. You go in, get your tray, and you go through the line. And they throw your food on the tray. So you see, the last one out, you better not be the last one out.

So you just woof your food down, and got some drinks, and ready to run. So they run you back over to the barracks, which was about, it's about mile, two miles over to the mess hall to the barracks where we live at over in training. So we go back over there that morning. Then go to the head. The head was the bathroom, was up above, you had to go outside to go to the bathroom. Up to another building. After that, say about 7:00, 8:00, they put you in formation, they drove you over to the barber shop.

So I went over to the barber shop, all the hair cut off. Whoa, I said, Jesus, what is this? Then you go to PX [post exchange], and they give us PX gear, a bucket, water bucket, soap, everything. Then you go to the supply. They ask you what size shoe. You said just give me some shoes to wear. What size pants you wear? They'd get, throw the pants to you, jackets and everything, you know. So you got your toilet gear, all your PX rations, and the water bucket.

Then you got your seabag on your back. They're gonna drill you back over to the barracks. Go on to your barracks, well, you're stringing out for about two miles, before you get to the barracks. They get to the barracks, strip you off, take all the clothing from you, . . . take all the civilian clothes, you get military clothing, and everything. And you go back the next day, you get your hair, cut all that hair off you and everything, and more. You're ready. That's your life. That's what boot camps are.

Glenn White When I got to Montford Point, the MP at the gates stopped me and he said, what can I do for you son, you come to see your father or shine shoes? I said to be a Marine. And when I told him that I said because I was a Marine from then on, 'cause it was yes sir and no sir and no, not too many no sirs. I did exactly what they said and that was all. We didn't give them no back lip.

The first time I had been on a boat and it was out in the New River going to the rifle range, they'd taken us to the rifle range [by] water so we wouldn't know how to get back. And when we got out there I guess the Navy played a little game on them; they made it like the boat was sinking. And then we went on to the rifle range. When we got there that's where we were using live bullets then. Wasn't using no fake bullets, darts or nothing like that. We was using real stuff, put you away. And they go through a whole lot of safety precaution, and we were through that everything was fine. We learned how to get into position, of course. They would teach you; then if you didn't learn, you'd learn the hard way.

The hard way was they sat on your back and put you in position, but other than that, if you obey and listen you made out. You didn't obey, you didn't listen, you know what happens. It wasn't no one to say that you can't do this. You had to do everything, try to do everything they tell you or ask you. And they could see you just obeyed and listened and did the best you could and you made out.

I was a jack rabbit; not only me, all of us in that platoon. You had two platoons together. I was in 549, and 550 was our sister platoon. And so everywhere we went the two platoons would be together, we would either train or we went in the classroom to study notes, ask questions, we all was together. Now they say I don't know, I definitely see it in this handling, knocking around.

Now if you got a little sassy, well you expect that but as long as you act right. I didn't see nobody that got hit or did anything unless there was a reason. Well, if it was a reason, you soon would find out, because you was on the deck or wherever you was, they didn't play with you. They let you know that we [drill instructors] are not your mother and father. They didn't say I love you, but they said we could look out for you. As long as you don't look out for yourself, we're not gonna look out for you.

We talked to each other and we read each other's mail. When one Marine or one recruit got a letter and the other one didn't, they'd let him read. You know, it won't be his wife letter, but all their [other] letters.

Andrew Wiggins I believe all of the guys in my platoon were very enthusiastic and were determined to make it through. And I don't remember of any person in my platoon who did not actually participate and make it through all of the things that we needed to go through. Even Jackson, who was the oldest guy in the platoon; sometimes he was a little bit slower than us, but he took all of the training and completed it. And, even the times when we were up past ten, eleven o'clock at night marching and things like that. It was more or less taken in the spirit of, this is what we've got to do, and we're going to do it. Nothing is going to stop us, and this is the way we face the situation.

We only got the opportunities to go through the training with the bayonet course and the rifle course and the marching through boonies, and mostly we finished all of this. Everyone went home on seven days leave.

When we returned off of the seven days leave, we were kind of put in a holding camp to, for assignments to go different places.

Joseph Myers They would form what you'd call depot companies, which is work crews, and ammunition companies who would handle the ammunition. But you had to go to school in order to be in the company. To learn about how to handle different ammunition, brands of ammunition. And how to handle it. How to keep it from blowing up on you and everything, you know. For safety precautions and all that. You had to learn all of that. Had to learn about the fire patterns.

After I got out of boot camp, I went to NCO [noncommissioned officers] school. And at the NCO school I became a drill instructor. And I remained a drill instructor in the 51st Defense Battalion. I was a part of the 51st Defense Battalion and training recruits. And after were trained, then they form what you call the 52nd Defense Battalion. And the 51st Defense Battalion would go overseas. But I remained back in the States as a drill instructor to train more recruits.

mpoverished, relatively isolated, and completely segregated, Onslow County was representative of many rural southern counties in the 1940s. According to the 1940 census, it contained not a single urban area, defined as a community of a thousand people. Of the county's 17,939 residents, the majority, 13,077, were white. The 1940 census classified 13,603 of the county's residents as farmers, and land ownership patterns revealed the racism that pervaded the region. Whites owned 1,822 of the county's farms; blacks owned 366. Large numbers of both whites and blacks labored as tenants on tobacco and cotton farms. Others eked out a living in the timber industry, felling pines or working in the sawmills of the region, accounting for many of the only 275 persons classified in the census as wage earners. Many rural residents, black and white, supplemented their income, and their diets, with seafood harvested from the Atlantic and the county's numerous tidal bays and creeks. Although schools for whites were vastly superior to those for blacks, many white county residents as well as black were barely literate; the county's males averaged only 6.1 years of schooling, its females a slighter higher 6.9 years.

Jacksonville, the county seat, had a population of 873 people in 1940. The county bureaucracy that labored in the courthouse and the lawyers who represented the county's citizens in civil and criminal cases comprised much of the town's population, along with a few professionals—doctors, pharmacists, teachers—and shop owners who served them. Blacks survived as domestics, tradesmen, day laborers, and, of course, teachers in the public schools, where they received a salary much lower than that paid white teachers. The community's paved streets ended at the railroad tracks across which its black population lived, graphically illustrating the region's segregationist code.

While the construction of Camp Lejeune and Montford Point threatened to disrupt a centuries-old pattern of rural life, it promised undreamed-of prosperity for the county's residents, which most were eager to embrace.

What Montford Point did not threaten was the South's, and Onslow County's, dedication to segregation and the overt racism of the white population, the depth and intensity of which is hard to imagine in today's world. The doctrine of segregation governed every aspect of life—employment, schools, churches, hospitals, restaurants, theaters, and transportation. Legislation compelled blacks to drink from separate water fountains and in court to swear on separate Bibles. The mores and folkways of the white citizenry rigidly enforced those aspects of racial segregation not incorporated in the South's legal system.

No aspect of daily life was overlooked in the white South's relentless determination to keep the region's black residents in a subservient position. Whites sought to deny African Americans their essential dignity as human beings, even in the most routine and ordinary events of everyday life. Thus they refused to address blacks by the titles of Mr. or Mrs., forced them to use the back entry to white homes, and required them to sit in the back seat of private automobiles just as they were legally required to sit in the Jim Crow back seats of buses and trains. For those African Americans who dared challenge the system, the threat of the lynch mob still loomed as the ultimate means of enforcing the segregationist code. Enlistment in the armed forces provided no protection, even from the possibility of lynch mob violence.

Al Banker I was on a bus, going to Kinston, North Carolina, from Jacksonville. And the bus was loaded with Marines and a few civilians. And this Afro-American Marine was sitting in a seat on the bus, and this white lady who wanted to sit down, the Afro-American Marine being in the rear of the bus, where we all had to sit. The bus driver told the Marine he had to get up and give the lady the seat. And he refused. But then the bus driver had a few words, said a few words to this young Marine and went up to his front seat and came back with a wrench of some sort. Like he was going to hit the kid. And a few white Marines on the bus warned the bus driver not to touch the guy. Not to touch the Marine. Don't put your hands on him. That was one incident. There were many others but that was one that stood out, 'cause I really thought we was going to have more trouble at that time. And the Marine sat there. He did not move. And the bus driver drove off. The lady sat up in front, he [the driver] found a seat for her. That was one of them. There were many others.

Melvin Borden When I went into Jacksonville I didn't have no conflict with no white at all, because, well, we went down to the colored section.

We went down to the colored section, called the Little Dixie Cafe, and we were sitting there. I was with a guy named Wallace. And 'cause he feel he was a bad Marine he always liked to pull a knife on a person. So, three guys come in there, civilians, you know, and we were sitting on with these black guys, everything in there, black. So, the guy said something. So, this guy told him, none of your damn business, you know, and the girl was sitting there. I said, don't bother us, guy. We don't know what he is. So, he said, what you say, he told him, he pulled out a little gun, looked like it was that [a foot] long. And, see, we sat there and he talked, told that guy what he thought and beat him upside the head and told him everything he wanted to have, say, when I say scat I don't want to see nothing but the bottom of your feet. When that guy left there, he took off.

I was raised in segregation. I know what the punishment was when you violate them, see. And, this friend of mine, he talking about what he wasn't going to do. The police took him down to the station. And his head was full of it when he come back. You did what they told you to do. He said yeah, yeah, actually, you got to did what they told you to do.

Well, the general feeling was both they [black merchants in Jacksonville] were glad to see Marines come in, the merchandising and the people, 'cause that's where they made the money at. And they had these places where you could go and get sandwich and different thing like that. And, though, go meet a girl, they had a movie where you go upstairs and the white downstairs. See, as long as you abide by the regulation they had, see, you didn't have no problem.

And so you come out there, they had a place where you get on the bus, you go to the back of the bus and you sit down, whatever the bus driver tell you, that's what you do. But I never had any trouble out of no one in Jacksonville 'cause I never went to a place where they [blacks] didn't go.

Joseph Carpenter This is my first time being in the Deep South and I was fully aware of the Deep South, 'cause we've heard of all the lynchings. All this was in the papers in D.C., and I grew up in D.C., District of Columbia. I had read about the Ku Klux Klans and all that, and we were in the South, in North Carolina.

I wasn't too anxious to go out on the town on liberty because of my experience of getting down there. But a group of us got together. We decided that we would go and, as I said, Jacksonville was a very small place. It did have a railroad track and just on the other side of the railroad track, I guess there may have been a dozen African American families lived on the other side of the railroad track. But there were thousands of us, so you can imagine how that turned out. And so, and of course, we worried constantly about malarial diseases, this type of thing, not malarial, but, but venereal diseases and this type of thing. So that, that concerned me particularly, so I said, well, I don't want to [be] involved in that. So I then started going to the District, 'cause I lived in District of Columbia, so, and I could catch the train and get there if I could get out.

And that was the disappointing part, because we only had that one bus station that would get us out of Jacksonville and that was the Trailway Bus. When the Trailway Bus would fill up, they would have two lines, one for the whites and one for the African Americans. So they would fill up with the whites as far as they went in the bus, and then if any space left over, any seats left over, we were then allowed to get on there. So we'd maybe start at 4:00, they may not get out of Jacksonville 'til about midnight because of that situation, you know, it was, if it had enough whites to fill the bus, we couldn't get on it.

And then when we got to Rocky Mount, if you're catching the train, when we got to Rocky Mount, we would have to catch the train. And of course, there was only one car, one coach for us. Fort Bragg [an Army base] was just south of us, so on the weekend, Fort Bragg soldiers would just about fill up that [African American] car. So when they got to Rocky Mount there would, maybe one or two seats. And of course, they had MPs there to stop us from getting on. So what we would do because the black car was way forward anyway, we'd go down the track and wait 'til the train pull off. Then that time, when the train pull off, they had a platform that they laid over the steps and then they could close the door. So before, when the conductor laid the platform down over the steps, we would then toss our bags at him, which made him move and then we would jump on the train. And of course, the train is going as we got on it. So that's how we managed to get out of Rocky Mount.

Now, to catch the buses, we had the Trailway Bus could take you to Washington. But if you did that, when it, where it stopped, there was no place for us to eat. They would stop for the whites to go in. But we made out on that deal because we were able to go around the back, or they sent us around the back of the restaurant and that's where the cooks were, so they would fix us all kinds of sandwiches, charge us little or nothing for it. So, we made out as far as the meals were concerned. But it was just embarrassing.

We were what you would call typical Marines, one for all and all for one. And wherever we went, we were that way. After I'd been in for a couple of years, the white Marines had begun to accept us and support us. 'Cause what happened one day, I was coming back and I just wasn't thinking. I was coming back to camp and I came to Rocky Mount, and I got on the bus coming into Jacksonville. I sat down in the front just because at home, I would do it anyway and I just wasn't thinking. And, the driver said, move to the rear. And this, like I said, I don't know where my mind was, but anyway, it mustn't registered on me what he was saying. So he says, move to the rear. So finally a couple of white Marines spoke up and says, you, you drive this bus and get us to Jacksonville or else. So he kind of left me alone and then we went on in to Jacksonville. And then after I got off the bus it dawned on me, he was talking to me.

Averitte Corley Yes, Jacksonville, they had very little to offer. And, as I said, in J'ville they had every, all the black community was across the railroad tracks. They had one little USO [United Service Organizations] was part library and the USO. And they had two or three juke joints, two or three old taverns that you go to, but going downtown you can forget that. Because people would not accept you downtown.

I can remember on the buses going on liberty, this is after boot camp. If the bus was full of black Marines and a white Marine didn't have any place to sit, they would tell the black Marines to get off the bus and give him your seat. It was overt prejudice. And I couldn't understand that. And a lot of the times it embarrassed the white Marines 'cause a lot of those guys couldn't understand it either. You know. But that was the custom of segregation, was the law of the land back then. And you just dealt with it. You, if you rebelled, you're going to get in trouble, now.

Charles Davenport Well, liberty, we have to go to Jacksonville to take the bus. And the surrounding towns—Kinston, Morehead City, Beaufort, and Wilmington—we had to sit in the back of the bus. We resented that. And some of the cities around there, the Marine Corps would supply the K-6 truck. They had seats in the back. They would take us to some of the cities in the trucks, and so forth, so you had to go where the truck went. You had to be on the truck to come back, and when we got to the towns, this was a new experience for the people of North Carolina. And seeing that everybody hated us down there, except the black females. And I said, we figured that they were more attracted to the uniform than they were to us, you know?

But the black servicemen around there, sailors and soldiers, they hated us, because seeing the girls were swarming around us, the black civilians, the white civilians there, they showed contempt at the restaurants and so forth. If they served you, they're saying you have to go to the back door, and this and that, and the other. And so, usually we would eat supper at the base, go into town, catch a bus, go on a truck, and we wouldn't plan on eating anything else until we got back to the base. And it's on overnight pass on a weekend, we got a dorm or a hall or someplace like that. They have black hotels and black restaurants there, so we didn't have too much of a problem there, except in the city, the white taxicabs would not take us anyplace.

We had to ride in the black-owned taxis. The people at the bus stations though, they were as fair as they could be, considering the laws that the state had enacted at that time. But they tried to be civil. And since they had interstate and intrastate bus and train transportations going through the towns, they had the black restaurants, and the white on the other side, and so forth. And most of them tried to divide the service, according to how many people got off of the public conveyance. If there were more blacks at the station, and they would have more of the help to go over to this black side of the station, to take care of serving us. Or if it was more whites, they had more of the staff taking care of the white passengers. And this expedited their getting people served and so forth, and back on their conveyance, so that they could attend to their journey. But it was demeaning, and, it was something that we had to accept, and then every once in a while, there would be a minor incident of some sort, and we tried to put that behind us, too.

I got to know Raleigh pretty well. I liked the people in Raleigh. In fact, in the black neighborhood, they used to tell me I was the unofficial mayor of Raleigh, North Carolina, because I went there so often. One night, I was with a friend of mine that had originated from my home town. He was in the Marine Corps, too. And we got lost in Raleigh. We were trying to get back to the black hotel, where we were staying, and we saw this hotel, and we walked in to try to get directions. And it was a white hotel, and there was a lot of white men sitting in the lobby. I don't want to say a lot, but about eight or nine white men sitting in the lobby. It was about 1:30 in the morning, and we walked up to the desk clerk, and these men looked at us, and they started whispering. And they got up, and they started to walk over towards our direction.

The desk clerk was a young man who looked to be about thirty years old, and he put his hand up like that, and he said, no, no, no, no, like that. He said, gentlemen, may I help you? And I told him yes, and I told him that we were lost, and where we wanted to go. So he gave us directions. And we prepared to leave, and he said, may I ask you a question? I said, yes. He said, I see black men in green uniforms at Raleigh. He said, I happen to know that the ccc [Civilian Conservation Corps] wore green uniforms. He said, are you men with the cccs? Or are you Marines? And I said, told him, the difference. I said, on our collar, they have the globe and anchor. And on our caps, we have the globe and anchor. I said, when you see that, they're Marines. I said, I don't [know] what the insignia of the ccc wears, but they definitely don't wear the globe and anchor. I said, also, we only wore one chevron then, on the left sleeve, I said, if you see chevrons, and I said, in time you will, I said, but right now, we're all privates, but when you see a chevron on the green uniform, that also has that insignia, that we are Marines.

Lawrence Diggs In Jacksonville, North Carolina, . . . when you get on liberty, you got maybe three, four hundred men coming out of camp to get on these buses. And if there were white on the bus, they, if they had most of the seats, and you started in the back and you get up to where the whites were sitting, you were not supposed to sit forward in front of them. So we had asked some of the white people to move up, there was some vacant seats up there, you know. And some would and some wouldn't. And a discussion would ensue, I mean, and if they didn't want to move up, well, naturally, we wanted to sit down and if there was one or two people that said, now, you should move up and this, I mean, you know. So some people that was just hard hearted, they'd say, oh, you can sit in the back. White persons would call the police because, say we're gonna sit in front of him unless he gonna move, you understand what I mean? And I think he was just being defiant, that's what.

It happened once with me. And there was about six or seven Marines on the back there and they just moved him [the white person], just picked him up and took him on up front, I mean, up further, where we'd have some seats. And he called the police. The police got on the bus and one of the sergeants spoke up. He said, yeah, we moved him and you don't want us to sit in front of him, so we'll push him up further, you know, anyway. But the police sometime, he'd raise a lot of hell, but I don't think he took anybody off the bus. 'Cause if he took the sergeant, he had to take eight more Marines with him; he wasn't gonna go alone, you know. So, that was that.

And New Bern, I went to New Bern, I went to several different towns. I went to Wilmington. We'd sleep in the cemetery at night. When the uso closed, you know, you only get so many people in the USO. They maybe have forty, fifty beds. Whether you know it or not, nobody's coming out in the cemetery. I mean, people just don't come out there. So we knew that and, we just, you know, five, six guys just take them big overcoats, go out there and lay them down and lay on them, you know. We went in New Bern and, I mean, away from camp. I'm trying to think of some of them little towns. We went to Durham; we went up to Durham, and they had several all-women colleges out there in North Carolina and we'd go to those towns where they had a lot of females, you know.

Hulon Edwards When I finished training, I went into Jacksonville. Anytime I wanted to go, I went in there. I didn't visit that town that much, but I went into town and relaxed, went to USO, and to places like that. The USO was great. I thought that was the best thing that they had going at that time. USO, we had beautiful places to sit and write letters, and read books, and listen to the radio, and watch the little, whatever they had for entertainment there. Play table tennis, and pool, whatever; we had a good USO, I'd say. It was real, really fine.

I would say being in Jacksonville, North Carolina, and then the state of Mississippi, Mendenhall, my home town, or anywhere in the state, or anywhere where I used to travel, was about the same. I'd size them up about the same. It wasn't any difference in the way we had our liberty spots picked for us. And our areas where we went and ate, lunch or dinner, whatever, was about the same. I couldn't see no difference really, there, so, it wasn't that pleasant to go to town. I just kind of stayed in the barracks.

Right after boot camp, fresh off base memories I have, I met a friend of mine, I ran into him, and he was from the same hometown I was from. I met with him, and we started going on liberty together. He had a car, and we had a little bit more fun. And we would ride into Wilmington, and we had nice, pretty nice places to go. Here in Wilmington, North Carolina. I recall, over here, I used to live up here on 13th Street and Orange [Street], at about, oh, I'd say about three blocks away, they used to have a place over there, a nice little nightclub, a nice place to eat, and it was a great place to go. I thought it was the beaches, out on the beaches where we went for recreation to swim in, beach houses, and so forth. So I thought, I thought it was pretty nice there. I went to Seabreeze [a black seaside resort south of Wilmington]. Seabreeze, that comes to my mind, that's the name of the beach that we used to go to often, Seabreeze. I enjoyed it. I enjoyed Seabreeze, nice space. Good, good swimming, a lot of people there. All black, yes sir.

James Ferguson Most of the prejudice that we experienced was not on the Marine base, even though we were a black camp. Montford Point, where we went, was all black, commanded by whites. And that was our camp. Conditions weren't no problem with the camp, since we were all black, but segregation, hostility, the minute you left the camp and went to Jacksonville, that's when your problems started.

And black Marines, wherever you went in many cases you were unaccepted. I'll give you the perfect example of one black Marine was on liberty in a midwestern town; I don't know where it was. It might have been Chicago. He was arrested for impersonating a Marine. Many people were not aware of the fact that there were black Marines, and people looked on black Marines as some type of hostility, such as, who are you? We didn't know that you were in our Marine Corps. And when I got liberty after I got out of boot camp, I got liberty in Washington [D.C.]. I went down on the corner of Fourteenth and Constitution Avenue waiting for my girlfriend. I had on my dress blues, which I bought. And I had never received so many hate stares in my life of people looking at me in my dress blue uniform and wondering, how in the devil did this black man ever get to be a Marine. Because the word had not gotten around that there was such a thing as the black Marines. And so, wherever we went, it was the first time that people had ever seen us.

Paul Hagan Well, what we would do is we would have the buses out there [Montford Point] that picks us up and carry us on liberty, all night. Because there were no white, the only white out there was the officer of the day. And he come down from main side [Camp Lejeune] over there where we were and after we got on the bus to go on liberty, bus come back at 11:00. Went out there around 5:00. And due to the fact when we got in town everything was white, colored. Bathroom and everything. And you always had two MPs in town. One was black and one was white. And they had a railroad tracks with a train go by. The black was across the railroad track and the white, before you get to the railroad track. And they had a white and a black MP, so when the black go down across the track, he sent a white MP right on down there with him. We wasn't allowed to go down there where the white was. That's just how segregated it was. And the USO, all black, that's where we had to go to the USO and a couple of clubs, and maybe one barber there now. That's the way we went on liberty.

We went on the USO during that time. They had a little USO there and we all black and, and was small, so small that sometime we would have to sit on the outside. And across that track it was a dirt road. After we crossed the track it was a dirt road there. It was paved on the white side. Because before you get to the track they were paved, and then after you get to the track it was a dirt road, and so the white wouldn't come there. But the black and we sure didn't go across there because we had MPs at all times to keep us segregated. [At the USO] Marines just played cards and drunk sodas, and stuff like that. We play in the USO. But, wasn't no gambling there. We just played cards and stuff like that and didn't have no bands or nothing like that.

But we could go to, like I said, they had two bars there when I was there. And one was called Ash and the other one called the Savoy. We could go there and drink beer and stuff like that. No alcohol like whiskey. But we go there and we have a good time and really enjoy ourself.

Ruben Hines I encountered a lot of incidents, racial and nonracial, in Jacksonville. We were really restricted to a certain area in Jacksonville. And that was across from the railroad tracks, yes, all the way down to Kerr Street. Kerr Street was about three blocks long. And it wasn't paved. There was no pavement. Dusty. Juke joints, whiskey joints, liquor joints, restaurants, all those. Prostitution was rampant, and all of that. And that's where we spent our liberty on that street. We go off the street, we were considered out of bounds. And so, that's where we were confined to that area. As a matter of fact, if you were caught across the tracks going uptown, you were put in jail. White police, white MPs and black MPs. Black MPs would run you back across down the tracks. Not only arrest you, they would beat you up. I got my head knocked more than one occasion being out of bounds, so to speak. In other words, I was not across the tracks. I was walking to the bus station. Just walking. Especially after sundown. You, if you were black you better not go walking through town after dark. Unless you worked uptown. If you did, you were arrested. And most often than not beaten by the MPs or the white policemen.

[The USO was] a very small building. Wasn't too much bigger than the room that we are in now. I can't remember Louise's name [a girl who worked at the USO]. We had hopes this is, you know, people, young ladies, trying to keep the Marines company and so forth and so on. And we had one small USO. And it was all. Most times than that, we couldn't even get in it. Because that was the only recreational facility we had. But most times we just spent going from the liquor joint to the juke joint and drinking liquor and walking the streets all night long.

I do remember a man particularly. His name was Merlin Jones. Sounded like a woman. But he was a man. And we called him Bill Jones. He ran the

Ash Pool Room. He was an African American. He took a, it wasn't a genuine, interest in the Marines. It was money-oriented. He knew most of the business, or so-called businesses, if you will, fostered that existence on the income they could get off of a Marine. Really, just like it is now, but especially then. For example, you go in a store. Not a store. Cafes you want to call them. They was nothing but old bent-down, beat-down buildings and maybe a table and two chairs. You wanted a fish sandwich; you'd get a piece of fish fried, fried fish between two slices of bread. And he probably might charge you two dollars for it.

I remember coming home once, I was arrested for impersonating a Marine, because people didn't believe there were blacks in the Marine Corps.

Leroy Mack Kinston, New Bern. Didn't go to Raleigh, too far away, too far away. I was in the fire department and hours was forty-eight on, forty-eight off. So we could go into Jacksonville. At the railroad tracks, there was this big sign that said, out of bounds to all white military personnel. The street was paved, or tarp, black tarp, up to the railroad track. But once you crossed the railroad tracks, there was nothing but sand. And that's where we had to go. And I don't know, I think there was two clubs there, but it may have only been one. But anyway, that was the only place that we could go. Now, down by the river was the USO, that was for whites. It wasn't for us.

And Wilmington, all of the towns were in a span of fifty miles. Wilmington was fifty miles from Jacksonville, Kinston was fifty miles from Jacksonville and New Bern was fifty miles from Jacksonville. Well, Wilmington was a pretty good place. Camp Davis during World War II [an Army camp located just north of Wilmington] had a lot of black military personnel there. They came to Wilmington, you know; they kind of treated us with open arms. Kinston and in Wilmington there were much to do. You had a nursing school there [in Wilmington]. It was right behind the American Legion and so, you know, the ladies would stay out until 11:00. They had to be back at the school, but there were so many other places. Castle Street had all kinds of clubs on it. The main road by the projects that came in front, there were Johnny White's, was a big nightclub. All the bands would make that watermelon tour [black clubs in the South played by black musicians]. They'd come and bands like Buddy Johnson, Lucky Miller, and Dizzy Gillespie. First time I saw him was in a tobacco barn in Kinston. It was so cold, everybody wore overcoats and nobody danced.

Johnny White, he had a big club at Seabreeze, a place called Seabreeze. Every Fourth of July, people would come from busloads, there would be thousands of people and everything was there. Restaurants, hotels, bars, dance halls; they had a pier that went out into the ocean, and at the end of the pier was a big pavilion. And we'd go out there and dance and oh, it was something. Wilmington was a good spot.

Now, Kinston; Kinston was just as good. They had, I think one big club that everybody went to and everybody enjoyed that. Going to New Bern, that was hazardous because they didn't want us up there because the guy told me. He said, Mack, I just don't want to see you up here because you might be trying to take our ladies and I don't want you to get hurt. So I said, yeah, okay, fine. So I never did spend too much time in New Bern. As far as going anywhere else, no, there was nowhere else to go.

Archibald Mosley And my buddies, we waiting to catch a train or something to go somewhere. And we saw a drugstore across the street. And, you know, in Carolina, it is hot down there. We went over, we wanted to get some ice cream to cool off. Went in there and ordered some ice cream. And the young girl, lady, asked us what you want? We said we want some tutti-frutti. Now that's what you said back as teenage boys. Today the same ice cream exists, it's called White House ice cream nowadays, because it has fruit cut up in it, and it's nothing but vanilla with a lot of fruit, cherries and any kind of fruit you can think of in it. And she when she handed the ice cream cone with a double dip on it across the counter to us, it was chocolate ice cream.

And [I] slapped it out of her hand. And it went all over her and on, all over the counter, and on her. And she screamed, and the manager came out of the back and called the police. And some Navy fellows were around. And they heard her scream, want to come to her rescue, want to take it in hand. And it was just about to have a Civil War right there in Rocky Mount. But it just so happened Captain Harvey [a white officer at Montford Point] showed up.

And Captain Harvey wanted to know what's going on. We said, well, police gonna get these black Marines. Captain Harvey wanted to let them know, all of the officers in the Marine Corps at that time were all white. And Captain Harvey, of course. All commissioned officers were white. Then Captain Harvey said, these are my boys. And that's one time I didn't mind being called a boy. And he said, these are my boys and nobody in those uniforms, those uniforms don't go to jail. Those uniforms don't go to jail. And, come on, let's go, boys. And I was so glad to see him. And that's the pride of the Marine Corps, the pride of the Marine Corps. It does not go to jail.

Herman Nathaniel I was born in the South. So, I didn't have a problem with the segregation part of it. So, I don't have any specific thing. Because when I was off base, we were out to just to have fun. And we knew where we didn't have a problem. Because we were brought up in the South. At least I didn't have a problem. Being brought up in the South I knew where to go. And it didn't bother me that much the fact that it was segregated.

You know, I can imagine people from other places that might have a problem with it. But it wasn't a problem then, because I had lived all my life in a segregated society. So, the main thing I wanted when I got off base was to have fun. And I knew where to go to have fun. That's about it.

Norman Payne This incident happened in New Bern, North Carolina. That was an experience. When I say it was an experience, if you take in my age factor, and the fact that I'm a long ways from my society, everything was new to me, okay? Not only new, totally strange. I think the hardest adjustment I had to make, sum total of my experience in this respect, in North Carolina, was black people. I never knew at that time that I didn't know anything about black people. I didn't.

There was an incident that I was involved in. I was walking along, and there were two whites in front of me, and two black women coming from the opposite direction. And when they stopped, the white said, now don't you black bitches know you're supposed to get off the sidewalk when a white man pass?

So I said, what did you say? And he said, nigger, I wasn't talking to you. And I hit him, and I knocked the hell out of him, okay. And the next thing I know, the sheriff was there, and the townspeople were there, okay? And they took me to the little area away from that scene. And one fella said, I told you, this must be one of them fellas from up north, 'cause they ain't had the education that they supposed to be having. And that was ringing in my ear. And the guy said, boy, where are you from? And I said, I'm not a boy. So he pulled his pistol, and he stuck it to my head, and he said, boy, I'm gonna ask you one damn time, boy, where you from? I said, from Chicago. I told you. I told you that boy wasn't educated. He never been educated as to what he supposed to be doing. And a guy, he told me, he said, well nigger, I'm gonna give you one more chance. He said, if I ever catch you again I'm gonna blow your damn brains out, you got that boy? I said, yeah.

Okay, when that failed though, I went back to the black community. My chest was stuck out I say, I'm gonna go back there, I'm the hero, you know? And the black people said to me, why did you come down here causing trouble? That hit me in the face like a brick, okay? Well, one thing I didn't understand it, okay? And I said, what do you say? Well, what I didn't understand at the time was the fact that he was saying, that the northern blacks were more defiant than the southern blacks. So consequently, what went on the agenda was the fact that, I'm gonna have to teach all of you, and make an example of you, so you don't do the same thing, okay? I couldn't piece all this together, at one time. You know, it was rolling around my mind, okay? And I think the first thing that hit my mind was, well, I said, I don't know anything about my own people.

Steven Robinson Some things that happen to you, you say this really couldn't be happening to me for that reason, because of what I look like. Because I don't even know, I don't know these people. I never done anything to them. Why could they have this, this kind of rage? Why could they have this kind of attitude or nature toward me when I don't, and I don't feel that way? In other words, I don't feel that way against them? If anybody should have that feeling, that attitude, I should have it against them. Not them against me, because I never did anything, I never did anything to them. And I don't know why they should have that feeling against, me but they did.

Other experiences I had it's just, it's with me today. I shipped out of Jacksonville with a legal company. I was a platoon sergeant. I had the 1st Platoon in the 34th Depot that shipped out of Camp Lejeune. I think we shipped out around late '40, '43, maybe early '44, I can't recall now, on our way overseas. I went by troop train from Camp Lejeune to Camp Pendleton, California. We came to Arizona and it was one of those generic type Arizona days. It must have been about 110 in the shade. I saw a thermometer that said 110 was the temperature there. You really could see the heat waves come off the highway. We had a coal locomotive that was pulling the troop train that I was on. And we got there, we're taking on watering hole. I think it was Phoenix, Arizona, and some of the fellows saw a sign across the highway. It was a sign of a Coca-Cola being advertised. It was a huge Coke bottle, probably about eight or nine feet in length. And it was painted to illustrate that it was cold. You could see the cold sweat from the bottle.

And one of the fellows asked me, can I go over and get a Coke? I said, it will only be ten or fifteen minutes, so you go over and you come right back now 'cause, I'm not going to look for you. So they jumped off the wall, the train was elevated from the highway maybe about twelve feet above the highway, maybe less than that. They jumped off the elevation, ran across the highway, and I figured they'd probably be gone ten, fifteen minutes. I looked up and virtually they were back at the troop train. And so I said, I didn't see any Coke or anything. And I said to the first fellow that walked past me, I said, did you guys get your Coke? Did you get your Coke? And I don't know if he ever answered one way. I knew he was disturbed about something so I didn't say any more to him.

The second man that passed me, I said, did you get your Coke? His name was Jimmy, Jimmy Wilkins. Jimmy was probably seventeen. He had to be seventeen to have been in the Corps at that time. But he was a very youthful-looking seventeen; he was just a teenager. He was seventeen, but he looked about thirteen or fourteen. And whenever he told you anything, words just tumbled out of his mouth. He was just an exuberant teenager.

So finally Jimmy stopped me and said to me, he says, Sarge, they wouldn't sell us any Coke. And I said, what do you mean they wouldn't sell you any Coke? He said no, there was a sign on the door and the sign said no Indians, Mexicans, niggers, or dogs allowed. And if you seen the hurt in the boy's eyes, and he just shook his head and never said anything and just walked on. The other two men never said anything to me. They just walked past with their heads down. And I remember when, well because Jimmy was killed on Iwo Jima.

George Taylor Couldn't even get a hamburger in town, no place. It was horrible down there. Just like one of my sergeants stopped a black girl to find out where the restroom in the office was. And she told him. And he come out. The police had him go to the car. Rolled the window down. And made him [the sergeant] stick his hand in there. And rolled the window up on him. And beat him. Why? Because that was their girlfriend.

And we went to try to get a hamburger at a place. Couldn't get that. You in a bus station, over that sort of chain across, you on this side, they're [whites] on that side. And they never cleaned the [black] bathroom. You couldn't go into the concession. They [whites] got a stove there where they stay warm and everything. You had nothing over here. Just a cold place when you're waiting on the bus to come. Then you got to get in this back seat. And that's where you're at. And then if it's crowded, with whites, you had to stand up. But that's supposed to be my back seat back there.

Glenn White It was real, well you know what to expect so you did, you didn't have to be told. You didn't. After you got there and found out what you had to do, you act accordingly and everything was fine. You stood in line and nobody bothered you. They had a place they called USO. We used to go there, especially the younger Marines which wasn't used to going out staying late at night. So we liked to go to the places like that where we could have fun, shoot pool, play cards, write letters. And talk to each other, sometimes you'd meet some friends, some later friends. And it was pretty good. I was so shook up they told us so much about VD. So I was scared to talk to her, to speak to the young ladies. They all was black. The USO was all black at that time.

Wilmington, they had more recreation than Kinston, because Kinston didn't have too many, well they had blacks but it wasn't too many of them. Like Wilmington. Wilmington always and you could come they had ballgames, you could go to Kinston had ballgames, you came to see the Kinston, I think it was the Kinston Eagles, something like that, a baseball game. So it was like I say, if you obey and listen, kept your nose clean it was nice. 'Cause I wasn't used to running around staying out all the time at night. At 12:00 in D.C. if you didn't have a job you better not be caught on the street at 12:00 at night.

There they [girls at the USO] played cards with us, danced with us, they talked with us. Some of them, some of the young Marines went home with them, but I didn't. 'Cause I never did go home. I was too afraid of them to go. So I just stayed out, would go catch a bus and come back to Montford Point. I'd just come on back to Montford Point. But most of the time I went over to D.C. and like that, places like. I didn't have no trouble. I didn't give them no trouble, so I didn't have no trouble.

Joseph Carpenter When we were sent to Norfolk, we were stationed right opposite, or adjacent to, the Italian prisoners. Now they had freedom of the base, freedom of Norfolk city that we didn't have; and when we caught the bus to the train, we had to sit in the back. They could sit anywhere they wanted, and they were supposed to be our prisoners. They had a fence; they were in a fenced-in area, but the gate was wide open—there was no sentry or anything on the gate. Our barracks were right next to that fence. It was a chain-link fence, and our barracks were right next to that chain-link fence. And in that time, you know, the blacks were always held with a separate part of the camp. That's where they put us 'cause the whites were elsewhere on the base.

[Prisoners of war had] definitely more privileges. They could go anywhere in town they wanted; we could only go in the black section. And of course, as I said, on the train, they could ride in the back of the train or anywhere on the train they wanted, but we had to get in the car right behind the coal car or the baggage car, whichever one was there. And buses, they sat in front and we sat in the back.

Harry Hamilton When I was in the in the States, when I came home on leave, I was just observing the prisoners of war that were sent to a marker, and then we used them as working the farms and different areas. And that's what I couldn't understand too much, whereas they had the freedom to use the washrooms and the restaurants, whereas I, being a serviceman, I, we, couldn't go out to those places at that time. It was still the segregated South as far as black men were concerned. Well, it was from Germany and from Italy, the ones that was captured during the Second [World] War in the European theater. [I saw them] In Mississippi when I came to visit my family on leave from the Marine Corps. I observed whereas they could go into the restaurant and to the washrooms, it was for white only. But we could not use those facilities at that time, the black servicemen.

Steven Robinson It was fifty years ago. It was like yesterday and it hurts you. And there's not a day that passes that I don't think about some of those fellows that I left. And you say, why would you think, I don't know. I guess it's in my psyche, it's in my mind. I couldn't help it. You think I would suffer this if I could help it? No. I can't. If I could take a pill, to do away with the anger, if I could take a pill to do away with the hurt, I would. I'd get it. I'd get it in a heartbeat. But I can't, it's there.

And the thing that comes back to me and I explain, I explain to them all, coming back to Arizona, Phoenix, I was on a Pullman train and I saw these men, white men, tall blonde men in khaki, some were dark. And I found out, I asked a Pullman porter, who were those people? I didn't think they were Americans, but found out that they were German prisoners of war. They were Italian prisoners of war fraternizing with American white women, going into clubs and hotels and bars that they wouldn't serve us a Coke in. This happened in Arizona. Tucson, Arizona. And it disturbed me to such an extent, I wrote [Senator Barry] Goldwater. [He] ran for the presidency of this country, he wrote an article in *Time* a number of years ago that I couldn't let the man get away, but he was a senator from Arizona. And I called him. I guess he have must thought I was a fundraiser because he took my call and I told him about what I saw in Arizona, in Tucson, Arizona. And he said to me, he said, you know that was the way it was. . . .

And my brothers and sisters looked up to me. And when I went back to camp, they took it hard. So, I decided rather than wake them up, I'd leave because it was hard to see them cry and Dad had gone. I had a habit for some reason or another of taking my money out of my wallet and putting it up on the dresser. And then my brother Ralph next to me. We slept together. And I didn't want Ralph to know, because he'd always wake up and wake the other kids up, that I was leaving. So, I took my money out of my wallet and left it on the dresser and then turned the light on. I thought I got all my money off the top of the dresser. And lo and behold, I left a $20 bill there. I didn't know it till I got to Roanoke, Virginia. I didn't have any money to go from Roanoke back to Camp Lejeune

I went into the station, walked up to the counter. I asked a clerk there if they had, what they call, travelers's aid they call it. And he said, no, I never heard of travelers's aid. He kept looking at me. He was a white man, probably at that time maybe around fifty, maybe in his early fifties. Travelers's aid, he said, what's your problem? I said I don't have money to get back to the base. I said, I left my money at home and even if I called home and had my mother wire it, it won't get here in time for me to get a ticket to get back to base. And if you don't get back to base in the Corps bad things happen to you, if I don't get off of leave on time.

He said, so you need a ticket. I said, yes sir. I think a ticket from there, from Roanoke, Virginia, back to Camp Lejeune was about eight or nine dollars. It was a lot of money then. You got to remember this was 1942 or 3. And the man studied me, studied me for about, I thought, forever, but it couldn't have been more than a minute. Just looked me straight in the face, right in the, right in the, full-flushed in the eyes. He went in his pocket, came out with his wallet and put a ten dollar bill into the till. He gave me a ticket, wrote the ticket off and put the change from that ten dollar bill, 'cause the ticket was eight dollars and some, just, maybe change of one dollar and a dime back in his pocket. He said here's your ticket. Now, you get, your train will be leaving in just a minute or so, so get through the gate and catch, and make sure you don't get left behind.

I said, well give me your name, I want to send the money back. Sir, I have the money. He said, no, just get to the gate and get on your train. I turned around, I walked through, I was walking away from him, I guess I got about ten or fifteen feet from him or maybe a little more. He said, just a minute, come here. I turned around and went back to him. And he went in his pocket, I guess the same wallet, took out two dollars and he handed to me. He said, you're going to need to eat on your way back.

Now, he was a southerner. He didn't know me from Adam. I never saw the man before. But from bad thoughts that run through my mind about southerners as a group, as a race, I thought about that man who didn't know me from Adam. But he knew enough to know that I'd be court-martialed had I not got back to my unit. Never will forget it. Can't.

t was not just in the South that Montford Point Marines and all African Americans faced racial discrimination; segregation reflected the racial attitudes and beliefs of the entire nation's white population. For the entire time black recruits trained at Montford Point, segregation was the official policy of the Corps, and it was the law of the United States. American armed forces remained segregated after World War II, until July 26, 1948, when President Harry Truman signed Executive Order 9981, finally ending segregation within the military. The implementation of Truman's executive order proceeded gradually, however. The deactivation of Montford Point as a segregated training facility occurred on September 9, 1949. Thereafter all black Marine recruits trained at integrated facilities. Segregated black units remained in the Corps, however, well into the Korean War. Segregation also existed throughout the South, despite the Supreme Court's 1954 ruling that segregated public schools were unconstitutional, which did little to disturb the daily routine of life in the segregated South. Elsewhere in the nation, especially in major urban areas, restrictive housing practices and employment discrimination continued to be common, forcing large segments of the African American population into segregated communities and lives of economic hardship.

After the Korean War the African American Marines who remained in the Corps, and later black recruits, found themselves serving in a fully integrated Marine Corps. When stationed in the South, however, once off base they continued to be forced to abide by segregationist state laws and face the racial prejudice of a white society still devoted to the doctrine of white supremacy. That situation existed well into the time of the Vietnam conflict, coming to an end only when African American citizens took their campaign for equality into the streets of the South's major cities. The 1963 march on Washington, in many ways the fulfillment of the planned march on Washington of 1941 that led to the establishment of Montford Point, and other struggles of the civil rights movement eventually led to the passage of the

1964 Civil Rights Act. This historic legislation, signed into law by President Lyndon Johnson as Marines trained at Montford Point carried out their duty on the battlefields of Vietnam, finally outlawed segregation in the United States.

Gene Doughty At the outset of Montford Point camp, when it was first established, quite obviously we didn't have black drill instructors. What headquarters Marine Corps sent it [Montford Point] to do was to get the most seasoned, most polished veterans in the Marine Corps, particularly those who had served in the earlier Guadalcanal campaign. And that was around November, '41. They were chosen to be drill instructors, because of their background, and I might add, most of these guys were from the South. Most of these guys were from Mississippi and Georgia. There were a few who really didn't want us in the Marine Corps, quite obviously, very angry about allowing us black folk to enter into the Marine Corps, the most elite, most prestigious unit. Kind of bothered them a little bit. They just didn't want us.

Now, I'm not saying the overwhelming majority. I would say there were just a few, understand, who just didn't want [blacks]. They really did not concern themselves with turning out an elite bunch of guys. Instead, they would rather see you walk out the door and never come back. So that was the attitude of the drill instructors. That made me bitter. That made me bitter. Because now, you know, what I'd looked at when I looked at the Marine Corps as a prestigious unit, you know, hey, loyalty and all that sort of thing, nonbiased.

And then to come down there and be part of this kind of response, social response, just didn't fit too well with me. There were times when I might have left. And that's exactly what they wanted. They would rather see us leave any time. But that kind of dissuasion, I had to meet with that, because, hey, I'm down here. And this is a challenge. With the help of some other peoples, my brothers, my buddies. Other people says, look, hey, we're down here for a purpose, and we're gonna stick, and we're gonna go through this thick and thin, regardless of what happens. So grin and bear it. And I remember those words quite well. Grin and bear it. And so I succeeded in graduating from the 48th platoon. I might add that I was very fortunate.

Ruben Hines When I first went in the Marine Corps at Montford Point and as a Montford Point Marine, I experienced definitely harsh, rigid segregation, rigid discrimination. There was no in-between. There were, quite frequently, racial slurs made, directed at us blacks in the Marine Corps. We could not go to the main side [Camp Lejeune, where white Marines were based], that was where they had the PX, except on designated days. We had a time to go in there and get what we wanted to get, and then we had to get out. It was just that way. Many of us rode trucks, and some of us were marched in platoons. That was about thirteen miles over to the main side, the main base on Camp Lejeune. And that was where we were given the "privilege" to go to the PX and buy what goods and services we could. Then we had to leave there and come back [to Montford Point]. That was anathema to me and to a whole lot of other people because we could go maybe once a week or once every two weeks. As far as the racial situation was concerned, I would argue it was no different than outside [in Jacksonville and the civilian world]. It was the same thing. You only had certain places you could go.

Generally, no [i.e., staff members at Montford Point were not racists]. But there were exceptions. And that's when we encountered the officers. I remember distinctly one person's name was, lieutenant by the name of Le-Pointe, who was very vicious in his reaction to us, in his demeanor and his language. I would say, I thought that was really inhumane. And there was another one, but [he was] on the opposite end of the spectrum. We had a warrant officer by the name of Mr. Augustine. Now, he was paternal in his treatment. However, there is no question that he was still a racist. Because when he used the term "you people," he used it so derogatorily it make you want to vomit. When he communicated with us, and spoke sporadically, a few words at a time about a job, he would say, you people are no people. And when I saw you people coming to the Marine Corps, only then did I realize there was a war going on. And it made us feel pretty bad. Made me feel bad.

LePointe. He also used the word "nigger." And he had no qualms about it whatsoever. Who were we going to complain to? Nobody. Nobody. There were some people who objected, but it was just brushed off. And I said, oh, well, that's the way with so and so, and so and so.

You have to understand that the Marine Corps at that time was very racist to be sure. But when you look at the composition of the Marine Corps, the majority of the people in the Marine Corps at that time were from the South anyway.

Fred Ash After we got out of boot camp, we went to an organization at Montford Point called H and S Company. H and S Company was where you did guard duty and whatever else that they had to do and also, at that time, we really wasn't allowed over at main side. Main side was, well, a section for mostly whites.

The only time I remember that, 'cause I went one time. And where you go over to main side, you'd be on a trash run. They had this fifty-five-gallon drums. You'd make about three or four trips a day, and every section wherever they had them [the drums] at and empty them in a dump truck. You even didn't eat over there. When you would take a break for lunch, you'd come back to Montford Point; and then the guy that was driving, he'd go back to the motor pool, and then when it was time to pick you up, he'd come back and pick you up and you'd go back on another run for the rest of the day.

When we'd be on these assignments and, actually it was a cleanup or garbage runs and whatever other [duty], we'd ever go over there, but we even go and cut grass with swing blades. While we were over there, we'd always knock off in time enough to get back to our camp, to Montford Point, to get our lunch or dinner, whatever it was. And they would tell us that we couldn't eat over at main side or in the mess halls over there, because we had to eat where they drew our rations at. That's what they told us. But to me, it didn't make sense. . . .

Well, I was so rejoiced over being a Marine it didn't matter too much. And then I would rather, 'cause if you would go over there, they'd look at you like you were something from outer space anyway. And then there'd be times that we'd go in certain areas. You probably wouldn't see the guy, but you could hear him, and they give us the name, not us but the Camp Montford Point, Monkey Point, and they would [call it] . . . some of the whites.

But anyway, we should go over there [to Camp Lejeune], and I just go into the icehouse over there, you know, to pick up ice for bringing back to the officers' club. I worked at the officers' club. That's when they integrated the bus, I believe. I can't think of the year that they integrated the bus, the Marine bus into Jacksonville bus area. I don't remember either riding on the Marine bus integrated until the buses was integrated in Jacksonville coming off the base. But you know, we always catch the bus when they [went into Jacksonville]. When you got on the working party, they would send you in a truck or something, you didn't have to worry about it, 'cause you'd be out of the group. If you go from Montford Point to Camp Lejeune, I think we rode a bus, couple of times, over there for a parade. We were in a parade, but that was all Montford Point [Marine], they were all black.

LaSalle Vaughn Well, I got orders in 1943. And I got orders to report to Parris Island, South Carolina. . . . And the thing about it, we got to Parris Island. We went to Yemassee [South Carolina]. They had a barracks behind the train station. We came in on a bus and they kept us overnight in the barracks, and somebody pick us up the next morning, take us to Parris Island. And as God is my witness what I'm saying now is the truth. And God is present right now. Let me tell you what happened. Came the bus, the MP got on the bus [was] white, didn't have no black MPs then. No black MPs. Didn't have a black MP there [at Parris Island] until 1949.

And you got on the bus, he say, boy what are you doing with my uniform on? And I was a guy, you know, used to fighting all the time. And I jumped up and the same guy out there, he the one who grabbed me. He said no bro', we called each other bro'. Said no bro', say, you know, you'll get in serious trouble.

Let me tell you what happened. They took us on the base. And they had tents for us, a lot of beautiful barracks [for whites]. I goes over there [to the white base] to the commissary just about every day. And big old beautiful barracks. They had tents [for us] and the weather was four degrees in the wintertime. Four degrees in the wintertime. We had a wooden stove in the barracks. Where other Marines were living they had gas stoves. And I'm a witness. . . . So anyway. We could not go in the PX. . . . We could not parade on the parade ground. Everything was segregated.

Frederick Drake Montford Point wasn't bad at all to me because I was used to kind of getting down. And from there, I along with twenty-four, total of twenty-five black Marines went to Parris Island. And Sergeant [LaSalle] Vaughn kept me under his arm, and we went on to Parris Island. The beginning was, we were something new there. The black Marines. And when we got there, we couldn't go to the [Post] Exchange; we couldn't go to the sick bay. They didn't even put us in jail. They built a jailhouse for us down on Battle Creek. As you're coming in the gate [at Parris Island], there's a bridge you go over. When you go over, go through the main gate, there's a bridge up there. They built us a bridge, right there on that creek.

And we went on in and we went to work. And they gave us a little Quonset hut, put us off to the side there, and we stayed in there for about six month. Now we couldn't go to the exchange, sick bay, and for a while we couldn't go to the movie. But eventually, they built us barracks. Up going toward Page Field. If you ever [had] the tour of Parris Island, you leave officers' country and you're going up the hill there, and you go across the river there. And they built us a barracks up there. 'Cause now, at that [time], we had our doctor to come certain days. We could have parties, because we was taking care of officers, and we knew what partying was. So we was able to have parties and had our little PX in there, right there in our barracks. So it wasn't so bad. I didn't stay up there very long either. I soon went to work for generals.

Roland Durden The 33rd and the 34th Depot traveled together on a troop train from North Carolina going south toward New Orleans, where we picked up German prisoners, two carloads of German prisoners. I always say they look like Rommel's troop, big, tall, blonde Germans. And we headed out west. When we got somewhere in the West, we stopped for either coal or water. The Red Cross nurses came out to the train to give us coffee and doughnuts. Our officer, our captain, who was white, he said serve the Germans first. Our Red Cross nurses said, no, we'll serve our boys first.

Steven Robinson I have to believe that it wasn't by accident [that the story of blacks on Iwo Jima was not told]. It was purposely done. I look back and you want to say, hey, they wouldn't do that. Yes, they did it. 'Cause I talked with a fellow, as a matter of fact, he's not young anymore. He was in my platoon. And he told me that he was on the beach and they were filming. They didn't have the TV coverage then. They were filming either some Marine replacements as they were coming to shore. He said he was on his way. They used us [black Marines] for grave registration. They used us for guard duty, brought guards on ammo dumps. The guards on the supply dumps, the guards on the medicine. As I said, guards on the water. He told me, he said, you know, they turned when they saw my unit. He was one of our squad leaders.

He said when they saw my squad leader coming past, they turned the cameras away from us. I said, well, it's just your imagination. And he said, no, they saw me coming, saw us coming and turned the cameras away. Then you had another instance where I know several the fellows in the redoubt had taken cover behind a tank. One was one of my corporals and two of the men in his squad.

I guess, maybe it was a conscious thing. I mean, they knew that they had really never fully accepted us, and I say, I talk about not just the rank and file white Marine, but I'm talking about their officers. They knew that. It had to be a guilt complex. Here these fellows, frankly, because I really can't think of any other race of people that would put themselves to the position to become cannon fodder, considering the way, you know, when the discriminations in the '40s were mind-boggling.

In the '40s [the *Philadelphia Inquirer*] was probably the largest weekly in the United States if not in the world, especially controlled and published by African Americans. And they had during the war a slogan, and it went, V for Victory. V for Victory home and abroad. In other words, we want to overcome the bigotry at home and we want to overcome the Totalitarianism, Nazism and all the other isms abroad. So it was, there were two fronts we were actually fighting the war on. We were fighting the war against the bigotry at home and fighting the war against the bigotry overseas. And we were fighting the war to liberate people who had more liberty then than we had. And we were in harm's way because we were in uniform and there were so many things that could happen. In other words, you couldn't get out of uniform without a court-martial. We were really in harm's way so I say that we were confronted with a lot.

As I said before, some things that happen to you, [you] say this really couldn't be happening to me for that reason, because of what I look like or because I don't even know. I don't know these people. I never done anything to them. Why could they have this, this kind of rage? Why could they have this kind of attitude or nature toward me when I don't, and I don't feel that way? In other words, I don't feel that way against them. If anybody should have that feeling, that attitude, I should have it against them. Not them against me, because I never did anything to them. And I don't know why they should have that feeling against me, but they did.

So they took that feeling not, not just [in the United States]. I was in Japan for almost a year, occupational forces. When the white Marines come over, they brought the same values they had in the States, they brought over with them. And we were blessed because the Japanese spoke no English. So that, in other words, they [whites] couldn't propagandize them [the Japanese] to the extent that they could do it maybe to an English-speaking country. Americans had some kind of an aversion of learning the language of the people who they come to occupy. So they didn't learn any Japanese. Japanese spoke, could speak no English. So the Japanese couldn't be propagandized by the fact that somehow they [white Americans] want to portray us of being you know, a subhuman species.

Averitte Corley Now there was an incident on Saipan I can tell you about. There was [an] all-island dance, and they dropped leaflets in each area. There was a white outfit top of Mount Tagoochau, I think eleven service companies. And we were way down the north part between Tanapag and Marpi Point, which was the Japanese airbase at one time. We were down to Suicide Cliff [where Japanese soldiers and civilians had jumped to their deaths rather than surrender to the American forces]. We were down in that area. And they dropped these leaflets, said we having an all-island dance. Everybody invited, come to Mount Tagoochau, at certain times, so forth. Well, we went up there thinking they going to have black Red Cross girls flown in from Guam. 'Cause they had some on Guam. In fact, there was a girl on Guam from Indianapolis named Catherine Hicks. Red Cross girl. They didn't have any black Red Cross girls. All white.

So, a black sailor asked one of these white girls to dance. And they had just laid this Quonset hut floor; it was a slick concrete floor. He asked this girl to dance and she said, how dare you ask a white woman to dance? And he hauled off and hit her and she slid on her behind all the way up to the island commander. His name was Captain Smith, I never will forget. Right at his feet. And he ordered his orderly, said, shoot that man. Well, that guy got out and run, run down the hill then. He couldn't get off the island and the orderly shot [at] him out[side], so we went out to hear the shots 'cause they were still Japanese up in the hills.

We didn't know what was happening. You know, they were still hostiles off in those hills. So, I ran out there and right by the island commander, of all places to end up, and I'm the first black thing he saw. And he said, take that man to the brig. And the orderly said, well, sir, he just came out. He said, take him to the brig. Said, we going to hold him till we get the other guy. I'm a Marine and this [other] guy's a sailor. But he got away, but he couldn't get off the island, they knew that. So they put me in, took me to the brig for three days in solitary confinement.

Benjamin Patterson Our first stop was Ellice Islands, went to a little island called Funafuti. And we got there and the other group hadn't left, so we slept out in open field at night, ready roll. So the other [white] group left, we went to take over the guns and everything. The first thing that happened to me, the natives walked up to me and said let me see your tail. The white Marines had told them that all black people had tails. The natives come and say, let me see your tail. I said we don't have tails. I said, feel back there, then he feels, oh, that's not what we hear. I said, no, we don't have tails. Quite an experience believe me.

Ellis Cunningham The troubles I had in town was normally not with the civilian authority. It would be with some of the white Marines, because we had just so many buses, and to run back to the base, and people didn't have cars like they did now, everybody would have to ride the bus.

Riding the bus then was a hassle. Because the black guys had to go to the back of the bus, but they'd be loaded last. They'd load the white guys first, and then load the [blacks]. The rule was that the whites would load from the front to the back, and the blacks would load from the back to the front. Wherever the line stopped. Well, if you have enough white guys that loaded the bus, all the way, that's the way it happened, they got loaded all the way.

And, so the black guys standing out there wouldn't even get on the bus, or you'd get on, but there wouldn't be any seats, so you would stand. I had that happen a few times. A couple of times I got a bus moving like that, it would be, maybe one or two seats left, and, if a white guy didn't object to you sitting beside him, then you sat there. And every now and again, you'd get a guy who objected to you sitting or standing, so, you'd mark that guy, you know? If he got off where we got off, whether that's what he intended to do or not, we'd get off there and teach him a lesson about this, about occupying a whole seat. Had a few incidents like that.

George Taylor My aunt used to work for her [a white woman] at her home. When I went into the Marine Corps, she [the white woman] gave me a little picture at this little party she gave. This lieutenant, Lieutenant Wilson, saw that picture. Trouble started. I tried to get a furlough home. I couldn't go home. So, you do the next best thing. You go over the hill [absent without leave].

And then, on my way back to camp, I got put in jail in Akron, Ohio, in 1943. Cleveland was the induction center. So, they came from Cleveland to Akron, thirty-five miles, and brought me back to Cleveland. And they examined me and everything. And gave me traveling paper to go on my own. And then, when I got to Camp Lejeune, I got twenty-one days on bread and water and a $21.00 fine. A lot of money back then.

So, three days into my sentence, they told me to mop up the barracks and everything. And he [the guard] went out and he come back. Puts his head down to sleep. And he snatched me out of the barracks. And I popped him. And throw me up against the wall. And I asked for the officer of the day. And the officer of the day came. What's going on here? Well, I told him, I told him to mop up, and he didn't mop up. Why didn't you mop up? I was the bread-and-water prisoner. And bread-and-water prisoners don't work. He forgot all about that. So, they let me out of the guardhouse.

So, when I get back to my barracks, two of my buddies, Green and Johnson, both from out of New York, saying, hey, how did you get out? And I explained to them what had happened. Let's go to Montford Point and have a party, 'cause we're getting shipped out in three more days. Which I don't drink, but I can drink Coca-Cola, you know, I never did drink. So, we go over there. I go in the door. Green go in the door. The black MP shoots.

Everybody said, now why you shooting at him? Why you shooting at him? Why you shooting at him? He don't say anything, being a sergeant, he get the officer of the day. Brought him over. Sir, why would our fellow Marine shoot at us? Get back where you belong, he said. I said, get back where you belong. Case is closed. You can't go nowhere else. That's it. So, we walked out the door.

And Johnson say, he was after you. I said, for what? You got the white woman picture on your locker box. I said, what are you doing shooting at me? He's from the South. Whatever that man tell him to do, he gonna do. So, my rifle's at quartermaster. 'Cause once you AWOL [absent without leave], they confiscate, and put it up.

We went back. And Lang slept next to me, from Chicago. We growed up together. I got his rifle. Johnson, he done got his rifle. Green got his rifle. We shot at the theater where the white officers and their wives sat at. Nobody got hurt. And went back and cleaned those rifles with hair oil. That's how, the sweet-smelling hair oil. And put Lang's rifle back.

Well, about forty minutes later, the four white officers came in. Get your rifles and stand by your bunks. Everybody get their rifle. Nobody know who did shooting. Nobody even know, at the barrack, didn't even know the shooting had gone on 'cause we're across the bridge. When they got around to me, Lieutenant Wilson say, Taylor, where's your rifle at? I said, sir, I think it's at quartermaster. What do you mean, you think? I said, just what I said. I think it's at quartermaster. What is it doing there? I said, just got out of the guardhouse. For what? I was AWOL. What are you doing out? I said, they let me out. Where are you from? Chicago. You're one of those Chicago gangsters, huh? Put it any way you like, sir. So they couldn't find nothing wrong with any of the rifles.

Going overseas, we hadn't got to the Equator yet. We just about getting to the Equator, when man, it's hot. I'm laying across deck, and this so-called Sergeant Davis came up and he kicked me on the bottom of my feet. And told me to pick up around the deck. I said, man, don't kick me like that no more. You're not my sergeant, and I'm not passing out stripes. You don't do no work on this ship. Then don't kick me no more. So, I stretched out again. He kicked me. I got jumped up and run into him. I tried throwing him overboard ship. And Major Bobby had the guard to stop me.

Hit me on the side of cap, and I hit the deck. Hit my crazy bone, and I'm screaming, Bobby, I'm gonna kill you. And the major listened to all of that. So, I'm going down before the colonel. The colonel said, What's going on? I said, they decided to kick me. [The colonel said] Shut up. I said, you asked what was going on. [The colonel] said, shut up.

He looks up at the sergeant, what's going on? I tried to give him an order and he didn't like it, and he tried to throw me overboard ship. I says, no, no. I [already] got three sergeants. I never tried to do anything to you. You kicked me. You don't kick me. And then the colonel hollered again, I said, shut up.

Well, then I'm thinking to myself. Heck, I'm going to the guardhouse for what? Was something that somebody else did. Not my sergeant, he wasn't even a sergeant. Nobody else knew him. They put him on board ship. And I'm gonna get even with him for kicking me twice. I know if I hit an uncommissioned officer at wartime, what it consist of. It can be a death penalty, a life in prison, or what have you.

But I had to hit him. 'Cause he kept you know, with a little grin on his face. And I hit him and I heard the colonel say, court-martial him. I was down on that floor. And I heard the major say, put those rifles down, and get him up off of it. So, they did that. I'm in the guardhouse on board ship. And we get on land, I go to the guardhouse. Then they get me two lawyers. Guess who one of the lawyers was? [Lieutenant] Wilson. I didn't need two white lawyers there. And he one. Didn't need none. Go before this board, all these white officers around this board. All these white fellows is witness. Which it should have been all black guys is witness, 'cause that's what I'm affiliated with. The two guards was outside the door. This so-called sergeant, they flew him back to the States. No other guy, no other sergeant knew him.

At the end of the day, the lieutenant at the end of the table says, to me, Taylor, if you can give us any information about the shooting back in Montford Point, we may consider being lenient with you. Look like something smack me in my face to say, they set you up. They had to shoot at me for them to pick me out. Felt that I knew why somebody shot at them. So, they figure, hey, he did it. Or he knows who did it. So, as we stood there and I was thinking, I said, hmm, they're gonna set me up.

And then the lieutenant said, you know anything? I said, oh, Lieutenant

Wilson, let's see, remember you came to our quarters and you asked everybody to get their rifles and stand by their bunks? When you got to me, you asked me, where was my rifle? And I told you I thought it was at quartermaster. And you asked me, what was it doing there? I told you I just got out of the guardhouse. You asked me, for what? I told you, I was AWOL. You asked me, what was I doing out? I told you, they let me out. Then you asked me, where was I from? And I told you, Chicago. You called me a Chicago gangster. I said, I didn't even have a rifle.

And the lieutenant dropped them papers on the table. And he looked back at the two guys back there. FBI or some officers, you know, kind of, found out. And they said, get him out of here. Then they brought the general court-martial down to a summary. Gave me sixty days on bread and water. But I've been trying to find out, for what?

Herman Darden Jr. We went with the 51st; they were our first stop cross country. We trained cross country, equipment and all. We went out with about four different trainloads; it was a whole battalion, 1,500 strong. We ended up at Camp Elliot, right outside San Diego. And there, we ran into segregation.

Brick barracks here, empty, tents up on the hill, where we were bivouacked. Open-air movies, and this was when things really got exciting, because, the first day we went to the movie, open-air movie, down in the ravine, and were told, sorry, but you boys gotta sit in the back. Uh-huh. What do you mean? Well, that's the rule here. You boys have to sit in the back. You got a green uniform. I got a green uniform. We're going over-[seas], we're going to fight the Japs; his bullet ain't marked white and black, why we gotta? Well, that's the rule here. There was one thing about the outfit [51st]; it was unified. If one person spoke, everybody responded to it, you know? So one man was speaking, so he says, well, we got to sit in the back, yeah.

Hey fellas. So we just got up, and went out, formed a ring around the place. And we still allowed to sit in the back? Yeah. Okay, fellas. We just began to rip up the seating, just logs. We just ripped them up, put on the movie, and went on back to our base. So, this is, it may not have been written in history, but this is what happened.

They relieved our original CO [Commanding Officer at Camp Elliot], Colonel Stevenson, put in charge a Colonel Leggette, who told us, it's a disgrace to be seen with boys like you. They got boys like you working on my plantation, down in South Carolina. They tell me you have no discipline.

You don't know what you're doing, but by God, since I gotta be with you, when I leave you, we're gonna see. And after almost that two years up, and his tour of duty was halted, he had another parade and apologized for his initial statement, and said, I want you to know, I didn't want to leave you. I'd rather, I'd like to go back to the States with you. But I can't, he said. But I want you to know, I've never served with a better bunch of men in all my life.

Roland Durden Well, our officers were definitely prejudiced, particularly our captain. We had, well, three white officers, a warrant officer, as well as the captain and lieutenant. My captain wasn't what I consider appreciative of his men, because he wrote in a letter home that he didn't like serving with the niggers, and he had one of our black Marines as the censor officer. We had to censor all the letters, and if he knows the gentleman, he chewed out the captain for writing that letter.

But our captain very suddenly showed up after our initial landing [at Iwo Jima]. It was our sergeant who really ran the outfit. Our sergeant was a sergeant major. One incident occurred. There was about four of us black Marines sitting around this white Marine, young, but battle weary. And I quote what he said. He says, I was taught differently, but now that I see you people here, I have respect for you. That's all I can remember of what he said. I'll never forget what he said and how he said it.

Oliver Lumpkin We [the 51st Defense Battalion] went from Jacksonville to Atlanta. And Kenneth Whitlock, he was in charge of MPs. We got to Atlanta and we started out the, what do you call it, where the trains were down below the ground? So we started up. And a MP from the Army told us that we couldn't come up that way. And so, we asked him, where is that in the Marine Corps manual? And he called the police. And we marched right on up. Eventually, there was almost a skirmish. But we marched right on through, and we went on to breakfast. We were going for breakfast in Atlanta. And we were coming out the chute, up through the white waiting room. And the MP told us that we couldn't come through there. And Whitlock, who was in charge, he was provost, and he just told us to go over, continue to march, and across we went. And of course, a lot of MPs and police came, but eventually we went, we went on.

Johnnie Givian And this was in 1947. The month, I'm not sure but it was about May or somewhere along in there when I infiltrated back 'cause

I didn't stay out [on duty] for about thirty days. Then I came back. I came right back to Montford Point, and Montford Point hadn't changed no kind of way. They still haven't change no kind of way. So I went back to Montford Point. The only difference was that when I got out of the Marine Corps, I was labeled as a steward.

I was waiting on tables and stuff like that, and when I went back they put me in what we called the motor transport, AAA Motor Transport Company. Right there at Montford Point. So I was in there and stood guard duties and everything. And they put up a sign that they was looking for people to go on a detachment. They mean, you know, like leave Montford Point and go somewhere else for a certain length of time. And my name appeared on there to go to California. I was happy about that 'cause I had heard a lot of good stuff about California. But we got on a train one day and rode out there and they put us in a barrack, fifty-two of us.

And they put us in a barracks. It was an all-white barracks, 'cause matter of fact, all everything was out there was white. The whole base was except us, now, as a unit. We was the Montford Point Detachment Unit, I believe it was. But they put us in one wing in the corner of that barracks. It's the oldest building out there; it's Hughes Building. But we was on one wing and, and we was in there and that's where we supposed to lodged at. Went to the mess hall to eat; they had an area roped off for us. We'd go in there, they were segregated. They weren't as nasty as some of the people around down in this area [Jacksonville]. But they was segregated. We had to go to the furthest row. We couldn't go up there and eat over here. We just had to eat in that one place where they had it roped off, and the same way in the barracks sleeping. The theater was roped off at a certain area where we would go. It was in Camp Pendleton, California. And I stayed there about seven or eight months. . . . As long as I'm minding my business I pretty well stayed out of trouble, because I minded my business; I didn't try to be something that I know I wasn't.

Thomas Cork There were other things happened to me down there [at Montford Point]. I went on liberty one night. They asked us if we go on liberty; try to go more than one, because the town wasn't very friendly to us. And other Marines didn't want you there. So, I go by myself. I get all the way down the street and I saw these young [white] Marines coming toward me. They were laughing and talking. They acted like I wasn't even there. So, you know, I am thinking I am going right on past them.

But when I get up abreast of them, they literally knocked me off that street and said, this is my street, so and so, you know what they called me, and went on about their business. Now, here come the MPs. They didn't bother those guys, they got me. And what they got me for, my cap had been knocked off and got dirty. And I had to go back to the base because my cap was knocked off by these two young men. So, that kind of, you know, upset me. Because I know I was innocent.

I am vague on the month, but it's latter part of '49. It's maybe around August, somewhere in that time. We started our troop train out at New Jersey, and we picked up Marines all along the way. We started out with just the guys from New Jersey. And on to Chicago, Milwaukee, St. Louis, and on down to California. So, when we get down to California, our troop train is long. I mean, we have all these Marines picked up along the way.

But we get in to Camp Pendleton. We started to get out of the train; the Marines down there are standing out waiting on us. And the first thing I heard out of their mouth, here come the nigger Marines. So, I, like I said before, that word didn't bother me at all there. Because I heard it so many times. And just knew that that's part of their makeup to say that.

But my training there at Camp Pendleton, as I said before, I picked up a couple friends and he and I are together. Two whites and one black. And we kind of went around to different places together. And some place we go in, some place we couldn't. Some places the white wouldn't allow us in, some places the black wouldn't allow the white in. So, we stayed friends, three guys until we got on the ship to go to Korea. We get into Kobe, Japan. There was a band playing, welcoming us into Tokyo, to Japan. This young man, one of my friends, was standing behind me looking over and at this band. And he said with no uncertain term, I didn't know they had a nigger band here in Japan. I stepped right down from him. I never spoke to him again. That was the end of my conversation with him.

I heard later that he was killed. Over the years I kind of mellowed. But now I wished I had confronted him about it. And some people say yes, some people say no. It's a matter of opinion. But that really upset me, to hear him saying it. If anybody [else], I took it in stride. But I never thought that would come out of his mouth, because we had been such good friends. We ate each other's sandwiches. We read each other's mail and just got to be close friends, as young men would do. But it came out. And it just hurt my feelings. It really did. And then, took me forever to get over that. And like I say, all the years I kind of wished I had did different. But it's, you know, it's kind of hindsight.

Reuben McNair When I returned back to Camp Lejeune [after combat in Korea in 1953], I most certainly had [trouble] at that time. You was no longer in combat. I guess that the whole world had began to see the changes in things. And I'll never forget that one time, my first sergeant called me in. And he tells, I wanna introduce you to your platoon leader who will be taking over the platoon here.

And I had a rifle platoon at that particular time. This platoon leader walks into the office and says, Sergeant McNair, this is Lieutenant so-and-so. And I reached my hand out to shake hands and he just looked at me as if I were a piece of dirt. He refused to shake hands. And the first sergeant, he jumped up. And I thought the whole world had come to an end.

He turned the desk over and everything was rumbling. Camp's company commander rushed over to see what was going on. He says, well, a man refused to shake hands with Sergeant Mac so I think there's something wrong with it. Well, you see, he was out of the company. So, you did have things that taken place there and we, most certainly, I seen some things.

Carrol Reavis This was when the Korean things got hot. It was going on when I was in Hawaii. A friend of mine, George Kidd, we went to Hawaii together, but then he went to Korea and I didn't go. I stayed there. So I was sent back to Camp Lejeune into the military police, the division military police, and my duty was assigned to Wilmington. Mine was assigned to Wilmington, North Carolina. It's where my assignment was on weekends. You go up on Wednesday, come back Monday or Tuesday. And this is where I got into military police, 'cause I'd had the experience. And [it] was very difficult, because they [the military police] rented a house, [from] a lady. Her son was in the Army, and she was there by herself so she leased her house and rented it out to the Marine Corps, and that's where we stayed in Wilmington.

And we either went out at night for military police duty. So I had charge of that group, but we worked over the sheriff's office. In the afternoon we'd get dressed, go down to the sheriff's office, then we go down to our post. Now, we could not go in the [white] city area. We could only do military police in the black area. And a place called Seabreeze, which was a resort place from 1917, an area for the professional black people at that time. Seabreeze was where we took care of that on weekends and the black area, I forgot the kind of road, but it was a road over there they called, where all the black businesses were.

That's what we did, police duty. Again, if we arrest anybody, we had to turn them over. We could carry guns then. This was in '52, I guess, '50, back in there, '52, '50, through '53. My experience with that was just like it'd always been. You could do this, but you can't do that. And if you do this, you, this is what's gonna happen. And one incident took place there in, I guess, the beginning of '53. That's when they Marines came back from Vieques [a base in Puerto Rico]. They used to go to Vieques for training, and when they came back they got a seventy-two-hour pass to go on the weekends, and they came to North Carolina. And a lot of them went to Carolina Beach [a white resort] in Wilmington.

And there was an incident that took place in one of the hotels over there and, of course, they called for the military police. I was in charge of them, of course. I went up there, and they say, you can't go up there. I had one white. White Marines walked the white area, although they came under me. So when I got to the hotel, they say, you can't go in here. You can't go. I said, well, I'm in charge. They said, well, you can't go up there. I said, well, if I can't go up there, get back on, we're going back. So we took them back. The next morning I was on my way back to Camp Lejeune to report to the commanding general. I got chewed out and that was the end of that. I never went back to Wilmington to duty anymore.

I got transferred back to Korea after that. So this same old story went on. When I went to Korea, I became the NCO in charge of CID [Criminal Investigation Division] for the First Marine Air Wing there. Again, you could do this, but you can't do that. And a lot of black discrimination was going on at the time, but the general wanted to know about everything that was discrimination. But if an officer was doing it, I could not interview an officer, or I'd have to get another officer who was not military police trained or anything to interview this officer through him. Well, it killed the whole thing. And some things I went through I won't discuss at all here or any other time because of my [security] clearance of the time.

Wilmore Perry I was thinking about an instance where we, one fellow and myself, we're going into Jacksonville, and we encountered these three white Marines. They suggested that we start a race riot. And my friend wanted to oblige them, so we agreed that they would have this race riot, and he took out a knife. And the white man, he didn't like that, and he moved out. The next time we saw them, they had about five of them, coming for us. So we in turn retreated, went to the area where most black Marines hung out, and we recruited some of them. Consequently, before we could get together, the MPs moved in, and took us all back to camp. I was put in the brig overnight, and as a staff NCO the next morning, had the report for the officer. I was to explain to the commanding officer.

Melvin Borden I never had any trouble out of no one in Jacksonville 'cause I never went to a place where they [blacks] didn't go. I had trouble on the base, though, Camp Lejeune. It was definitely racism. When you go to it with a working party [from Montford Point to Camp Lejeune], my wife worked at a cafeteria, but that's after we got married. I got married in '53. Anyway, what happened when they would tell you, they say, you don't go in no barrack. You take one of the hole, pothole, if you want to go to the bathroom, go in there. You're on the working party. You put your feet in one of them barracks, you're discharged, you going home, see. There wasn't nothing but white [barracks]. See, we went on down on working parties. I was at Montford Point. '50, well '53, '48, '50, '51. I worked at the officers' club from '51 to '52. Then they sent me to general quarters. I started working in general quarters. I worked in general quarters, then that's when I was stationed back here on, on the main side. We were stationed on the main side, they stationed us down there at the officers' club. And they had a barracks behind there for all of us stewards to stay in, after you got out of boot camp. I stayed there.

I went to work for the general, first time. General Hart, General Listenberg. I worked for them, you know, with the other stewards. I was just a helper; when they need help, I work for them. They would always tell me what to say. It didn't make me no difference 'cause I was raised up under that law [segregation]. So, that didn't hurt me to follow that law. And I worked there; I got married working there.

You couldn't go into the white barracks. You had to have your own potty stool for if you had to go to the bathroom. You had your water fountain, had your water, you know, your drinking water. But you didn't go in the [white] barracks. They had a thing, you know, when go in the working party. They had a tank of water that you can go for black and then they had a toilet facility for blacks. Early '50s. On Camp Lejeune.

Johnnie Thompkins I served at Quantico. I stayed three years and then I moved on to Lejeune. And I was there from '53 to '58, and had a problem there. I don't think they had gotten the word, I don't know. I went to advanced supply school for staffing COs, and I finished that. While I was in school, there was three of us [blacks] at that school. There was another guy that I knew, I can't call his name, he's black. And then we had a black woman Marine, and it ended up that she had her a room, she had an apartment out there. The guy, he was married and he was living in the married quarters. And I would go out and see them from time to time. And it ended up that me and a bunch of the white guys, we got together one weekend, they said, let's go out to the beach. I said okay.

We went out to the beach. The beach, Onslow Beach, which is a base beach, it's a beach on the base. And we went out there, and we went to the first building there, and it said Enlisted Club. And we went up there, and we had beers, but I noticed, I'm looking around and, says, goodness, I didn't see a black person in the place other than myself. And I says, now, I know all those guys. Somebody [black] supposed to [be] here. So it ended up we had good time, but I heard James Brown [the black recording star], and I looked up the beach and there was a little beach house way up from this enlisted beach, and, oh, they're having a giddy old time up there.

And I went back, I had finished my course, and they assigned me to special services. And I went back to my colonel there, special services, he was a, a lieutenant colonel, and I told him, I said colonel, I said, what's going on here? He said, what are you talking about? I said I was out to the beach. You got a enlisted beach. I said it wasn't no blacks out there, they were all up at one end, and I come to find out that all of them up there were all kind of ranks, from private to sergeant, top sergeant. And he said, I don't know.

I said, well I'm looking in the paper here, and it says it has, down here, dancing at the master pavilion, you know, and it says, Thursday night, colored night. I said, don't you know that blacks don't party on Thursday night, they party on Saturday night. And he looked at me and laughed, you know. And I said, this isn't supposed to be. I said, this supposed to be integrated now, and that means your dance, anything on this building here. Blacks are supposed to go to it if his rank let him.

And he said, you know what he said? He said, are you sure? I said, you better talk to somebody. So, he went over and they had, the generals had a meeting, and he told them what I had told him. And about a week later, they had integrated that place. They took the beach where the blacks were and made it staff and NCO beach, and let them come on down to enlisted beach.

So, I had people on my case then. And I said, why? I don't know why you people sit around here and let these people do this to you. I said, I tell them all, if I got the right to go there, I'm going. They don't tell me nothing on the base. I said I might take stuff out there in Jacksonville, but I ain't taking nothing here.

Fannie Coleman I read about Montford Point my nursing years, was from '48 to '51, so it had to be a timeframe say '50 or '51 because we were not allowed to do things until you become a junior or a senior. The way I really learned about it, I guess it was the general or commanding officer would allow a bus, just the regular bus that they have out here [at Camp Lejeune], they would send them to Wilmington to pick the student nurses up. The city girls, [black] ladies, were not allowed to ride on the same bus as they were. Yeah, we were not allowed to ride with the so-called city girls. We were the student nurses [in Wilmington]. So the student nurses were not allowed. There were two buses and they would say, this bus is for the nurses and this bus is for the other ladies that are going to Montford Point. There were parts of Wilmington that we were not allowed in. We were on south side. We were not allowed on the north side because there were ladies over there, I guess, that part of Wilmington was not what they wanted us exposed to. So as a result, when we got ready to get on our buses, the black girls, the black city ladies, got on one bus and we were allowed to get on our bus. They call your name off like a roll call, you got on your bus, you were seated, and then they would drive us over here.

When we got to Montford Point, we parked at the building that we were going, which is still standing. I think it's their gym now. We were allowed to go in, be seated, and then they had bands, big name bands here at Montford Point. I think Louis Armstrong was one of them. Cannot remember the others at this point, but I think Louis Armstrong was one. Maybe Count Basie, I'm not sure. But they were name bands that we hear records of today. Then, we would go in there as the music began to play. Of course, the young Marines would come and pick the lady that they wanted to dance with. We could dance with any Marine. We could get in a group with the city girls, but once we finished, then we were called off, got back on our bus, and we were taken back to Wilmington to the nursing home.

As a young female, first exposure to a whole building of young men, and they were willing and ready to dance with you. Once you got one and he decided you were his partner for the night, every dance that came on, either slow or fast, that was your date for the night. And with that, of course, give me your name, give me your address. They could write to us. Could not visit except a certain time at our dormitory. But that is how, it just, like I said, group of young girls, I guess first time away from home, being exposed to a whole building of young men. It was exciting.

Well, a lot of the conversation was, where you from? The things that you enjoy doing. Why were you there? Where did you come from at this particular time to be over here for the evening? Usually, it was on Friday evenings that we were allowed to be brought over here.

When you're getting ready to leave, you're holding hands, you're laughing, you're throwing kisses 'cause there was no contact, throwing kisses and saying, I'll see you again. This type thing. It was just such a good feeling. And on the way back to Wilmington, everybody was laughing and talking and singing and until we got back to the nursing home, then you, we had to be quiet, had to be counted to go in for the night. As a result, I ended up dating one of the Marines for a while, and for somewhere along the way, we went our separate ways. But they could come and visit us to the dormitory, so he came to visit me several times.

William Vann What I consider a truly integrated unit I served in was [in] 1952. I served in Charlie Company, 3rd Regiment. That was a tent camp. They called it tent camp three-and-a-half under Camp Pendleton, and the 3rd Marine Division was from it. I was a combat veteran and I was pretty sure of myself, and another gentleman who was reserve happened to be Caucasian and he knew the commanding officer. I think they were in the same unit. We would do night training in the infantry, and this sergeant said that he was going to be the platoon sergeant. I said, how can you be the platoon sergeant, I'm senior to you, plus I'm a combat veteran. So, he said, well, I think I'll get the job.

So when, later on, after I heard about it, I wouldn't tolerate that. I said, here I am with a clean record and sergeant in the Marine Corps, combat, survived North Korea. I said, I'm going to request [to see the] commanding officer. So I would request the commanding officer. He said, you do the job, we don't have no complaint with what you're doing. He said, but if we want to make a change, I think you should consider it. I said, in any part of the United States the senior man get the job, and I'm the senior man. Plus, I'm a combat veteran, this gentleman never been overseas. So, he said, okay. I said, I want to talk with the battalion commander. He said, okay, we'll arrange it, so you can talk, and I talked with the battalion commander and I explained to him what was going on.

I said I have a clean record so this should not be, they want to put a reserve in charge of the platoon. I should get that platoon. And he just listened to me. I said, I'm a combat veteran. I said, I'm ready to go right to Korea to fight for my country because the Korean War was still going strong. He said, I'd rather go back, too, sergeant. He said I'll take care of this situation. So, he called the office, and I never heard no more about it. It was taken care of.

So, I put in for a transfer to C Company, then when I got transferred because I felt resentment was still being held. So the company commander said I heard about some of the things that happened, my new company commander in C Company. My new company commander, he said that in this company you will be in charge of not only the platoon, you will have the company. So, we have a parade coming off and you will drill the company at the parade where we're going to be taking pictures. And he said, other than that, you are our platoon sergeant, that's what you will be. I take my test and I passed the test. I got promoted to Staff Sergeant shortly thereafter. And I went back to Korea.

or the men trained at Montford Point, just as for white Marines trained at Parris Island, engaging the enemy in combat was the ultimate goal. They understood the dangers of combat, and feared combat, but feared even more the possibility that racism would deny them the opportunity to experience it, a fear that was well grounded. Like the combat troops of any culture, they held courage on the field of battle as perhaps the ultimate virtue. And while proving one's personal courage was important to them, even more important was the need to prove that African Americans were as capable and courageous under fire as were white troops. It was an obligation they all felt.

Beyond the need to prove that on the battlefield they, too, were Marines, the men of Montford Point sought to demonstrate that they, too, were Americans. They understood that participation in combat was the ultimate expression of their loyalty to their country and to its values, even though that country had chosen to treat them as second-class citizens. It is against this background of their need to be accepted as Marines, of their determination to enjoy all the rights and privileges of American citizenship, and of their hope to obtain a full measure of respect from their fellow Americans that their service must be viewed, especially during World War II.

The Ellice Islands, Marshall Islands, and Occupied Guam

In February 1944, the 51st Defense Battalion arrived at the Ellice Islands, located in the South Pacific to the east of the Solomon Islands, to relieve the 7th Defense Battalion. Divided into two units, men from the 51st occupied three of the nine islands in the group—Nanomea, Funafuti, and Nukufetau—which served as a staging area for operations in the Pacific to the north. Boredom, not the enemy, challenged the men of the 51st until they were transferred northward to Eniwetok Atoll in the Marshall Islands. There they again relieved a white unit, only once more to settle into the boredom

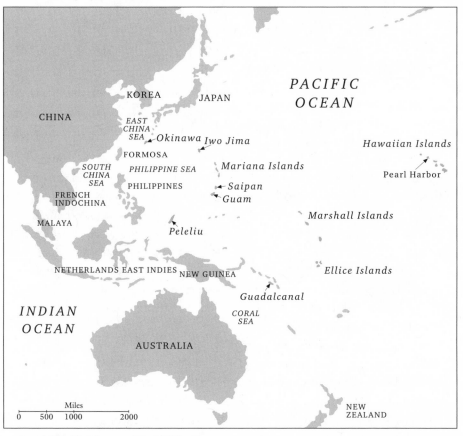

KOREA   JAPAN

CHINA

EAST
CHINA
SEA   Okinawa   Iwo Jima

FORMOSA

SOUTH
CHINA
SEA   PHILIPPINE SEA   Mariana Islands

PHILIPPINES   Saipan

FRENCH
INDOCHINA   Guam

MALAYA

Peleliu

NETHERLANDS EAST INDIES   NEW GUINEA

INDIAN
OCEAN

Guadalcanal

CORAL
SEA

AUSTRALIA

*PACIFIC
OCEAN*

Hawaiian Islands

Pearl Harbor

Marshall Islands

Ellice Islands

Miles

0   500   1000   2000

NEW
ZEALAND

South Pacific Theater, World War II

of preparation to defend airstrips from Japanese air attacks that never occurred.

Organized at Montford Point in December 1943, the 52nd Defense Battalion, like the 51st, was assigned to previously secured islands in the Pacific and never engaged in combat. In October 1944, units of the 52nd relieved a white antiaircraft unit on Majuro Atoll in the Marshall Islands, which American forces had occupied the previous February. The white unit, the 1st Antiaircraft Artillery Battalion, had been part of the landing force and had remained to protect a Marine Aircraft Group stationed on the island from potential Japanese air attacks. Other units of the 52nd drew a similar assignment at the Kwajalein Atoll in the Marshalls. In March 1945, the Corps began transferring units of the 52nd to Guam, which American forces had invaded in July 1944. On Guam, Marines of the 52nd participated in mop-up actions against Japanese stragglers. Rumors that the 52nd was slated to be part of the force being assembled for the invasion of Okinawa in April 1945 briefly raised the spirits of the men, but morale dropped when they learned the battalion would remain on Guam, where it spent the remainder of the war.

Walter Maddox We went over as a battalion [the 51st Defense Battalion] in January of 1944. We left [Montford Point] Christmas of '43, and they had a troop train for us. Took us all the way across country to San Diego. . . . The Marine Corps had a range at Lima Vistas, up in the mountains there, and they had a tent city. That's where we put the battalion. We left from San Diego on pier two, heading for the South Pacific. We didn't know where in the heck we were going. We were out in the sea for a couple of days before they informed us where we were going. We were going down to a group of islands. We found out that it was 750 miles north of Samoa. They were called the Ellice Islands. We relieved a [white] defense battalion down there. They'd left their gun emplacements, and then we took over. Those islands, group of islands were called the Ellice Islands. And the main island was Funafuti.

We had one alert whilst we were down there, and it was on the seaward side, and we had 155 [mm] long guns. Somebody said they saw a submarine and they got off a couple of rounds on it, but they don't know whether they hit it or not. That was at Funafuti. We left Funafuti going up the Ellice Islands going north. We didn't know where the heck we were going then. We would find out later, when we were at sea, we were going up to the Marshall Islands. We went up through Kwajalein. We dropped off an attachment at Kwajalein, and then we ended up at the Eniwetok in the Marshall Islands.

We later found out, years later, that Eniwetok was one of the staging areas for the invasion of Iwo [Jima]. Which we were scheduled to go. They had a battalion on board ship out in the harbor there that was scheduled to replace us. But since we had all the technology of the guns and the placement and everything, they decided to send them on in on Iwo. Fortunately, or unfortunately. If it had been us, they lost 50 percent on the beach going in. And that could have been our group.

I've been reading and keeping up with military history. I found out there was reluctance [to send blacks into combat], said we weren't ready, but we knew better. But all the training, it just went for naught. And this is proof that throughout the years, they were wrong. They were wrong. Not that we didn't want to go. You've heard that the black American newspaper out of Baltimore, what was it called? The *Afro-American*? They used to have big headlines, get our boys into combat. And we said, the hell with that. We didn't want to die. But that's the thing, we were gung ho. We were Marines. Marines from day one.

Harry Hamilton We went to Pacific by the way of Hawaii; we spent a couple of weeks there, and then it took us thirty-one days to get to the island. They was dodging the Japanese during that period. I was with the 52nd Defense Battalion. That was the second fighting unit that they formed in the Marine Corps at that time. Before that, they were forming the Steward Branches and ammo companies, working details, more or less. And we [American forces] won Majuro; from Majuro, we set up our camp there.

At that time, the Japanese wasn't coming back, and we didn't have to worry too much about that. From there, we went to Guam, and we relieved I believe it was the 14th [Defense Battalion]. It was an all-white unit that we relieved, and we stayed on Guam until latter part of '45. On Guam, we did a lot of reconnaissance. We was on detail, we were sent out looking for the Japs that were still on the island. And we did a lot of guarding of the prisoners of war, the Japanese. They would take them on work details, and we did a lot of guarding of them. And also, some of us had to help unload the ships when they came in. Before we were sent back to the States, we went to Saipan. And that's when our group was broken up. We had the guys that had more points [for time served] than I did, was married. I came home and they wanted me to reenlist, but at the time I didn't want to. I wanted to get out and continue my education. And I eventually got out in June of '46.

Walter Thompson Jr. What we [the 51st Defense Battalion] did, we patrolled. We patrolled. We picked up Japanese overseas, when we got overseas on the Marshall Islands. See, what they did, they bypassed a lot of islands. As they [American forces] was going through the Pacific, they bypassed [Japanese-held islands], because they could starve them out. They wouldn't have no chance on losing no men and they starve them out. Then the natives would snipe upon them and catch them.

And then, we go in and get them [the Japanese]. And we run up on four or five of them bunches. They scattered all over the islands, you know what I mean? We captured supplies and the greatest thing in the world, being on patrol found us some women. And so, we started looking for the women. And we brought seven [Japanese] back one time on a boat.

Had to stand guard on them all the time. All the time. Their eyes are slit like that. They look like they asleep, baby. Watching you like a hawk. And you be nodding and counting on the boat, and rocking, and watch them. And when we got back to the base and turned them into the stockade, the guy told them. Said, man, say, we almost had a good time. There were three, three of them seven was women. I didn't want to believe it. I'd say, no, no. But when we got to the stockade they were women. They were women. And there was a terrible excitement. Because, I mean, terrible deal on us because we was out there looking for the women. We know there were supposed to be some out there. And you run up on them and didn't know it, you know. Didn't know it. But that's what we did. Whenever, then we moved the natives from one island to another one. See, they bypass them, they didn't have no food or nothing. So, we go in with them LSTs [landing ship tanks] and put them on that LST, LSCs, that's the landing craft support. And bring them off the islands.

Joseph Walker We [the 52nd Composite Defense Battalion] were first split up in two groups. Group A and group B. I think I was in A 'cause Group A went to Majuro in the Marshall Islands. Oh we left, good gracious, we left out in California, San Diego. Next day we looked out there and half of those ships were gone somewhere else. By the third or fourth day wasn't nobody out there but our ship. I've forgotten the name of it right now. It had a little sub chaser, and half the time during the day we wouldn't see that sub chaser. We were actually afraid. I knew I was. When we got to Hawaii, that was another blessing. We stayed in Hawaii, on board ship, that was a miserable place too, nice and hot. Everybody's things were so close, and then of course, we left out going to Majuro in the Marshall Islands.

And they dropped us off and that's when we really got afraid, because the day before we stopped in Marshall Islands, Majuro, Marshall Islands, we didn't see any ships out there but ours. But that night we went in on Majuro, no lights. We didn't know where we were, but the guy told us when you hit the beach you're gonna have to find your hole and get in it. We didn't have any bombs or anything like [pre-invasion bombardment], this island had been secured.

But there were still submarine alerts and that kind of thing. So when daylight came up and you know what was sitting out there in that lagoon? The battleship *North Carolina*. And to make it sound as a big blessing, that rascal ship looked like she just pours, could knock down anything that came around, that was the best thing that ever happened to me.

Other than that we had a nice time on Majuro in Marshall Island. We'd go on patrol. We go scout the islands we'd see that any natives were over there or were there, any Japs had been there. And we saw signs of it [enemy presence], but we didn't encounter any shots fired or that kind of thing.

Saipan

Marines trained at Montford Point received their first taste of combat and suffered their first battlefield casualties with the invasion of Saipan in the Mariana Islands. After intense naval and air bombardment of the island, American forces invaded on June 15, 1944. The Montford Point companies that accompanied the invasion force on D-day included the 3rd Ammunition Company, the 4th Ammunition Company, and the 18th, 19th, and 20th Depot Companies. Landing craft loaded by Montford Point Marines came under fierce enemy shelling as they headed for the beaches, and once ashore both depot and ammunition company personnel dug in and helped repulse enemy counterattacks. After three weeks of intense fighting, including hand-to-hand combat, on July 9 American forces secured the island.

Turner Blount Well, after we's at sea for about ten days, we were told that we was going to take part in an invasion. And that invasion was the island of Saipan, in the Mariana Islands. And that took place on June the 15th of 1944. Being in the Montford Point Marine Depot Company, we was just in a supporting unit, who supports, to make sure that supplies and everything is available. And that we would keep the front lines and whatnot supported with the proper supplies they needed.

I recall air raids and things like that. We lived in a foxhole everywhere we went. We had to dig in and stay, never lived in a hut, a tent or anything like that. We just in foxholes, as we moved. And I spent a lot of time and doing guard of supplies. For instance, supplies have to go to the front. I don't care what time of night it would be, you would have to be on the truck to guard the driver, so the driver wouldn't get ambushed. And you would have to get on the truck on the supplies, sit on the outside, on the supplies. Just and guard supplies, as well as the driver, as you take, move forward with supplies.

I stayed in Saipan until the end of the operation there. After the operation there, we went to another island called Tinian, which is in the Mariana Groups, as well. And, of course, we performed the same duties there. I've guarding the prisoners or I had got prisoners on several occasions there. In Saipan and, of course, Tinian.

Fred Ash Well, we did security, 'cause we had Japanese prisoners, and we was guarding the prisoners, plus we was actually building the camp. We really didn't have a camp. And we had work details of blowing up [land] mines and marked mines, and then some of them [land mines] we had to search and find and look for them ourselves. We had demolition people that, you know, would help us, and we knew what to look for. So we'd seek them out, blow them up, and we had a lot of antiaircraft weapons. We didn't have nothing else to do, we'd polish them up.

Peleliu

In what is perhaps the least-known major battle of the Pacific island campaign, American forces stormed ashore on Peleliu in the Palau Islands on September 15, 1944. The amphibious landing came after the standard naval and air bombardment of Japanese positions. While the Americans encountered some resistance approaching the beaches, at Peleliu the Japanese commander reserved most of his 6,500 troops for a counterattack after American beachheads had been established, hoping to drive the invading force into the sea. The result of this strategy was one of the most fiercely fought battles of the Pacific war, which lasted until the end of October and claimed the lives of 1,252 Marines, almost 300 Army personnel, and practically all of the Japanese force. In addition, more than 5,000 Marines and 1,000 soldiers were wounded in the battle. Montford Point Marines participated in the invasion as members of the 11th Marine Depot Company and the 7th Marine Ammunition Company, in support of the 1st Marine Division, with both companies taking casualties.

Lawrence Diggs They shipped us out to Guadalcanal, and that's where we finished what they call jungle warfare training. So I went to special weapons school over there for different machine guns and mortars and what have you. I was with the 7th Ammo [Company], that was my unit. The 7th Ammo, in my view it was a supply company for a division. We got attached to the 1st Marine Division and the 3rd Battalion. We were replacing evidently some other unit that they had lost during the fighting out there before I got there. So, I was just one of the replacements, evidently.

When we boarded the ship at Guadalcanal, we really didn't know where we were going until after we'd been out to sea for, oh, maybe a day. I think they set out in the water maybe a day or two before they told the truth where we were headed to. And then they briefed us about what you were supposed to do when you get there, or go to the island. Because we set out there in the sea even when our Navy bombarded the island. We could see the island, but they smoked it over and cut down most of the trees.

Peleliu, and when we got ready to go shore, they assign you to whatever duties you're going to have and they sent my crew, I was with 7th Ammo, over toward an ammunition ship to start unloading as the first few waves of troops went ashore. Well, after we worked on the ship in different sets. We were working about seven or eight hours and then the [next] crew would relieve you. You wouldn't go ashore; you'd back on a rest area on the ship and then the next morning, if your crew had to work there, you'd start all over again. But, it was taking so long to take the island. They came over and just took the people that they knew had been trained to go ashore. And picked them up in amphibious ducks [a floating vehicle with tractor drives] and took them ashore. I was one of the groups that they took ashore.

When we got ashore, first thing they do, you dig yourself a foxhole; you dig, try to get in the sand deep enough to where you wouldn't get hit. And they just move you up as a group then, I mean, as you could move up. Now, the only thing that was keeping us down, they [the Japanese] had mortars that would come out on a track, and they just drop mortars all over the place. And you got your foxhole dug. Now when we dug the foxhole, we sit back to back, two guys in a hole and you sit with your back to each other. On that island, now they had land crabs as big as your hand, them land crabs. And at night, the land crabs crawled over and fall in that hole, he's crawling all over the sand, he'd fall in that hole with you, don't dare jump up or do anything. You just grab him and stab him, throw him back out of the hole. Anyway, I thought I was pretty well protected 'cause I had a guy at my back and I'm facing this way. You could sit in that hole just about all night and you wouldn't fall asleep, I mean, it's just too much going on for you to fall asleep.

The only way that we were able to get the enemy out of those caves up there was that we had different groups that was trained to scale a mountain, the sides. They would go up the mountainside with a tank on their back, with a flamethrower, you know, with the gelatin [napalm]. And we would start firing on the cave just to arouse those people [Japanese] that was back in there. To keep them from coming out and they would come down the side and that took two or three days. And when they come down the side and got next to the hole, they'd shoot that flame in the hole and if they didn't have an out on the other side, it'd burn up all the oxygen in it, in the hole. And that gun would be silenced. That happened on several occasions on that particular island. I think we only had three prisoners that was taken. Since I know now that the Japanese had a policy that they don't surrender, I mean, they'd rather die than surrender, or kill themselves rather than surrender. . . . I wondered all the time why they didn't surrender.

I was a rifleman, and I've had hand-to-hand combat with people. One of the people, once we got tents, once we got a beachhead on the island and moved in far enough where they could start the putting up tents for you to sleep in. You'd sleep in that hole for weeks. The Japanese would come down looking for food. The island was in pretty good hands then, and we had a great big guy from North Carolina named Oliver, and the Japanese came down and stumbled and fell in the tent on him. He tried to, and they didn't make a sound; it's just Oliver, Dillingham, and myself was in the tent. So when they fell in there, he [Oliver] just grabbed him and just choked him to death, just laid there with him all the rest of the night. And they had to give him a shot in his arm to get his hands loose from the, from the man's throat the next morning.

There was a lot of things that happened on the island that is not, I don't think, you'd tell on TV. But we finally got it secure. And the Japanese had a great big bulldozer that we couldn't get started or to move. I mean, one of the guys that like I said, the guy named Dillingham, he was a mechanic. His father in North Carolina had a logging outfit, trucks and what have you, so he was a pretty good mechanic.

He went out there one day, we had to bury the dead around there in order to put up the mess hall. He went out there one day, and it was a air-cooled motor, to start up the big motor. So he finally got it started; then he drove it, leveled that ground off, buried all those bodies and then we put a mess hall up, I mean, that 's where we put our mess hall up is right on the edge of the island.

We got a rubber boat and sent four or five guys out fishing with concussion grenades, and they'd drop them in the water and paddle like hell to get off them. And when it blow up, you know, the fish is numb, so they'd go by there and pick up a lot of different fish and take them up here and the doctor would tell you whether that you could eat these fish or not. We started eating pretty good after that. All the other time we was eating C ration before that.

I was nineteen. Mainly, what I was thinking about was survival. That was my constant thought, is try to be able to survive. This was a journey that I never [thought] I'd take, I mean, going out on an island in the Pacific or some place. I mean, it just looks like it was out of this world. I mean, it's somewhere that I never even dreamed of going. And once I'm out there and the group that I'm with, I had been taught that if we work together, we could survive. This was something that I thought about all the time. I mean, of course, being able to survive.

Now, the fear I guess wasn't any worse than it was any other time. As far as man-to-man [combat], I tell you, I was capable of handling just about any hand-to-hand combat fight if I got into it. 'Cause my life was at stake and I'm fighting dearly for dying. So, I guess I wasn't afraid. I just was looking for the unexpected all the time. I don't know what other way I can put it.

I can tell you one incident that, that happened that shouldn't have happened. We all had on colored underwear, you know, green for the jungle warfare. We had a scout, he was from New Jersey somewhere, named Douglas, and he could speak some Japanese. He was a black kid. He was a scout for the company. He went out and scout all around the island and went to the Japanese, where their soldiers were and told us about where to engage, where the mess hall and all that other stuff were.

And he stole a bike, come back on the, on the Japanese bike. And when he came into camp around dusk, he just went back to where he and his buddy was in the foxhole together; this is before we had tents. So now, that night, a land crab crawled in the hole where he were. He had on white underwear, you know, irregular Marine Corps supply. He didn't have on the dark underwear. We got all of that stuff just before we got on the ship, and he evidently didn't change. Anyway, when he hollered, they shot a flare up, the Japanese did, and you could see that white underwear. So they start shooting all across there, you know. In fact, he's lucky that some of our people didn't kill him. He survived. He gave our position away, though. But it was funny enough just [after it was] all over. It wasn't funny that night 'cause for about forty-five minutes to an hour they just, it was raked [by machine gun fire] all over. But you'd get down in that hole and get out of the way, you know.

I think it was around twenty-seven, twenty-eight days or more, and I really didn't keep track of the days. Once the island got halfway secured, we had cleanup. We had to bury all the dead and all this different days, you know, because it was, it was horrible. I mean, as far as the stench, stink was concerned. So after we got that done, we start trying to migrate around the island, but you went in five, six at a time, you know, together.

Reuben McNair I'll never forget, we were there in Peleliu in September of 1944. We were supposed to go up on the front line, take ammunition up, bring the wounded. And if you had the opportunity, you could bring the dead. But we was more concerned about the wounded, was to bring them back to the rear. At one point, we were sort of in a little tight position there. And we began to pull out the rifles and we [were] taking charge and secured the area. We had a group of white Marines; they was very happy. And as they returned back, they stated to [other white Marines], as to what happened. They said the black angels saved us. As you know, at that particular time, we felt a little uncomfortable when you called us black. It wasn't like when James Brown come along, singing I'm black and I'm proud. This is something that come along afterward. At that particular time, we felt a little uncomfortable.

However, to know that the black angels, if they throw out that we were black angels, I felt well, black angels saved you. So, we brought those people back, and they says, well, the black angels saved us and this is something that's in history that went down. So, we later hear James Brown say he was black and proud and that particular time, I guess we felt that we are proud and we was black. And I feel proud for that.

Lee Douglas Jr. We were left, and wind up in Guadalcanal. Guadalcanal Island. We went there, and every day we would go out training. The men would march, and then they would go out training. Getting ready, they call it snapping in. But we would get ready for an invasion. We knew that we were going to another place, invading a island. So, that's what we were getting ready to do. They would take us up in the jungles. They the worse jungles that you want to see in the Guadalcanal, but we would go up in the jungles, and we had to study the jungles. How to mark the trees, and how to be able to identify your way out. And this kind of training is what we had, preparatory for the invasion. Those in heavy equipment and transportation was out with their vehicles. Or traveling on the rough terrain so that they would understand how the terrain would be. And the troops would be out marching and testing their skills.

My outfit, the 7th Ammunition Company, was then attached to the 1st Marine Division. The 1st Marine Division did not have any blacks within its structure, and the only way that blacks get to get to them, it's like you grab a pot and place it over side the wall. They attached us to that division 'cause our job was handling the ammunition as it come off the ship. We were assigned an area on the island [Peleliu] where we would be, where all the ammunition comes to us, because they could not have that ammunition all over the island. You just had to be in a certain area.

D-day One, we were ready to go ashore [onto Peleliu], but they said that we could not go ashore, because they was having a lot of difficulty with the invasion going in. A lot of bodies was floating in the ocean, and they needed, right at the beachhead, a lot of bodies. And they assigned the 7th Ammunition, our group, to the bodies, to go and take the bodies out of the water and put them on nets and pull them back on the ship. The next day, they assigned us to the same job of securing the bodies from the waters. Whereby the propeller, the ship wouldn't cause trouble.

The third day, we went ashore. We went ashore in the barges to beachhead. Because you must go in. You got to get in the barges and go in with your rifles and everything. The ammunition stuff doesn't take place until after you take the island and settle. But you got to go in to do that . . . once you go into the Marine Corps, regardless of the assignment, you must learn the rifle, the pistol, the range, your combat, you have to learn all of that. You may be a mechanic. You may be a cook, but the rifle comes first. You must learn that part of combat. So, whenever you get overseas, your second job, that's all it becomes, second. First becomes the rifle. The invasion is first.

My company, when we went in, we went with our rifles blazing. There is no secondhand nothing. We had looked forward to taking the airfield in a day or two. And was no such thing as that, you know. They were dug in, the enemy was dug in so strong, until everybody was held up at the beach.

Iwo Jima

The photograph of the raising of the United States flag on Mt. Suribachi on February 23, 1945, has become an instantly recognizable icon. It is fitting this powerful image of that moment amidst the carnage and destruction wreaked by two armies locked in a struggle to the death has come to symbolize America's sacrifice and ultimate triumph in the war in the Pacific. Iwo Jima is a study in the horrors of war in the industrial age and of the courage of the men who endured it.

The all-Marine invasion force shoved off from the supporting fleet and headed for the beaches of Iwo Jima on February 19, 1945. The landing craft immediately encountered a barrage of enemy shell fire that signaled that the pre-invasion bombardment of the island had not significantly reduced the ability of the Japanese to resist. Mortar, machine gun, and rifle fire rained down on the Marines as they waded ashore and attempted to dig into the shifting, powdery black volcanic sand. The 8th Marine Ammunition Company and the 36th Marine Depot Company went in on D-day. Men of the 33rd and 34th Marine Depot Companies soon followed. The battle for

Iwo Jima raged until March 17, when the Marines finally secured the island at a cost of 6,821 killed and 15,308 wounded, including men from each of the Montford Point units. Of the more than 22,000 Japanese troops defending the island, only 1,083 were taken prisoner.

Ellis Cunningham I left Montford Point in August of '44 and went to Hawaii. And there we started loading, first separating the ammunition from various dumps we had there. We would pack the ammunition on skids, another form of packaging, and load them on ships. And we did this from September until January, not knowing at the time what we were loading all these ships for. We just loaded ships . . . until January, and we got on some of those ships, and left Pearl Harbor on the 19th of January, I believe it was. And started going toward Iwo Jima, and we got in the area of Iwo Jima, right after the day before the landing.

We'd already made a stop at Saipan. For a while, I thought it was Guam, but I was told that was Saipan where we stopped and rearranged the ships, because from Pearl Harbor we carried big pontoons on the side of all those ships. They were for two purposes. They was transporting the pontoons to make docks out of them, once they got Saipan and Guam. They floated pontoons to make docks and also to keep the ship afloat, in case you got torpedoed, or bombed on the way there, those pontoons on the side of the ship would serve as flotation. We cut them off the day before we got to Iwo Jima. And also that same day about six transport ships, the huge transport ships that carried the landing forces, and the numerous carriers and the destroyers and other ships, warships, were there.

D-day got people up early. I don't know why, but they got up early. On the LST that I was on, all of us slept on the top deck; anyhow, very few people slept below deck, because below deck was loaded with ammunitions and trucks and stuff like that, so there wasn't any sleeping space. Down in the berthing compartment was for the crew of the ship. We were just on our cargo ship, so we slept up top. We got that we could see early in the morning, the bombing and strafing from the ships and from the aircraft. Flew a lot of these aircrafts, bombing the island and strafing the landing area.

We watched that for a little while, but in the meantime, from these transport [ships], they were loading the assault troops. They [the landing craft] were circling on the water, and that's when the first wave took off heading to the beach. Later in the afternoon, it was our turn. We pulled up the LSTs, right up to the beach, the landing, the initial landing. We were running little landing craft. Most of them did, anyhow. And you got some of them were

Combat

Photographs of Montford Point Marines in combat are difficult to find. These shots, from *Pictures of African Americans during World War II*, an online exhibit of the United States National Archives and Records Administration, convey some sense of the men's combat experiences. (USNARA)

Marines catch a smoke on board a troop ship headed for the South Pacific.

The confidence and camaraderie of Montford Point Marines is evident in this shot of troops shipping out for the South Pacific.

A unit of Montford Point Marines in battle dress assembles on the deck of a ship in the South Pacific, February 1944.

Members of a 51st Defense Battalion gun crew on duty in the Marshall Islands

Waiting for orders to move forward on the beach at Saipan

Relaxing with a captured bicycle after the fall of Saipan

Two Marines prepare to drink to victory on Saipan, using one of the island's coconuts.

Marines on the beach at Peleliu

Two Marines using damaged ducks for cover during the invasion of Iwo Jima

Transporting the wounded at Iwo Jima

Three Montford Point Marines relax on the sands of Iwo Jima.

Somewhere in the Pacific, Sergeant Timerlate Kirven (left) and Corporal Samuel J. Love Jr. receive Purple Hearts for wounds received during the invasion of Saipan.

Montford Point veterans salute the colors at the 2004 convention
of the Montford Point Marines Association held in Arlington, Virginia.
(UNC Wilmington Television)

riding in amphibious tractors, and, especially tractor company, half the guys was riding on those. And there were three companies that were amphibious truck . . . they started ashore. Now all of those trucks was blown up before they got to the shore. And those trucks carried their weapons, primarily concerned with carrying troops. They were carrying ammunition and guns. The truck was equipped with a boom that could lift a 105 mm howitzer from the ship that they were carrying them onto the truck, and to the beach. That's how they got the initial howitzers to the beach. And they couldn't use them right away anyhow, because there just wasn't any room for them.

The LST that we were on pulled up right to the beach itself. Opened the front, that's where we would head out. Didn't make it very far on the beach, just yards, a matter of a hundred yards or so. Because the beach was soft, so much sand, so a vehicle could not run through it. So before you get a vehicle like a truck or a jeep anywhere, they had to go up the incline, you had to lay down mats, this steel matting, before the truck would run up there. And how you get the steel matting up there? You get a bulldozer to pull them up there. The bulldozers, most of them was operated by Seabees [Navy construction units]. And there's a special pilot to do that, pull these mats up so the truck would go up on them. Our job was to dig with the bulldozers again, with the Seabees, dig the bunker real quick, and put the ammunition into the bunker for distribution, for the assault troopers right in front of us. You had to get this to them because each man could only carry enough for maybe one day, depending on the intensity of the fight. He can only carry so much ammunition with him. So, it had to be replenished, depending on this ammunition company, to get the stuff to him, and that's what we did.

Yes, I did [see the flag raised on Mount Suribachi]. At the time, I didn't understand the significance of this, but I saw. I was maybe 200 or 300 yards from it, north of it; the flag was on the southern end of the island at Suribachi. When the flag was raised there, everybody was naturally looking south, and I saw the flag. But at the time, it didn't dawn on me that this was a significant event, so I wasted no attention looking at it. It didn't mean much to me until later on. My wife and I went back in 1995, on the fiftieth anniversary of this flag raising; we went back there. Now this time actually brought tears to my eyes. Now I understand the significance of it, and the meaning of it. So, you know, made a lot of difference then, but in 1945, it made very little difference.

Gene Doughty I had the first squad of the 36th Depot. And on our way to an island that I thought really, in our minds, and it's like everything else there. When you're embarking, or when you're en route to a undisclosed island, those who were really interested in the geographical location, you know, we've got our maps out, and we looked at, and says, you know, I bet you they're going here, I bet you they're going there. My feeling was the island of Taiwan, at that time I believe it was under another name. This island, for some reason, was isolated. There was no battles, no warfare. And I couldn't understand why this huge island, right off the coast of China, was not invaded. It's Japanese held. We couldn't understand why, and I thought that was the island we were going to.

Needless to say, when we did land, we landed on the island of Iwo Jima, which was part of the volcano islands. Its origin was a volcanic ash. There were four all-black companies [that landed]. There were just two [black] companies, the 8th Ammo and the 36th Depot Company, which I was part of, that landed on D-day. Eventually, the remaining part of the depot companies landed on D plus three, D plus four, etc. But there were two all-black companies that landed on D-day. We were pinned down for several hours going into one and two days. The island I would describe as out of the pages of H. G. Wells, if I may. Very eerie, there were no trees, there was no shrubbery. Just black sand, hills and dunes, that sort of thing. Extremely tough terrain. Even amphibious [vehicles], tracked amphibious units, to really ascend upon, you know, going into the area, they had their problems.

There were Army ducks, of course. There was a black regiment that took part in D-day. The unit escapes me at the moment, but we had a black [Army] regiment who also went on D-day. Part of their responsibility, history may not note this, and may not be in the books, but part of this Army regiment's responsibility was to help with the transportation of Marines from the vessels. And onto the shore. Army and amphibious, black amphibious units bringing in boatloads of Marines. And needless to say, they met with extreme, very harsh attacks from the Japanese there. Some of them never even got ashore. I give them praise . . . to these brave men from the U.S. Army, all-black units, who assisted the Navy department in hauling in Marine infantry troops.

There were three [Japanese] airfields on Iwo. It was Motoyama airfield one, two, and three. Only one of the three airfields was partly completed, it wasn't even completed, by the Japanese. So that when we landed, there was just one landing strip there, partly one landing strip. I was located right there. Our position, once we got to the beach, and secured, my company was asked to guard [the airstrip]. So we became a security force in that regard, around the first Motoyama airfield. That's where, on D plus five, when I saw, in the distance, the flag raising. So I was not really, not even at the base on Mount Suribachi, where the flag raising took place. I was further towards the shoreline, instead, where the airfield was at. To see that, I guess I would say we took part in the jubilation, the likes you'll never see again. You know, one time, to see these men just take off their helmets. Now, here the Japanese are still entrenched back in the hills. And these guys were taking off their hats and tossing them up in the air. And here's shellfire coming all over the place there. Sure, there was a flag raising. But that didn't mean that the Japanese security forces had been defeated. It was just a flag raising. There was still much to go, some thirty-three days left before the cessation of hostilities on that island. But, yes, we took part in the jubilation, and it was like we said, well, I guess it's gonna be the end of the war. We'll be home pretty soon. That was the attitude.

Roland Durden We stayed at Pearl Harbor for about three or four months and then we got on an LST, the 33rd and the 34th Depot [Companies]. . . . I slept under a truck, the top deck, from Pearl Harbor to Guam to Iwo Jima. The whole fleet formed at Guam and sailed north to Iwo Jima. . . . We arrived there the night or the early morning of February 19th, 1945. I got me a seat and I watched the war going on, the bombing, the firefights, and the battleships and cruisers that encircle the supply ships, the troops ships, the medical ships, and the other ships, and fire over the ships into the island.

On the night of February 23rd we hit shore and we loaded the front, the ramp, but the Japanese mortar hit us about five times. We were loaded with ammunition in the hold, so the captain pulled away from shore. The next morning, February the 24th, my birthday, we stepped on the island. Our job was to bury the dead. . . . We weren't told we were going to be in a burial detail until we got there. Until we saw the bodies. So, we weren't prepared; in fact, I don't think any war prepares you for some of the duties you will have to [do].

The way that was done is that we had maybe a Seabee or an engineer operating a caterpillar, dig a long trench to hold twenty bodies, ten in a row. And where the section put down gently and had their head facing the flag, the flag wasn't there yet, but they showed us where the flag would be. And we picked up the bodies that they were in all kinds of condition. I remember working with my partner, I always called him Combat Kerry. We had picked up a body and put him in the little area where we had dug up for the bodies and had to go back and get the leg. But bodies was in all kind of condition, the brains out, the intestines out, you know, some bodies way beyond recognition. After we had put twenty bodies in a trench, we'd have the chaplains, Jewish, Catholic, and Protestant, say their prayers over the bodies, which include ashes to ashes, dust to dust, and after the prayers are said and we had the trumpeter blow taps, whatnot. Then the operator of the caterpillar would cover up the bodies, then we go to the next trench, day in and day out.

I didn't see the flag when it went up, actually, I was still on board ship, so I didn't notice whether the flag went up or nothing, I couldn't say I saw it.

Archibald Mosley 36 Marine [Depot Company] got first, where we saw combat and bullets . . . in fact was Iwo Jima. All of us that embarked onto PA 33 [a troop ship] . . . instructors, all sixteen of us, and I hate I can't remember all sixteen of the names. But some that come to me, my memory now is Sergeant Hughes, Sergeant Cookie, Big Dunbar, who taught me how to curse, because I didn't know how. Captain Harvey had him take me out to the boondocks and teach that boy how to talk like a Marine. And some of the others, Epson, some of the others I could name, we were all attached the 36 Marine Depot Department, which one of our greatest conflicts out of all was the famous battle that'll never die in history, the invasion of Iwo Jima.

An island eight miles square and had a big mountain on the end of it called Mount Suribachi. Which created the island, the eight-mile island, by volcanic ash and soot that came up out of it when it erupted. And all of the soil was sandy soil, like from Suribachi. And actually, it was difficult to even dig a foxhole. Because once you tried to dig in it, the deeper you would go, the, the foxhole would cave in because it's nothing but sandy soil. It was difficult to hide in it.

Now one of the things I told you, we were on PA 33, which is a huge ship. But you couldn't make a landing on Iwo Jima with that. So we had to disembark off of the big ship onto what is known as a landing barge. And the landing barge would pick you up, get up high speed so as to try to go up on the beach, as far as it could. Because what you're bringing is the equipment and that's the reason your outfit is called 36 Depot [Company].

Depot applied to that you're bringing supplies. And sometimes we tried to impress on everyone our importance, not only to ourselves but to others. Because people were to think, well, because you are the workhorses, you carry the equipment, you carry the ammunition, you carry the fuel. It was the most dangerous thing in the world. Because sometimes if you were to look back at the landing barges coming behind you, there may be some of your comrades. And if the enemy shooting mortars get a direct hit on one of those landing barges that has fuel on it. Just imagine it blowing up and you're in it. Or one of the landing barges turn over and here you are sinking in the Pacific Ocean and the water all around you is stained because there's so many bodies. So, if after two and three days, you haven't even gotten up on the beach far enough to be known as you have made a beachhead, but yet, you've got to carry and drag this equipment on up. . . .

When the battle was declared to be over on Iwo Jima, five or so white Marines were on top of Mount Suribachi, raising a flag. That's become a great symbol. And, actually like we like to tell them, white boys couldn't have climbed that mountain if we black boys wasn't at the bottom giving them supplies and ammunition to be able to climb it. And one of the significances of symbolism that's being portrayed by the raising of that flag on Mount Suribachi is the victory of gaining the island. Why was the island important? It's because what we were supposed to do is build an airstrip on top of this island. And the purpose of that, the importance of that airstrip is so that the planes could come and be refueled and continue on and over to bombing the homeland of Japan. Even with that symbolism of the flag being raised on Mount Suribachi, we thought that this means it's all over now, and we can get a good night's sleep.

So many of us went to sleep that night, and that was when, I'm sure you've heard about, the great Bonsai Attack on Iwo Jima. The night of the Bonsai Attack is where a lot of old Marines referred to it. What that means is that you would put a bayonet on the end of your rifle. And the reason you don't fire the rifle, but attempt to kill the enemy with the bayonet is because if you're attacking in close, everybody's around and fighting, you don't know who you're shooting at night, in the dark, because that's what happened that night. The enemy came out of those caves. I'm sure you heard about how they were dug in on that mountain in that island. And that even for days and weeks, that island had been bombed and everything. And they thought they killed the enemy.

But they were down in caves, sometimes two and three floors down. I could remember one of the stories about that. There was one of those caves that had the outfit pinned down. And, the squad was ordered to go and see if you couldn't get it, and knock it out. And they come back and [Captain Harvey] ask did you knock it out? And he said, yeah, we threw some hand grenades in there and knocked it out. And he [Captain Harvey] said, well, did you go in and see if it [was destroyed]. I knew as a teenager, that I wasn't as dumb as grandpa and them thought I was, 'cause I had better sense than to go in another person's house, through one door, and I don't know whether there's another door to get out. Because if you go in one of those caves and he [the enemy] come in behind you and you don't know how to get out, you hung. 'Cause some of those caves were more than one story down and some of them would go way back.

Actually, one of the lessons that I learned from Captain Harvey, I asked him, I said, you mean to tell me you would send a squad of nine men up to a place like that, knowing they wouldn't come back? You would order them to death? And he said, well, young man, I'm not required to explain anything to you, just give you an order. But since you're my boys and you've been so faithful, let me tell you that you, which would you rather do? Would you rather sacrifice a few to save many? And that is one lesson that I will never forget. And want to give the old gray-haired man credit for, 'cause in my life, I've had to make some decisions like that. Sacrifice a few to save many.

I'd like to explain and tell you about when I was telling you about the landing barge going up on the beach. And to carry all the way from our landing barge going up onto the beach and not getting up there because you get off in water and describe to you what that water looked like. It wasn't clear. I'd like to take you from that on up to when we went off of the island. But some of the things I don't even like to remember.

But I do want to say one that I do remember. Because it correlates back to my first night at Montford Point. I told you when I said my prayers and the boys laughed at me. Well, the one incident that I'd like to share with you occurred in the night of the Bonsai Attack. Babyface and, and I hate I can't remember Babyface's real name. We called him Baby, that's the bad thing about nicknames to people. But the reason we gave him the name Babyface, he was only sixteen years of age. You say, well, how did you get in the Marine Corps? Well, he lied about his age and got in there. And he wanted one of those uniforms, too. He was like me. He felt, well, we, black fellows, you called us black, if you put some red around us, we're gonna look good.

But Babyface didn't wake up, when Babyface got injured. But what did wake me up is my foxhole buddy, Wilbur. And Wilbur woke me up fighting the enemy. But Babyface got hurt, and the gang, we all went to him. We couldn't help him. And we were calling for the corpsmen to come get him. But, so many people was hurt, and they were trying to carry off so many other bodies and other people. So in the meantime, while they would come, the corpsmen would come help Babyface. My colleagues said, Archibald, Archibald, come on, man, come on, Moses, pray for him. And you know, I didn't think about it at that time. I just went to Babyface, touched him and prayed for him. But you know, in my old age, you look back and now I'm mad. I say, you know, those same dudes that laughed at me and made fun of me saying my prayers that night, finally, at Iwo Jima, when it got tough, they wanted me to pray. But I'm glad Mama taught me how to pray. 'Cause those bullets and all were coming, they didn't say these bullets for whites and these bullets for blacks. Those bullets, you know what was on those bullets? To whomever they concern. And those bullets were just as much concerned to us as they were to everybody else.

My wife will tell you, I had to quit talking about it, 'cause I'd have bad dreams at night. She would wake me up and talking you're still fighting the war. I didn't get married until a year or two after I got out of the Marine Corps. But when I did get married, I was still fighting these battles.

Steven Robinson We landed on Green Beach. I got to tell you about when we landed. We landed D-day was February 19, 1945. The landing date was supposed to been 09:00. But the sea was so rough, and we disembarked in Higgins boats from the aft of the ship. We had cargo and that's going into the Higgins boats. One of the first people to go down into the Higgins boats were, of course, the platoon sergeants and platoon guide. We had to go down to secure the nets as the men came down the cargo net because you got to visualize that the barges are even, you know. As the waves go down, the barge drops. As the waves go up, the barge will rise. And he would have to tell the men as he lined up on the cargo net, tell him when to release to embark into the barge.

They had to release, when I say release, you had to release at that point in time because if they didn't, they may fall another six or seven feet. All of them had probably, all together with the ammunition, I'm talking about the bandoliers of ammunition, hand grenades and packs and your rifles and shovels and this stuff. They had probably close to 135 pounds of gear on. You fall in that distance, six or seven or eight feet with that kind of gear, you'd break an ankle, break a leg. We had to be certain that they were able to get into the barges without being injured.

And once you got into the barge, the sea was still rough, we rendez-voused for maybe about ten or fifteen minutes, I guess, to the other people were down in their barges. We headed into the shore. We landed on Green Beach. Our group was assigned to what they call shore patrol, and I was 28th Marine 2nd Battalion. We were Able Company, Company A, and we landed, of course, we had to instruct the fellows as they come down to the barge, that was our first operation. Don't harness up. Keep your harnesses open so then you think like you get a hit in the barge, turn over so you can just change, you can always get another rifle. Just change your gear, change your ammo, save your life. And then we had to instruct the other fellows that look, if your buddy get hit, just keep going, and find someplace safe, you know, until we regroup, until we move in further.

That was when we landed on Green Beach. Was February the 19th, 1945. When Jimmy lost his life, if it probably had not been Jimmy, it would have been me 'cause he was only two feet off my right shoulder. We got this [Japanese] mortar and it hit us. Jimmy had gone down to the beach. Jimmy was looking for sandbags to construct this foxhole. I didn't know where he was and he come past and I was chewing him off for not having dug this foxhole because I figured we were going to get sit upon [by] the barrage pretty soon. Jimmy was on my right shoulder about two feet when he got hit. And he was killed. One of the, I didn't know, I was blown up in the air about eight or nine feet. I remember being unconscious in and out of it. I would black out, come to, black out. I could smell the gunpowder in my nostrils and finally fell back to the deck. Corpsmen were running, people were screaming and hollering. And finally, the corpsman came to me and he checked me over. Found out I had some shrapnel on my left side. And found I had some shrapnel on my shoulder. And he kind of kiddingly said, well, he said, you're okay, but I can't send you back. I can't write you up and send you back to the ship. He said, you'll be okay. So I just consider you the walking wounded. And he looked down there for information, my rank and my unit and so forth, for a Purple Heart. And then I watched him. He took all this information down 'cause I said they're [the Japanese] going to barrage.

And [the Japanese] dropped an 88, I guess it was 88 or 105 [mm shell] on a pack house unit of probably about twenty-five yards away at the most. And they took an awful hit, a direct hit. These guys and their guns took a direct hit. When I saw them, they were up in the air, some of the bodies were up and their body parts were up in the air fifteen, twenty, thirty feet. I thought they were sandbags. I didn't know at the time, it was a body of Marines and they were blown apart. This corpsman, who had treated me and treated my foxhole buddy, he got over in time to get hit by one of these mortar shells and just, of course, completely devastated.

I think I witnessed the raising of the flag. It had to be about around the 23rd or 24th of February. I could see the men working away up the base at Mount Suribachi. You could see the artillery fire. You could hear the small arms fire. I said to, think it was my platoon guide. I said, they must be halfway up Mount Suribachi. They're going to secure that mountain probably today sometime. And about that time I saw the flag go up.

As a matter of fact, the thing that interests me was, I didn't know at the time, but I learned later that there was an Indian fellow. He was of Indian extraction, Native American. His name escapes me now. I saw him every day on the ship, we were on the same PA. I saw one of the corpsmen who was in the raising of the flag and another Marine. So there were two Marines who were on my PA and one of the corpsmen of the six to raise the flag on Mount Suribachi. I didn't find that out until later. It was just something that we had secured [part] of the mountain at that point, because the front was very fluid. The Japanese, you'd be maybe a couple hundred yards in today and they'd push you back, maybe a 100 charge the next day. That's the way it was. The front was just very fluid.

That sticks with me, and I [got] just more to the story about Jimmy. When we got to Pearl Harbor, we were unloading our gear. Jimmy was on a working party and he got his hand infected on some of that rough lumber. He didn't have it treated and it festered. As a matter of fact, it just about gangrened on him. It swole up. . . .

So I went to CO and I said to him, Captain, are you consider shipping [Jimmy] Wilkins back to the States for treatment on his hand? He said, yes, going to get a replacement. So I went to Jimmy. I said, Jimmy, I said, this is your ticket home. You're going back to the States so you can get better treatment. He said, no I don't want to go. He said, can't you talk to the captain and see if I can't get a chance to go with you fellows. And I said, this is your chance to go back to the States. So I went to the captain and talked to him again. And he said, well, he said you talk to the doctor. If you can convince the doctor that he should stay with your unit, he said, then he can go down. So I went to the doctor and I explained to the doctor. He said but you'll probably be aboard ship. He said we got doctors aboard. He said they can treat his hand. I have no qualms with him shipping out with you folks because I think by the time that you get where you're going, his hand will probably be well enough. Send up to be back to duty again.

So I went back to my CO and explained it to him what the situation was, and we didn't order a replacement and kept Jimmy. But we talked to Jimmy. Look, go back to the States. And he said, no I want to stay with you folks. I totally said to him, why, why? And he said to me and I'll never forget. I will take it to my grave. He said because you're my family. You're my family. And he stayed with us. I said, Jimmy was more than that. Jimmy was kind of like, he was like a, like a pet. He was kind of like, everybody liked him, everybody liked him in the platoon. I mean, he was just a likeable seventeen-year-old young teenager. And I might add, a good Marine. He was a good

Marine but, you know, he was a youngster, that's all. And Jimmy was the first, I think the first, that we'd lost in my company. Jimmy was killed, and we lost three others in my company. . . .

I got up at night, pitch, nights out there were so black, pitch black, not a star in the sky. Somebody come into my foxhole and said, Sergeant, you're needed. You're wanted on Post Number Three. They got trouble down there. I come up out of my tent, got in my jeep. I didn't even know [where] Post Number Three was because, as I said, I didn't post too many down there. I put the ocean on my right, inland was on my left. So, I said, I'll drive down.

They give me the general directions of where the post was, and I said, I'll drive down and I'll find this post and see what's going on. I got there, had barbed wire strung all around the area. I couldn't find a way in. I finally found a place, a defoliated spot, and I got under this wire, this barbed wire, and I come up on the inside where there should have been a guard. And I challenged them. I asked for a guard. Guard Post Number Three. Nobody answered. Guard Post Number Three. And I realized I was standing up, so the thought come to me because we had heard of Japanese trying to disguise themselves as Americans to lure you into a trap or ambush, so I decided I would get down off the [horizon], so I wouldn't be a good target. I kneeled down to get off so I wouldn't be a target for whoever it was there. So, finally a voice come back, he says over here, over here. It didn't sound like any voice I knew. And what had happened was this man had gotten back beyond this tarpaulin and he under the tarpaulin and the tarpaulin was distorting his voice.

So, finally, when he came out from under the tarpaulin, I recognized him as being a man from my platoon, Booker James. So I said, what's the problem? He said, I just killed three Japs. I said, killed three Japs where? And he was kind of, he was upset and he kept saying, instead of saying at two o'clock or at three o'clock [locations corresponding to numerals on a watch face], he was giving me over there, a motion like that, over there. And then he'd go back up under the tarpaulin. So I said to him, I could see where he wasn't going to be much help. So I'm going to try to find these Japs, because he shot three Japs.

So I got down, not to be a good silhouette, and I started duck-walking around the inside of the [ammunition] dump, to try to find these bodies. I couldn't find any Japs. So I thought maybe they got away. As I started back to where James was, I stumbled over the foot of a man and which I found out it was a Marine. And when I got back, I turned him over and it was a

Marine. It was a white Marine. I checked his pulse. He had no pulse. He had no heartbeat. He was dead.

And I said, well, James said it was three. And I hadn't gone very far, maybe another maybe eight or nine or ten feet, and I stumbled over a second body, another white Marine. I checked him out. He had no pulse, no heartbeat. He was dead. And I said, well, he said three. And about the time that I was about to stand up and walk back toward him, I heard this fellow groan. So, I went over another maybe eight or nine feet and there was another body, white Marine. He wasn't dead. He was still alive. All these men were running away from James because they were all shot in the back.

James had a BAR [Browning automatic rifle]. When I got to this man, he was still alive, barely breathing. I looked and he'd been hit at the back of the skull. I took my aid packs off. We had sulfur at those times. I sprinkled sulfur on the wound and tried to stop the flow of blood the best I could, co-agulate it, and to get the man down to the aid station. And I did all this, I said to James, he is a pretty big fellow, he's about my size, weighed about 200 some pounds and I had to get him back on the stretcher to get him back on the jeep.

I said, James, you're going to have to help me get this man up on the jeep. And James said to me, I'm not touching him. That's a Jap. And I said, James, it's not a Jap. He's one of our fellows. I'm not touching him. So, finally I said to him, I didn't know whether I had a problem with James before. I didn't know whether or not how far I could push him before James would turn his BAR on me. Who's to say what happened out there? Just he and I and if I'm gone.

So finally I said to him, James, get down and look at that man. I said, he's one of us. He's a white Marine. He got down and I said, you see he's not a Jap. Help me get him up on a stretcher. I couldn't get him up there alone. So, finally he helped me get him up on the stretcher. I said, now let me get him, take him out now and put him up on the jeep, get him down to the aid station. He didn't want to do it, but finally he come around and he helped me put him up on the jeep, and we got him down to the aid station. . . .

I went out in the back, and it was pitch black. Not a star in the sky. Inky black. And finally my eyes become accustomed, and there's nothing out there. And I said, well, I don't want to sound stupid by going back and asking this doctor where are the blankets? So, finally I noticed in the dark, maybe about fifteen to twenty feet away, there was something out there. So I walked over there and these were corpses. These were men wrapped in blankets. I imagine they were probably about stacked up at least five or six feet and probably at least thirty or forty feet down. There had to be at least 200 bodies. It hit me with such force that I, when I knew anything, I was kneeling on the deck. I tried to get up a couple of times. The strength had gone all out of my legs. Tried to get up, I couldn't pull myself up. So then I said to myself, what are you doing here? I kept, I don't know how long I was down, probably not that long, maybe a minute, maybe two.

And I went over there where these men were and I tried to get a blanket. The first man I tried to get a blanket from, he probably weighed over 200 pounds and the blanket was tucked too close around him. I couldn't get the blanket out from under him. So, I found me a couple smaller corpses, and I took blankets because I figured that they didn't need the blankets. I needed them because it was cold. And I wasn't going to take my blankets off the young Marine that I left in that aid station. I got back to my area and I just sacked out. I didn't wake up until afternoon about 1:00. . . .

But there's another side to that that it disturbed me for years. I had to go back, I guess it had to be about D[-day] maybe D plus eighteen, D plus nineteen. It was less than D plus twenty. I had to go back to the other side [of the] island. If you ever been on Iwo, they got these sulfur pits where they had this sulfur water. And as I come up over this ridge, there were Marines. I know they were Marines. There was about eight of them. As I come up over the ridge, this one Marine held his hand up for me to stop. I was in my jeep. So I stopped. I wondered what did he want me to stop for? But, I figured, well, I mean, just something momentarily, 'cause there was nothing. All I saw around me was a recon. And I thought it was a command post and for some reason he didn't want me to leave there, for whatever reason it was. It was stop. So, after what was about two minutes, I started, and he held up his hand again stop. I said to myself, well, what does he want? I couldn't figure why he wanted me to stop.

And these Marines, some of them had their rifles at port arms. There were a couple that had 45's on their sides so I figured they'd be the NCOs or officers. A couple of them had BARs; some of them had Thompson machine guns. And I looked to see what they were waiting on. Out of this rubble, which was a pillbox, were these Japanese prisoners, I mean Japanese soldiers, digging themselves out of this rubble. They were not in uniform. They didn't have a stitch on them but a loincloth. So, you could see that they wasn't armed. They had no arms, they had no hand grenades, they had nothing. They were just down to bare, naked skin.

All of a sudden I hear this small arm fire, so I reached for my carbine on the seat beside me, and I recognized who was doing the firing. The Marines were firing on these Jap prisoners that were coming out to give themselves up. And they were emaciated. You could see they were dehydrated. These guys didn't weigh any more than 110 pounds. And they hit them with a round from that BAR or that Thompson, and their bodies just scoot across the road. I couldn't believe it. I looked at this Marine and made eye contact with him. He looked at me and I looked at him. And I said, and the look that he had on his face was not one of friendliness. I thought I'd better get the hell out of there. So, I just gunned my jeep, took off and was gone.

Never told anybody about it for years and years, because I didn't, number one, I didn't believe it would happen. I did not believe something like that could happen. I didn't believe a Marine would do that, if I hadn't seen it with my own eyes. Now, I'm not going to go back, I don't know, I mean, as I said before, I don't know why. I mean, I know people change. I don't know why they did it. I'm not going [to] try to explain why they did it. I'm just telling you what I saw. I didn't think that the level in me, even at that point, a rage, or hatred, had risen to a level [they] would shoot down on an unarmed man. And I saw eleven unarmed Japanese soldiers executed there on Iwo.

Okinawa

American forces captured Okinawa planning to make it the staging area for the invasion of the Japanese home islands, located less than 400 miles to the north. Both Marine and Army forces began the invasion on April 1, 1945. Three Montford Point ammunition companies and four depot companies hit the beaches on D-day, to be joined by four additional depot companies by the end of the month. The Japanese continued their attacks until American forces finally secured the island on June 21. As on other Pacific island battlefields, the fierce Japanese resistance resulted in staggering casualties. The Japanese lost an estimated 107,000, of which 42,000 were civilians killed by American artillery bombardments, while the United States suffered casualties of 11,260 killed and 33,769 wounded. More Montford Point Marines, over 2,000, participated in the battle for Okinawa than in any other World War II engagement.

Turner Blount Well, Okinawa, I was mostly in a supporting group, of course. And make sure that all the supplies and everything was moved to the front. And guard prisoners, as well. Well, it just that, we went running for safety when there's air raids at night, during any hour, trying to run for cover. And, of course, stand duties at night, for the enemies. Make sure that you're not ambushed or anything of that nature. After Okinawa, I was sent back to the States in 1946, due in February of 1946.

James Ferguson I was in the Battle of Okinawa, attached to the 6th Marine Division. I think it was May something to June something [1945]. I was in combat on Okinawa. There were 2,000 black Marines that participated in combat on Okinawa. Thirty of them were wounded, four were killed. And the reason we had four, because in 1998, they found three dead Marines who had been declared as missing, they found their bodies in a cave on Okinawa. So that meant that four black Marines were killed on Okinawa. I was on guard duty, we guarded Marine supplies and in many cases we would guard supplies on a ship.

So I was guarding the Marine beer and whiskey and supplies on a ship known as the *John S. Rawlings* in June 1945. And while we were guarding that ship, that ship was torpedoed by a Japanese torpedo bomber. And the ship was damaged so severely until it subsequently sank. Now, on Okinawa, most of the Japanese planes were suicide troops, suicide planes called kamikazes, in which they would ram the ship, blow up the ship and committed suicide. But I considered it very fortunate that this was not a suicide plane. It dropped a torpedo and ran.

Occupied Japan

With the end of the war, a number of Montford Point units drew assignments in occupied Japan, primarily at the former Japanese naval base at Sasebo on Kyushu, the southernmost home island, which had been designated for occupation by the Marine Corps. Three ammunition companies —the 6th, 8th, and 10th—and six depot companies—the 24th, 33rd, 34th, 36th, 42nd, and 43rd—arrived at Sasebo in September and October. While stationed at Sasebo, some Montford Point Marines also helped begin the task of clearing debris created by the atomic blast that destroyed Nagasaki, located about forty miles to the south. With the cessation of hostilities and the successful occupation of Japan, the United States quickly began the reduction of its military forces, and both the 24th Depot and 6th Ammunition Companies were disbanded at Sasebo before the end of 1945. Other ammunition and depot companies were transferred to Guam and deactivated in early 1946, while still other companies made it back to Montford Point before being disbanded. With the deactivation of the 8th Ammunition Company and the 49th Depot Company on Guam on September 30, 1947, all the companies formed at Montford Point were disbanded.

Joseph Myers I went back to Hawaii [from Iwo Jima]. And I began training men again. Because for the invasion of Japan. We was on our way to invade Japan when the cease-fire was ordered. So, instead of sending us back to the States we all said, we were singing, California here we come. But they didn't let any California because they said Sasebo, Japan, here we go. So, we end up in Sasebo, Japan.

And I was picked as one of the sergeants to go out with John Gayer to accept the surrender there in Sasebo, Japan. I was fortunate enough, I was lucky. I always in the right place at the right time. I was lucky enough to be chosen by my CO to go up and stand with the general. What they did more or less was, they got us all lined up. Including some boats and jeeps and trucks. And they marched us up in Sasebo, Japan. Down at the navy yard. Where they had the submarines and things. And then, we had to line up. And the general and the admiral came down to accept the surrender of Japan. Not of Japan. It was with the navy base at Sasebo, see. We had to line up behind them in, in four-man honor guard. And I remained there on base duty, guard duty more or less, till I got to come back from there. And they shipped me from Guam back to the States.

Ellis Cunningham When we were on our way to Japan, we got on a transport this time, a transporter designed to carry troops. And when we got to Japan, or got near the port, they took us off of the transport and put us on landing crafts, and took us to the beaches like we were going in for an invasion. Got to the beach and lined up on the beach were the Japanese soldiers and sailors, lined up there like they were ready for a parade or something. Or inspection.

We were told not [to] interfere with them, to go around them and do what we had to do. Charge up the, up the hill just like we were making an invasion. Of course we didn't do any live firing, because no one was shooting at us. But we went up and took up firing positions, but within a couple hours the camera secured us from that. And went back down to the beach, and were assigned to the jobs that each of us went to do.

The ammunition company was assigned clearing the ammunition that the Japanese had stored in the caves and elsewhere around the city. So that's how we spent most of our time. Gathering and destroying the ammunition in some way or another. We got assigned barracks that the Japanese,

I guess the sailors used to live in, or the soldiers, and stayed there during the destruction of ammunition and weapons.

The depot companies, there was a endless list of things to do ashore. Because the people needed to be fed and get housing for them and everything. Because they were bummed out, they had nothing. So they would gather every day. A lot of our people learned to speak Japanese, because they were assigned the duties of supervising small groups of Japanese. And they did that as long as we stayed there.

Archibald Mosley When the battle was over and we had victory in Iwo Jima, we were sent to the homeland of Japan to Sasebo and Nagasaki, Japan, to clean up the ash from the dropping of the atomic bomb. When we got there, I have never seen before and have never seen since such a devastating sight. Things were destroyed and torn down, burnt. The best way I could even describe the ground is like when I was a little Boy Scout and we were doing Boy Scout camp and you made a bonfire to roast hot dogs and marshmallows that you put them on a stick. Well, when you put the fire out and you kick the ashes and all away, the ground looks crushed and burnished. That's the way the whole land it looked when we got there. I haven't been able to go back and see it since. But I'm wondering how many years it took for that soil and that land to come back. Because when we got there, you couldn't have, being a southern Illinois boy down in foreign land, I bet you'd have to plow and fertilize land before we could grow some corn again, after the way that land looked.

Not only the land and the buildings and everything burned, but even some of the people. While we were there, I remember we were there during November [1945], because we had Thanksgiving dinner there. Turkey, and I couldn't enjoy my turkey Thanksgiving dinner, you know, you have this platter and plate they put it on. It's because I looked out the tent and out there in the back I saw little Japanese kids going in the garbage cans, where we were emptying our platters into, getting drumsticks and all and, and eating on them and so forth.

But some of them, the sides of their faces were scarred, where you would see they were burned, and so forth. And even the hands of some people were burned and all. And one conclusion I came [to] from that is, and it might be why I became so sympathetic and wanted to choose an occupation of the ministry. And after finishing college, go to a seminary and study for the ministry is to have some compassion on people because it's one thing that visit to Japan taught me—that war is hell.

Why human beings would ever want to go to war, drop bombs and all on one another and cause the next generation and children and all to suffer? The Marine Corps made me tough, it made me violent, yes. But because I was conditioned, programmed into it. And that's one of the things you program us into war and fighting, but when we were discharged, nobody deprogrammed us. The only deprogramming I got would be from a loving wife that has been with me for fifty some years.

he experiences of the men who trained at Montford Point and served in Korea and Vietnam were nothing like those of the Montford Point veterans of World War II. Nearly 20,000 black Marines had served in World War II, but at the outbreak of the Korean War, less than 1,500 African Americans served in the Corps, nearly a third of whom served in the Stewards Branch. Although combat-trained black Marines represented only a tiny fraction of the Corps's manpower, it was they who integrated the Corps at unit level as the Corps used the Korean War to implement President Truman's executive order to end segregation within the military. In Korea, for the first time, black Marines fought side by side with their white comrades in fully integrated combat units.

An even smaller number of Montford Point Marines fought in their third and final war in Vietnam. The harsh realities of combat remained the same, and racial tensions continued to exist, but the Marine Corps had changed dramatically. In Vietnam the Montford Pointers served in a Marine Corps they could only have imagined as raw recruits in the 1940s. They fought in a fully integrated Marine Corps, at times in units commanded by black officers. The vast majority of African Americans with whom they served in Vietnam had trained not at Montford Point, but with their fellow Marines at either Parris Island or Camp Pendleton. It was a Marine Corps their courage, determination, and sacrifice had created.

Korea

Because some of the most ferocious engagements of the Korean War came in the early stages of that conflict, men trained at Montford Point fought on Korea's bloodiest battlefields, especially in the Inchon landing and the Chosin Reservoir campaign. On June 25, 1950, North Korean troops swept south across the 38th Parallel, since the end of World War II the division be-

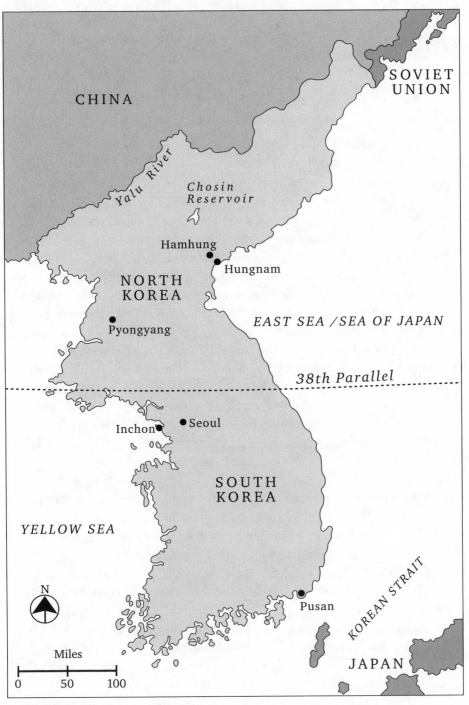

CHINA

SOVIET
UNION

Yalu River

*Chosin
Reservoir*

Hamhung

Hungnam

NORTH
KOREA

EAST SEA / SEA OF JAPAN

Pyongyang

38th Parallel

Inchon Seoul

SOUTH
KOREA

YELLOW SEA

N

Pusan

KOREAN STRAIT

JAPAN

Miles

0   50   100

Korea

tween North and South Korea. They easily captured the capital city, Seoul, and pushed South Korean and United Nations forces to the tip of the Korean Peninsula. Drawing on American experience in the Pacific island campaigns of World War II, General Douglas MacArthur, commander of all United Nations forces in Korea, in a daring and brilliant maneuver, on September 15, launched a successful amphibious landing at Inchon, a harbor town on the Yellow Sea approximately fifty miles west of Seoul. Led by American troops, the invasion force recaptured Seoul in less than two weeks.

Moving northward, United Nations forces began to drive into North Korea, capturing its capital, Pyongyang, on October 20. Despite Chinese threats to enter the war in support of the North Koreans, in late October MacArthur launched a major offensive. Vowing to sweep to the Yalu River, the border between China and North Korea, and end the war before Christmas, MacArthur ignored the explicit instructions of President Harry Truman not to send American troops into the vicinity of the Yalu. On November 23, in the brutal cold presaging the Korean winter, thousands of Chinese soldiers stormed across the Yalu, overrunning American and United Nations positions and forcing MacArthur's forces into a general retreat back to the 38th Parallel. The war settled, along that line, into a bloody stalemate, which MacArthur proposed to break by bombing China with nuclear weapons if necessary, a position that led President Truman to relieve him of command in April 1951. The stalemate and the fighting continued for two more years, ending in an armistice signed on June 26, 1953, which left the dividing line between the two countries essentially unchanged. The Korean conflict left over 54,000 American troops dead and more than 100,000 wounded.

Calvin Brown And finally, in June 1950, Korea broke out. The Marines, naturally, were being called [back to active duty], right and left. At that time, all the black Marines that had gotten out were called back; they were going in line companies [combat units] left and right, because they were going where they were needed. Several of my buddies I know that got hit and killed and whatnot, and all like that. The Army unit called the 24th Infantry was trying to hold them, but they couldn't. The North Koreans were barreling through, coming down to South Korea. And so, we went to Korea, and I had this laundry unit, I had a black and white crew. All over Korea, I went and set it up, and used it, and set it up, and used it, and took it down and went to another place.

I made the Inchon landing. We left Inchon, we went to the capital, Seoul. Then you left Seoul, and went to another little place, Dijongbu. And from Dijongbu back to Seoul. And then from Seoul up Hongchon, then from Hong-chon to Hamhung. A place called Hamhung. That's as far as I got, but the rest went up to the Chosin Reservoir at about twenty miles this side of China proper.

You couldn't expect the Chinese not to intervene, since I've grown older and looked at things in the world, because they were all Communist to-gether. And so, when the Chinese swept down on us, I think MacArthur and the president knew that that was gonna happen. I believe they had an idea it was gonna happen, anyway. We had several alerts once. They had moved the machines inside a building in Hamhung. And we got an alert one night, and a captain came by and as he passed me, [he asked] do your men have enough ammo? I said, well, we've got an initial amount. He said, well, come to the truck. I came to the truck and he gave me two boxes of .30 caliber, and he gave me a machine gun. Now, I had never really received no train-ing on a .30 caliber machine gun. Nothing happened that night.

So the next day, the same captain came by with an Army man with him. And he said, he's gonna show you what to do with this gun, in case you have to use it tonight. He said, we expect them to come through. So then, we were in the city, but there was a little canal, like, that ran past the area where we were at. So then he told me how to set the gun up, and put sand-bags around it, and all that sort of stuff and whatnot. And he left. About twenty minutes later I heard some firing, but it wasn't close to us. It was maybe, say, half a mile.

So I alerted my crew, and we all took a watch on the gun, but nothing never happened. The next morning the city was still the same. Then when the Chinese barreled in for real, they got within twenty-five miles, I think, but they never came close. So then when the Chinese, the steam blew out of their effort and they stopped, then we all moved to New Maison, that's where the whole division went, to New Maison.

So then I was put into a graves registration unit. I drove the truck for them. We went up and picked up the dead bodies and brought them back to Maison, and they buried them, and so forth and so on like that. And I stayed in Korea until July the following year, 1951, and I made staff sergeant in May, I think, of that year. Since it [the Corps] was integrated, and Mac-Arthur was out, and the new general took over, I can't recall his name now. But he said that we will have an army of men who will be proud to fight be-side each other. We have a common enemy.

I left there in 1951; in July 1951, I came back to the States. I stopped in California, and I came back to North Carolina.

Thomas Cork When we got into Kobe, Japan, they switched us off to get on the LSTs. And we went in to Inchon. Now, by this time, I am the only black in the outfit. The rest are white. And at first they didn't accept me. Wouldn't talk to me, wouldn't say anything to me. But as time went along they realized that I am part of their outfit, and they are going to have to deal with me from then on.

In California I was trained on the light machine gun. That was my job. When I got into Korea, that's what I had to do with that light machine gun. That was my duty. And went on into Inchon. From there on, we would kind of move along, but those times the segregation part never crossed anybody's mind. Because we are in this thing together.

Never heard another word about calling me any kind of names. I became a Marine like the rest of them. And that made me feel good. I felt welcome with them. Because here I am, a nineteen-year-old, man, being in combat the first time. Don't know what to expect. And when you got people around you, they don't want you there, you got problems there. But as it turned out they really accepted me. And they treated me like any other Marine going into combat together.

I'm a gunner and I had assistant gunner. Our life depends on each other. He has to feed the ammunition to me, make sure I have the ammunition. I don't have time to load it. Only thing I do is load it and cock and let it go. His job is to feed it to me. His job is to haul the ammunition up to me. Now, what's normal with a machine gun, I found out this later, I didn't know it at the time. The life of a machine gunner is very short. Because the enemy knows, they can see the fire coming from a machine gun, they know there is firepower. So, they concentrate on the automatic weapons, especially machine guns. But, fortunately, I made it through.

This is in Inchon. Young men going in combat. The first thing that popped in mind is now looking [at] the Marines that were ahead of us, we went in on, I think, about the thirteenth wave. The one before us, a lot of those guys were killed. And those bodies were just stacked up, you know. And you see these guys getting killed. But strange thing about it, you really don't think about death. I mean, your job now becomes survival. And our job, once we get on land, we start moving north. And little by little we took town after town after town. We all went to Seoul, went to Seoul twice. We lost Seoul and had to come back out and start all over again. There were some hills above familiar to a lot of people. Pork Chop Hill, and, and those hills. We take them today, and tomorrow we might come back down and had to re-take them again.

And one thing stands in my mind most, well, we got on the hill one time. On the other side of that hill, there was another hill. We kept seeing these people going and coming out of this building. They go in real fat and come out skinny. Go in real fat and come out skinny. So, we called back [to] the recon[naissance] and told them what was the experience up there. And they said to sit tight. We'll try to find out what's going on down there. So, I guess by the third day, we see these people still going out of the building. Actually, we found out later it was not a building at all. They were enemy going in out of that building. And a lot of them were dressed like civilians. . . . because they weren't in uniform like we thought they will be. They were military people, but in civilian clothes. It was an ammunition depot for them. So, the recon called up and said, go for it. So, we started firing on it. Next thing you know, there was all kind of explosions. Because we had gotten this ammo.

The colonel came up, you know. He calls us out and gave us commendations and then talked to us about that. And then, start moving on. We moved on. And now we began to move pretty fast. We went all the way into the Chosin Reservoir. Now, Chosin Reservoir is a story within itself. We were sent and went there. And we had thought the war was over. My captain said you young men will be home for Christmas, okay. It didn't happen that way. Moved so close to China that we looked across the [Yalu] river and see Chinese on the other side just walking around like. Think nothing about it. So, the Marines were sitting in the middle. Eighth Army on the right. And what they called the ROK Division, which is Republic of Korea, on the other side. Well, what happened, the Chinese came across. They came across on foot. And everything they were carrying was like a weapon. They had all their food on them, what little water they needed. Everything, rice, whatever they are going to carry in combat they had on their body. So, how they got past us, they were literally walking past. And we had no idea there was any enemy in front of us, because we had gone as far as we could go. But those Chinese came across in thousands and thousands, and thousands and thousands.

We got from the recon back there said they had found some Chinese back there behind us now. Then we began to tighten up and found out where these Chinese are coming from. But by that time they had us surrounded, completely cut off. Now, it's about thirty some below zero. The only clothes we have was those scout boots. And they were good boots. Nothing wrong with that. But the problem was, your feet sweat in those boots and freeze. So, that's what happened to us there.

We started coming back. And I think there was a general made a statement about we are not retreating, we were attacking in a different direction. Which, in fact, that's what we was doing. We had to turn around now and start back. One of the things happened to us. We didn't have supplies. Only supply we had, like, one-day supply. So, they had to drop our supplies to us. But when they dropped the supplies, the Chinese was getting them before we'd get to them. So, the Marines devised a decoy. They would drop dummy stuff down. And the Chinese would go for that. And then they'd drop ours down to us. And ammunition and food was a premium. Because we just didn't have it. Water was a problem. If you all tried to make a cup of water out of snow, that's a project in itself. Because you got a cup of snow and you get about a teaspoon of water. What we had, water, came from the snow.

When they finally got us out of there, they broke through and the first person I saw was a British Marine and a Turkish Marine. They had a little flag, like waving it. Because I had no idea, I never seen a British Marine or a Turkish Marine. Had no idea who these guys are. I am thinking they are the enemy. And so, they are making sure that we didn't shoot them. Because they started waving a little American flag. And they got us out of there. And what they were doing, they were trying to take out the ones they thought was in bad shape.

What they kept asking me over and over again, how do your feet feel? As long as you felt, you had feeling in your feet, you are pretty well. But when your feeling disappeared then that means you're frozen. When the guys were taking me out, I said, I am okay. I don't have feeling at all. They said, you are the one we want. Because we know what's happened to you. Your feet are frozen.

So, went and got me back to Tokyo. This is another story. I mean, I don't mean to sound humorous. But some things just got to be humorous to you. There was a hotel that was a hospital used to be a hotel. And had these big mirrors around. They brought me on a stretcher. And I went past this mirror and I looked and saw myself. And I am telling you, I was scroungy-looking. I hadn't shaved and bathed and whatever. And I said, as I asked later, who was that? And they just said that's you. And they started cleaning me up. And, getting, you know, clean clothes and food, and all that bit. But the problem with my wound is my foot. When they took my boot off, it was frozen. And the boot came off and part of my foot came out with it. That's why I lost all my toes in that.

I stayed in Tokyo I guess about a week. Then they sent me to Midway. Then they sent me to California, Travis. Then they flew me all the way across the United States to Westover, Massachusetts. And then, down to Saint Albans [Veterans Administration Hospital in Queens, New York]. One of the problems they was running into, they had never had that severe a frostbite. Not only myself, there were others. They never had that much frostbite condition. They didn't know how to handle it. And what they was trying to do, they was afraid that I don't get gangrene. Which I did to a point. But not serious as they thought it would. So, every hour on the hour, they was taking my blood to make sure that gangrene didn't go too far. So, now they had to take the part of the foot that was all the way frostbitten.

Hulon Edwards I served in the Korean War, in, let's see, '50. I served there for fourteen months; that's the way it was. I was hit up there, with shrapnel on the south, and I refused a Purple Heart, because my mother was kind of ill then. I was in infantry. I had a machine gun section, that's the light machine guns, .50 caliber. I was section leader, and I was directing fire, placing units into positions, and [taking] out patrols, and whatever, fighting off the enemy.

And most of the time, we were hit, bombarded all night. One night everybody was chased off of there, and I come to [be] commander. I was the highest-ranking person that [was] left off that hill. There was eleven of us. Eleven of us got off of there, not being KIA [killed in action], WIA [wounded in action], or MIA [missing in action]. Walking wounded. Walking, you know, just shrapnel. I said, walking wounded. I didn't take the Purple Heart.

I made staff sergeant over there, by the way. I fought in the Pyongyang area, around the Hill Eighty-one, I think. And armed the resistance, that's where we dig in, and stop the enemy, and hold them back from there.

Ruben Hines Yes, I went to Korea twice. I was in motor transport. And we were near the [Chosin] Reservoir when the Chinese crossed over. That's where the Chinese entered the war during that particular period. I never will forget. I mean, it was nothing easy and it was nothing wonderful. Was cold all the time. Freezing to death and all that. I didn't see nothing good about it. But, you know, I was there.

I never will forget one particular incident. When the Chinese broke through, I had a buddy from Louisville, Kentucky. His name was Rudolph Hyde. I was visiting the hospital, visiting him rather, in the hospital. He had feet in a basket [from frostbite]. And the colonel broke through the tents and was telling us to run for it. Run for it, run for it. Run for what [I asked]? He said the Chinks coming, the Chinks are coming. I knew that's the nickname for Chinese, you know.

And so I started getting my gear and getting ready to head up, so to speak, like everybody else. And I remember Rudolph asking, what about me? What about me? The colonel told him, said, hell, go for yourself. Wasn't about ten to fifteen minutes later with, Rudolph and me, see? And about ten, fifteen minutes later who was running behind [me and the colonel]? Rudolph, with those, frostbitten feet. He lost his feet later. But I never will forget. He forgot all about that pain and discomfort that he had and he started running with us, you know. Oh, it wasn't too good. But I remember him with a lot of fondness.

Henry McNair I went in at the Inchon landing in 1950. The 1st and the 5th Marine Regiment[s] landed on the 15th [of September]. The 7th Marines landed on the 21st, and we landed and moved out and supported the 5th and the 1st Marines securing and taking of Seoul, surrounding Seoul and all the way up to the 38th Parallel. My job at that time was 3.5 rockets and flamethrowers. We didn't use the flamethrowers too much but rockets we used, 3.5, and we had some of the 02.36 rockets. I was a rocket launcher, rocket man.

I was in the Chosin Reservoir campaign, 7th Marines; we spearheaded all the way up to Chosin Reservoir, Yudam-ni, fighting Chinese, 124th Black Diamond Division. They overran my unit twice. We followed them with bayonets, and the most of them would just keep running past us. You know, it's hard for me to remember. This thing was fifty-five years ago.

At that time we had word to go ahead and pull back. At that time I was at Yudam-ni. That was about twelve miles from the Chosin Reservoir, because we had shifted across from the Chosin, and we were trying to help Dog Company, 2nd Battalion, 7th Marines. And all of us had to pull back what was left. My unit come out. We had forty-two of us. Dog Company had seven men. Fox Company had thirty some men. All of us wasn't in fighting conditions. Most of us was wounded, but we had no choice. They couldn't evacuate us out or anything. We walked out holding the railhead. The railhead is a big old road along mountains where the vehicles would fall, troops would fall. In the meantime we was fighting Chinese, mortar fire, artillery fire, all the way back down the hills, all the way back down the mountain. The weather was real cold. It was about forty to fifty degrees below zero, real cold. Half of us was froze with frostbite. Some of us couldn't hardly move, but we continued to move. We pulled out of the Chosin, and we made it back to Hamhung, North Korea. [When] we pulled out [for deployment to the Chosin area], my battalion, twenty-seven, when there were 1,300 men. We got reinforcements while we were there, and when we come out, there was 283 of us left in fighting conditions. The most of us were still wounded.

Reuben McNair Lo and behold, the Korean War come on. And during the Korean War, I most certainly was eager to be there. I had looked forward to this. And it's sad that you have to look forward to a war to prove your ability to do. However, when I arrived in Korea, being in a rifle company and a line company, there was never more than two black staff non-commissioned officers in a battalion. Needless to say, I didn't see that many of my people at any time.

During that particular time, March the 26th in 1953, the Chinese overran our outpost. We had outpost, Vegas, Carson, Reno, and there was three outposts out at that particular time. Unfortunately, myself and another staff sergeant was out on the outpost. Chinese, about ten o'clock that night, lit the skies up just as bright as day. The next thing we knew, we could hear Banzai yelling and screaming and then a bugle blowing. They estimated it was perhaps about a battalion of Chinese come in. Within an hour and a half, they overran our post that I was on, which was Vegas. Joining about 500 yards from Vegas was Reno. And about 500 yards from that adjacent, there was Carson. They [the Chinese] did the same thing at the same time. We assumed that most of the troops there was taken out, knocked out. There was eight of us left alive at that particular platoon. We eventually made our way back to the MLR [United Nations Main Line of Resistance]. During this particular seventy-two hours of fighting, our rifle company was Fox Company Second, batch seven, lost all of their troops except forty-two, forty-three, I believe. We realized that there were replacements. But I'd never knew that there was that many men lost out of our Fox Company at the time. So, I was well baptized at that particular time.

Johnny Washington One of my squads went out from my platoon, and they got hit. And they went ahead and got hit, they went on patrol, and hit some mines. We feel that the North Koreans had reversed where we had put the mines out. Figured that they had reversed it, and we got our truck, a squad got hit. And we lost about sixteen, eighteen of them out there, and we lost about about four or five KIAs there. We had to go out and find out where they were and bring them back in. It was a horrible thing. It was a hard thing.

Glenn White I was getting out that morning. When I got to the gate they told me to turn around and go back and they gave me a new set of clothes and everything and I came over to Korea. Well it was a black unit until we got to the ship; then we all mixed up after we got over the ship.

That's where we made the landing at Inchon in '50, I think, 1950. We made the landing at Inchon with the 5th Marines. And the 1st Marine they made it down, then we all got together and went up north and that's where we got, I want to say chased out, that's where we got sent back.

When they [the Chinese] came in, we was playing softball. I don't know the place, it was way up north you could look over in Russia [China]. Well, when they first came in we didn't, well they surprised us to tell the truth. At least me. All of a sudden our tanks, they would hear bullets hitting off, and well there wasn't supposed to be no bullets, nobody to fire no bullets.

We was cut off for two or three days, three or four days, something like that. We didn't know we was cut off though. Our outfit, we had to stay out there to do the best we could. When we got out, we got together and then we come back down south. At that time you ran across combat everywhere you went. 'Cause we didn't, we couldn't tell a North Korean from a South Korean until we got to him. And then it was too late, most of the time. You just could trust nobody. If he wasn't American or he didn't talk like an American, you had to be more careful.

Johnnie Givian And people were being shipped out and everything, and I came back into the base [Montford Point] and I got in our motor transport at that time. I met my wife; she wouldn't marry me. So I got mad with her and anyways that's not part of the story, but I volunteered to go to Korea. I went over there; when I got there they had invaded Inchon, probably about three to four months or something like this. It wasn't long after, because they were still talking about it and everything. I moved in about thirty miles north of Inchon and that's where the DMZ [Demilitarized Zone] was set up in. That's where I went, up in there. That's the main line of resistance.

I had worked in the fire department at Camp Lejeune a little bit, and when I got over there they sent me to Pusan, that's right on the tip of Korea. And I went there and there wasn't no fire department. It was a truck with a hose on it, that's it. But that's what they call a fire department. That's where I was at and I was just bored. And I volunteered 'cause they had a list there at the camp. Every day they put a list on the board. Anybody want to go up to the front sign here, and I signed. And I went up where they were fighting. It was about thirty some miles northwest I believe from Inchon, and it was about a mile from Bunker Hill up in there 'cause it's always on the line up there, the DMZ, which is the line of resistance. I was sent up there and they put me in a company called Line Company Third Batch Fifth Battalion and that's where I was in. And this was a line company now, this was a fighting unit. Thought I would die in Pusan, but now I'm on the line where they're fighting at, that's what we call the DMZ. Up there where that line was where the North Koreans stopped and where the Americans stop at that's where the line of resistance was. So now I got in the line company up there and now I'm a fighting Marine altogether. And that's where I spent the rest of the time, which was about fourteen months. . . . I ended up on Bunker Hill.

When they invaded Inchon they went on inland. When I got there they was about twenty miles inland like, you know, west. Going this on lateral like and that's where I was in this area. And that's where the bulk of the fighting was at this time. It was south of the Manchurian border coming out of China. We was in that area right in there it was about, oh, middle way of Korea from this side to that side. And it went all the way across Korea this line did. What we did when I first got there, we were put into a defense force. We were at the line of resistance. And what we did daily for two, three, or four months we would go out at night as a patrol. It was squads like, platoons set up, and they, squads, would go out. One would go in one direction, one would go in another, and this was because they were trying to keep the surprise of an attack, you know, from coming up on us. So we go out and search out and find out what's going on out there at night. And then in the daytime, we would try to catch some sleep or get something to eat or try to do a little shower, bathing or something. And the getting ourselves ready to go again at night, and we went this just every night.

We would go out and leave and go out and come back at the dawn of day on tomorrow. And we would go check out what they call outposts in between our line of resistance and their lines of resistance. Sometimes it would be thirty feet and sometimes it would be 300 yards. And sometimes it would be a half a mile over there, you know, and the distance between the two lines. That's where we'd be over to see if they're camping up on some of these little knolls and hills out there. And taking them out at night and that's what we would do.

And this come routine, this combat. People would die. And they would get killed, and the next morning we'd find out their squad had two deaths. Because they ran into an ambush or something. Fear was there, yeah, but you got to brave yourself for that. If I must say I grew up during that time, I grew up to be a man, all that stuff at Montford Point was tough and bad and ugly but I grew up because I had to face death and really did. We ran into gunfire. We got ambushed out there in the squad that I was in. We had a man by the name of Freak. He was a student at Penn State College and he was drafted in. He voluntarily went into the service, and he was a sergeant. I was a corporal at that time, and he was a strong man; he was a real strong man and, and he got killed and I took his place. Racism didn't show up then; nobody every talked about it, it was almost forgotten. I was the only black at one time there in our regiment of people, that's 300 some people. And I was in the squad, and the company commander made me squad leader with that squad when Freak got killed. So the racial problem wasn't over there then, you know. I know I was black but that's all.

The fighting part was the problem and we had to survive. I mean we had to survive and, and we were coming, you forget who you are, you know. And live everyday. I used to lay there when I got back off of patrol and meditate on how I was gonna get through that day or that night. 'Cause they become separated from everything else, just surviving, and that's what we did. We ran into a lot of opposition. We had what we call outposts. And this hills that are like little small mountains, and it was sitting in between us and the Chinese line. At this time it mostly was Chinese over there. We used to have to go out and stay on this outpost for seven days, to make sure that we're not gonna be surprised with an attack or something. And then that outpost would get attacked. I was in a severe one.

One time, we was out there, it was a Marine company and the support which was two corpsmen, a radioman, and a chaplain. And the CO [Commanding Officer] reminded to sixty-nine people out on that hill that's how many was out there and we got attacked one night. And the next evening, or night rather, we came up the hill. When I got back to our line, which was about a half a mile away, maybe a little further, when I got back to our line, I find out that it was seven of us walked off that hill. The rest of them didn't make it on foot.

The first time I was wounded we was on the line where we got this trench dug. Our line, you know, where in front of it is war. Behind of it is [where] you try to get peace. But anyway on that line, and we was up in there one day and this captain, Hoke was his name. He had sent and told somebody to fly some ice cream up there on the line. It was about 105 degrees. And they flew it up there, so he called up to me, I was the squad leader at that time. I had this guy; I liked him but he was pretty rough. But anyway I, when I got the word, I said, get ready we're gonna have ice cream 'cause there's a little thing. I took out the door to go, 'cause he asked, you know, the squad leader always want to go get it.

And I took off and the guy reached and got me back in, pulled me back, and he took out. He gonna get it. And they ran out and a China mortar came in. It was half a can of gasoline, it was sitting in a mortar can where the rounds come in. It was a tin can and we used that for our tanks for these little Coleman stove we had. And that mortar round hit that can and it went up in the air. And this guy went down. He was ninety-eight percent burned, fire burning like a torch. I was right behind him 'cause I was gonna pull him back again and get out there, but I didn't have time. That's when the fragmentation from the thing got me, my sight, lost my sight.

They flew him out to Japan; me, they flew me back down to Pusan. They had a medical thing set up down there. My eyes were blind, but then they figured out that it was just the blast, the heat from the blast, and I was just full of shrapnel because a small part of that shell was right there. The big part flew way over and we was right up under and we caught all that.

Then after so many days I went back up to the unit. . . . The next time [I was wounded] we was out on Bunker Hill . . . that was the name of the hill, and we got attacked. That's the one where seven of us walked off of there. When I came down you know I had been ripped open under my arm by my ribs, like somebody took a knife and cut it. I didn't know nothing about it till I got down there 'cause I wasn't even thinking about that. That was the second wound I got.

I left Korea fifteen and a half months after I got there, and I came back with the draft that I went over there with. It was 4,800 marines that was in this draft and went back it was 1,900 of us. I came back and landed, we landed there in California. When we got off the ship, went through down and got processed and everything, went through the medical things [examinations].

Vietnam

On March 8, 1965, the initial contingent of 3,500 Marines sent to Vietnam landed at Da Nang, a huge airbase on the east coast of northern South Vietnam, close to the Demilitarized Zone that separated North and South Vietnam. Da Nang, with both naval facilities and an airfield, quickly became the supply and support hub for American operations in northern South Vietnam, with Army, Marine, Navy, and Air Force units stationed there. Marine

CHINA

NORTH
VIETNAM

● Hanoi

LAOS

*GULF OF
TONKIN*

DMZ

● Khe Sahn

● Da Nang

THAILAND

*SOUTH
CHINA
SEA*

CAMBODIA

SOUTH
VIETNAM

● Saigon

N

Miles

0   50   100   200

Vietnam

units assigned to Da Nang protected the base, flew helicopter missions to support and supply troops in the field, and operated fighter aircraft that harassed the enemy. By 1968, the airbase at Da Nang was considered the world's busiest. By 1970, the Da Nang area hosted forty-five American military bases, in addition to over sixty South Vietnamese installations. In 1972, in accordance with the American policy of Vietnamization, the United States withdrew its troops and turned the giant complex over to the Army of the Republic of Vietnam.

In 1967, Marines captured Khe Sahn, a town in northwest South Vietnam strategically located along the Ho Chi Minh Trail, over which the North Vietnamese supplied their troops in the south. The Marines converted Khe Sahn into a firebase, from which they constantly shelled the North Vietnamese. In preparation for the Tet Offensive, on January 21, 1968, some 20,000 North Vietnamese troops began a siege of the 5,000 Marines at Khe Sahn. The besieged Marines held out until April, when American forces finally drove the North Vietnamese into Laos.

On January 31, 1968, with the Marines besieged at Khe Sahn, the North Vietnamese and their Viet Cong allies launched the Tet Offensive, overrunning and occupying provincial capitals throughout South Vietnam, capturing the old imperial city of Hue, and attacking the United States Embassy in Saigon. American forces secured Saigon within a matter of days, but the offensive continued in the provinces for nearly a month. Extensively covered by the media, especially television, the Tet Offensive shook the confidence of the American public in the possibility of a military victory in Vietnam and in many ways began the long process of American disengagement from the Vietnamese conflict. By the time the United States finally pulled the last of its forces from the country in 1975, almost all Montford Point veterans had retired from the Marine Corps, with most accepting jobs in the civilian work force.

Adner Batts I did two tours in Vietnam. I didn't ask for either one of them, but I did them . . . both of them was twelve months apiece. By that time, I was an engineer operations chief, and by that time, unlike Korea, we had vertical envelopment. We was using helicopters then. Everything from all of the logistics, as far as off-loading ships and helicopters, moving troops, setting up LSAs, logistical support areas, and things like that. That came under you. Sending out companies to their different fighting areas, from the LSA, you was moving troops and supervising lifts. So, 105[mm]s, and 155[mm] howitzers, that was out of different support bases, that came under you, as an engineer, a support man. My rank at that point was a gunnery sergeant.

'66, that was when the NVA [North Vietnamese Army] first came down, in the first big operation, Operation Hastings [a Marine offensive launched in May 1966 to prevent the North Vietnamese forces from taking control of Quang Tri Province on the northeast border of South Vietnam]. And I think the other one must have been about '69. [I was] back in the States about a year, and [then] back over there. I was at Khe Sahn. You were right up there, on the DMZ [Demilitarized Zone, which separated North and South Vietnam]. We didn't have anything above ground up there. You had to live on the ground; it was called Rocket Alley. We got incoming [shell fire]; there wasn't a day passing we didn't probably get incoming. But as far as going out and meeting the enemy with a rifle, no, I didn't do that.

I remember [during Operation] Hastings, that we was getting ready to go for Europe [another firebase], and I would hear about the NVA, when they first come down from [North Vietnam], if it would end up it was a Vietcong, but we got, now, hardcore northern soldiers. That came up on waves, and fell down, and fired just like they had protection in front of them. And [American officials] radioed from Europe that was saying how heavy their casualties was. But ours was very light.

F. M. Hooper I received orders to go to Vietnam, and I went to Vietnam. I was attached to the Marine Corps air wing, and I served in South Vietnam in the supply field doing aviation supply. I was dispatched from Da Nang, and I went to Marine Corps Air Group Number 12, which was stationed in South Vietnam. I had to go to Da Nang for schooling, certain classes; I went to Da Nang for certain classes periodically. A one-day, two-day course. I was dispatched a total of exactly thirteen months from the day I arrived to the day the plane left [for home].

From the time that I arrived in Vietnam all I could hear was shelling and planes taking off. And I didn't hardly sleep one night. When I was able to rest, it was only when the planes stopped flying. I arrived in Vietnam in 1967, and I did not leave until after the Tet Offensive [in] '68. The day that we received word through communication that our base would be hit tonight we had made preparations all day and all that evening. And we even had skirmishes, outposts. I was involved. And finally we got an all-clear signal, so we returned to our base camp area, and just about the time I was ready to jump in a bunk and pull the cover up, all hell seemed to break loose. That was really the most outrageous time of combat because I jumped up, grabbed my helmet, and jumped into a bunker. Damaged my shoulder, but I survived, even though rockets and mortars and were falling all around, I was able to survive. The time that I departed, like I said, was thirteen months later the Tet Offensive was over, but it was still a lot of fighting going on. After I left Vietnam we got stationed at Camp Lejeune. I stayed there, and I was still in the supply field until I retired [in 1971].

Johnnie Thompkins I took the first MI6s [rifles] into 'Nam. That was in '67, and dropped them off. We first got hold of MI6s, the Army had MI6s, when they went into 'Nam, but we didn't. I took the first MI6s in there. And the funniest thing there was that I asked for some water, I needed water. And they had a free night, there was free day, it was all day and all night they had. And the guy said, I got all the whiskey and all the beer you want, but I don't have any water. This is in Da Nang. And I said, you don't have any water? He said, no, don't have any water. I just told him that it was something that the Lord have always looked out for me, it look like.

I volunteered to go to Korea, and my captain stopped me, and said, no, take his name off the list because I need him here. And from there when I went to Okinawa, I was going to 'Nam, that's where I was scheduled to, and the guy got on the plane and said, I want Master Sergeant Thompkins to get off here.

But they gave me two trips to 'Nam, and I took the MI6s in the one time. I volunteered to take in the first load, and then about a couple months later they asked me if I wanted to go back again. I went back again, and this time I went up to one of the outfits and dropped off my weapons, and the guy says, they didn't fire on your airplane? I said, no. He said, well, they're right down at the end of the field there and usually airplanes get fired on.

I met some of my boys that I knew, and they said, hey, say, you gonna stick around? I said, well, I'll stick around a few days, maybe I'll get to pop some fire around here, you know? And they said they get hit every night, so I'm gonna see me some action. The first night, nothing. Second night, nothing. Third night, nothing. I said well, sir, it's Friday night, we're getting ready for Saturday night. I said I'm going back to Okinawa. Told him I wanted to go to Okinawa. The guys came over to see me about three months later, they got R and R and came to Okinawa. They said, Thompkins, you know, that night, that day you left, that night they hit us with everything but the kitchen sink. I said, you know, that shows you that the women here won't let them harm me when I'm in the area. And he said, oh, we know better than that.

Turner Blount I was stationed at Camp Lejeune, and I was ordered to Okinawa as a duty station. When I reached Okinawa, they reassigned me to a aircraft unit, helicopters, of course, MAG [Marine Air Group]-16. And said, instead of you being as personnel here at Okinawa, you'll be going to Vietnam. And I really didn't understand what was going on. I was in Vietnam where there was very little contact with the Vietcongs, wasn't at first. . . . 'Cause we was free to go just about anywhere we wanted to in Vietnam. Da Nang, itself, I could walk down the streets of Da Nang just like I could in Japan, I mean in, Jacksonville, when we first got there. That was in '65. And they said, we rotate our squad, our aircraft from every six, spend six months in Vietnam and they come back for six months. But this time they were going until the war's over. So I spent about three weeks, maybe a month, in, on Okinawa. And from there, I was shipped out. I flew to Vietnam. And we landed at, in Vietnam. And we took up boarding in a little place that the French had when they were in Vietnam, some buildings, their old buildings that they had there.

In Da Nang, I was with a helicopter squadron and my duties there to make sure that the helicopters was protected, especially at night, with security, and make sure that they had the proper equipment, fuel, whatnot to fly. We, after in Vietnam for about, oh, five or six months, the fighting still escalated and we couldn't go off base, like we used to. And we just had to fight at night; it be attack each night.

We moved to a camp called Marble Mountain [part of the Da Nang area defenses]. And that's where this helicopter squadron was to stay. And, of course, we were attacked nightly. They'd be trying to destroy our equipment and our helicopters. That mean that a lot of Vietcongs was killed within the camp area because of that attacking us on a nightly basis. We had our camp area up front with our machine guns position set up. In our rear was a little river, so we didn't worry too much about the river. But just the front. There's a lot of sand dunes and things out front, too. So they would try to slip through the sand dunes to avoid our machine guns. They would come in with their saki charges and with their weapons. Their weapons was attached to their arms with a hand to be free, where they could use the hands.

And they would drop saki charges down the smoke stacks of our helicopters. Oh, they would attack us each night because they was trying to get to the helicopters. And this particular night, they had an opportunity to find us. We had the sand dunes, was pretty high to come through. And, of course, they came in. That was almost like hand-to-hand combat because they were so close, you know, at night. They was able to destroy several helicopters and we killed about maybe thirty or forty Vietnamese within their camp area that particular night, so that's a night to remember, always remember.

I spent a year in Vietnam there. And we was there [Marble Mountain], I would say about eight months. Now after those Vietcongs and well, the Vietnamese, we call them Vietcongs. They were bodies, had to be destroyed. It was left up to me, with my men, to have all those bodies picked up. And the ones that was still alive, they wanted to interview them, of course, then see what kind of information they could get from them. I had seen that those was disposed of. That was a sort of part of my duties that I never will forget. The bodies that was already dead.

I came back to the States after that assignment. I was assigned at Camp Lejeune at that particular time. I stayed in the Marine Corps from the time, 1966, when I came home, until I retired in 1969.

Johnny Washington October of 1966, I went to First Marine Division. I was first sergeant in the Third Battalion, Fifth Marines. And I stayed there for a year as a first sergeant. I had a lot of troops. I lost a lot of troops in that battalion, in my company. I lost a hell of a lot of troops in Vietnam. Still today, I keep contact with about three or four guys from New York. They call me monthly. We talks about the battles and so forth, that we had in 'Nam. And during my tour at 'Nam, after I was there nine months, they brought in some new first sergeants and we had a lot of casualties.

The colonel asked me, says hey, I need a personnel officer. I said, hey, I'm no officer. He said, I need a personnel officer. So he says, we'd like for you, since you got only three months to do in Vietnam, we'd like for you to come and be a personnel officer. So I went in, take up personnel officer in the battalion. The job there was casualty reporting, and so forth. You did the casualty reports. We wrote letters, proofread the condolence letters. My job was also to go to the morgue and identify a lot of bodies. This is a sad type of duty. It's nothing proud. It wasn't nothing happy about it. You brought a trooper, you come in, you talk to him, and hey, you go down there next couple weeks, and there is the body bag. You got to go down and check him for I.D. by his dental record.

I really found out some tough situations. Vietnam is one. It was a tough situation that I found myself in. It was hard. It's tough. Thing I did is pray. Talk to my troops, and tell them to keep the faith. And you know that somebody got your back, and you got theirs. You could make it. Thing I depend on was the Marines. Because I know I had a company that was gonna stick with me. I know I had other Marines, if something happened, we was gonna have support. And this the way you got out those situations.

Ruben Hines I did three full tours in Vietnam. I went over, the first year I went over '61 and '62. And nobody knew anything about Vietnam. Because when I came back, they asked me where I've been. I told them and people have never heard of it before. Matter of fact, I didn't know what it was until I looked at the map and found out it was old Indochina. That's what it was. Parts of old Indochina. I was in helicopters then. I changed my MOS [Military Occupational Specialty, or job title]. I couldn't get promoted in motor transport and changed my MOS to helicopters. And I was a helicopter mechanic in Vietnam in '61 and '62, [stationed at] Da Nang.

Is when I encountered agent orange, by the way. They would not give us gas masks when we were doing the spraying, defoliating, they called. They wouldn't give us gas masks, or did not issue us gas masks on the pretext that these chemicals were harmless. Little did we know that twenty-seven, twenty-eight years from then it will come out. And by the way, 90 percent of the guys I served [with] in Vietnam during that particular time, they are dead from agent orange. I'm just a survivor.

The next tour was '63 and '64. I went back. And I was stationed again at Da Nang, but we were flying out in different areas where the troops were stationed. Most of the people were stationed that was in the Army at that time. We were, do re-supplies for them. Special forces was there. And we were there. Sad part about it, in '61, '62, we couldn't sign a statement saying that we were American military. We could not admit that we were American military personnel. Our money was being transferred to banks in the United States, because we weren't allowed to have money. '63, '64, they had admitted that we had military personnel in Vietnam. I never will forget. We left Vietnam and we went to Thailand for some reason. I don't know what for. But we stayed there a day and a half. We was on orders to get out of there. And we had to get out of there fast, and we had to come back to Vietnam, where I finished my tour of duty.

That [my third tour] was '67 and '68. '67 and '68, we were stationed first in Da Nang. We went to what we called the rock pile [Khe Sahn]. This fellow from Jacksonville, Griffith Smith was his name, the master sergeant who got the Bronze Star for being under fire the longest [in a] Marine unit in the history of the Marine Corps, was [there]. We flew in and out of his unit at the so-called rock pile. Matter of fact, I got hit numerous times, not physically, but my plane did. One time we came out, had 110 holes in it. About every time we went into the rock pile, we got hit. Matter of fact, I flew over 200 combat missions.

When I served in Vietnam, there was a stark difference in so far as racial attitudes and racial treatment were concerned. By that time, of course, the Marine Corps was totally desegregated in all aspects and in all areas. There was no such thing as segregation. We could go where we wanted to go and with whom we pleased. There was not racial animosity "exhibited" in Vietnam. We were all Marines, we were all buddies, we were all looking out for one another.

Maybe on occasion, when a guy might have too much to drink, he would resort to racist epithets, racial slurs, racial remarks. I had a guy, his name was Willie Williams, and every time he got drunk, he would bring up something about race. For example, he asked me one day, he said, Pappy, can I ask you a question? I said, what? He had been drinking. He said, you sure are a funny acting nigger. He said, you don't act like other niggers I know. I guess I became very emotional, as a matter of fact he outraged me, and I hit him. When I hit him, it was a funny thing. He wanted to know, What did I do? What did I say? But nobody interfered. There was no racial side to the thing, you know, blacks against whites, whites against blacks. It was just me and Willie. . . .

Willie came back the next morning, and he apologized when he got sober. He said he was sorry he did that. But the quirk about the whole thing is that every time Willie got drunk he would come into the barracks and holler, Where is that nigger? That would get it on again.

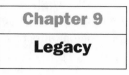or the men of Montford Point, the memories of their ex-
periences together are deeply personal, powerful, and un-
forgettable. Montford Point shaped them into a unique
brotherhood, men who share and identify with the Marines' reputation as the nation's mythic warriors. They are
proud of their service in three wars. They understand the significance of
their victory over racism and the price they paid to achieve it. They know
that what they endured made possible a career in the Marine Corps for
future generations of African Americans and helped bring an end to segregation in the United States. Whether they remained in the Corps or returned
to civilian life, Montford Point shaped their character and careers.

Montford Point Marines are justly proud of their accomplishments and
fully aware of their place in history. Concerned that their legacy continue
to be recognized, a group of Montford Point veterans met in Philadelphia
in August 1965 to form the Montford Point Marines Association, which was
chartered the following year. The association is open to all honorably discharged veterans and active-duty personnel from all branches of the service, without regard to race, creed, or color. Its purpose is "to promote and
preserve the strong bonds of friendship born from shared adversities and
to devote ourselves to the furtherance of these accomplishments to ensure
more peaceful times."

While the association's initial members were Montford Point veterans, its
membership now is composed primarily of African American veterans of the
Corps who enlisted after 1949 and active-duty African American Marines. Its
members currently belong to twenty-nine chapters located in cities throughout the nation. The association also sponsors a Ladies Auxiliary open to the
wives, daughters, sisters, and mothers of those eligible for membership. In
addition to preserving the legacy of the original Montford Pointers, the association works to support educational programs, veterans' programs, and
community service organizations. It maintains its own scholarship fund, as
do some of its chapters, publishes a national newsletter, holds an annual national convention, maintains a website, and occasionally publishes material

on the Montford Point Marines. The association also oversees the operations of the Montford Point Marines Museum, located in one of the original buildings on the grounds of Camp Montford Point, now called Camp Johnson, at Camp Lejeune, North Carolina. The museum bears the primary responsibility for preserving the legacy of the men of Montford Point. Its mission is "to collect, record, preserve and display, in a museum setting for public education and viewing, the largest collection of photographs, documents, papers, and artifacts, forever capturing the unique history of African American Marines from 1942 to 1949."

The men of Montford Point attend the association's annual national convention in steadily and rapidly decreasing numbers. There they renew old friendships, reminisce about Montford Point, recall hardships endured, and remember those no longer in their ranks. They also meet association members who joined the Marine Corps after 1949, men whose careers they made possible. To those Marines who came after them, the original Montford Pointers are legends—honored, respected, and admired. To their fellow Marines and their fellow Americans, they are symbols of courage and honor, of sacrifice and achievement. Among the ranks of the original Montford Pointers there is a readily evidenced pride in having served as a Marine. They cherish their Montford Point experience and their almost palpable sense of camaraderie with fellow Marines who share it.

Al Banker I got quite a bit out of it. One thing, I am respected every place I go. The Marine Corps taught me that. Discipline in anything I do. My work as a civilian, if it wasn't for my Marine Corps background and training, I never would have advanced to the position that I held in Grumman [Aerospace Corporation]. In the civilian world trust, confidence, honesty— all those things help. If I had to do it over again, I would, number one, further my education. I did graduate from high school and had a course in business administration. But I would have gone further. But with the education I did have, it helped me to get where I am today. And I don't regret going into the Marine Corps. And being one of the first Afro-Americans in the Marine Corps and making history. It wasn't easy. We had problems and there's still a few wrinkles in the sheet that have to [be] ironed out.

Averitte Corley The training in the Marine Corps instilled in me that I could do anything. You know, said, I can do this. I've gotten through much tougher stuff than this, you know. There's something about the Marine Corps training that instills that in you. I don't know what it is. It's intangible but it's there, you know. It makes you proud to be, having been a Marine.

David Dinkins I think it gave me a confidence that I could do almost anything. It toughened you a little, for sure. And my life has been pretty good. I attribute a lot of it to the Marine Corps. I felt it was a privilege. I'm very proud of having been a Montford Point Marine.

James Ferguson My experience in the Marine Corps is one of the greatest experiences I've ever had. I think the Marine Corps did a lot for me because it was tough. Being a black Marine was even tougher. But I've appreciated what the Marine Corps did for me because I think it made a better man out of me. Because there's an old saying, once a Marine, always a Marine, and the change is forever. Whatever the Marine Corps instills in you, it never leaves you. It becomes a part of you, and I think that, had it not been for a Marine that I wouldn't have the pride that I have in being a Marine and myself, because it puts you on a higher level, having been a Marine.

Harry Hamilton My experience with the men that I served with was very, very, very fine to me because I think that being at that camp, being segregated like we were and all the challenges that we came through, it made me a much stronger person. I cherish the memory now that I had with all the fellas that I served with while in service. Some memories that I'll never forget.

Ruben Hines The most important influence and how it affected me was the discipline. I didn't stop my learning experience while I was in the Marine Corps. Because I took twenty-two correspondence courses and went through eight Marine Corps schools. I was, I'll say, academically oriented. It served as a motivating factor. Not only the discipline, but it served as a motivating factor for me to further my education. When I got out that's what I pursued all the way till the doctoral program. I'll always be very, very proud of the experiences and the exposure I had in the Marine Corps. Because it helped me along the way. It made me realize that I could do the so-called impossible, and the miraculous takes just a little while longer.

George Taylor I would go back in the Marines. I was proud of the Marines. We did something that a bunch of us guys came out of nowhere and we trained one another. And I liked that. You know, we was together. We had that togetherness, you know. And, hey, you know, we gave a hug and embrace. And that was a thrill.

Johnnie Thompkins I think the Marine Corps saved my life. If I had gone back to Winston-Salem where I lived at, it was about fourteen of us grew up together, and we were all born in '26, '27, '28. We all were around the same age. Out of that group of fourteen boys, I was the only one that finished high school and the only one that went to college. And they all have passed, and they either went to prison or they got on drugs or just got in fights and got killed.

Herman Darden Jr. To tell you the truth, I have choked up many, many times. I recall, I think it was a couple of years ago, at Marine ball here in the District [of Columbia] I looked and saw all that brass, [black officers] walking around. In my lifetime, not counting recently, because I know that other generals have come on board, I've had the privilege of meeting and talking to at least thirteen black generals. And when I stop and think that in 1943, when I saw a black with one stripe on, boy, I felt great. But when I saw all that brass, the generals and the colonels, and the majors and all, I cried.

Reuben McNair Each day, I tell my young people as I walk around, I paid for the things that you got here, receiving today, and the opportunities that you have. So you don't have to go out here doing what I did in the Marine Corps wishing for war to prove to someone that you can make a change, that you do the same thing that everyone else can do. You don't have to take the abuse or sit on the back of a bus to go into Jacksonville, or any other place in the world. We don't have to do that anymore. And I tell them, you don't have to prove it. I've already gone through this, and you don't have to prove anything to anybody in the world.

Steven Robinson To create a legacy of young, black African Americans that will have an important role to play in this nation whatever discipline they elect to follow in a life as a professional career. They've earned that right because they put everything that they had at one time on the line. And I served with them; [they] would have given a life in a heartbeat for people who never respected them, never cared about them. And it's those who I hurt for.

I really don't hurt for myself because I had a good life. I come out of service. I was able to go to school. I was able to graduate from college. I would even get a master's degree. I was able to get bachelor's and law degree, doctor's and law degree and practice law for fifty years in my county and my state and become an affluent, wealthy man. And send my five youngsters to college, three of which have become professionals, and all that came by the fact I was able to serve. And that's the kind of legacy I would like to see other African Americans to enjoy and experience.

And I think that well, it's fifty years ago, the feeling is still there, you still feel it. You still feel the hurt. Hurt doesn't go away. I see that Jimmy Wilkins never came back. I buried him on Iwo, and I always regretted the fact that I was never able to contact his people to tell them how he died. And tell them what a good Marine he was. And any of the other men that died on Iwo. Black Marines that were, that were brothers, so to speak. Never gave them credit for what they did.

I mean, when you were there, you saw this and you saw it every day. I was on Iwo Jima for 106 days from February 19th, I think until May the 6th. Then go to Okinawa. You smell it, you smell it, you smell the death, you smell the decaying meat. These young Marines that died on the beach and died in the bunkers and you smell it, and it was fifty years ago.

I've been very fortunate. August of next year [2002], I will have practiced law for fifty years. I've been so fortunate. I come out and met my wife on campus at the University of Pittsburgh. We were married. And she gave me five beautiful kids. And I have five beautiful grandkids, talented, all kinds of potential. And this is what it was about. You bought the legacy. It was about these fellows.

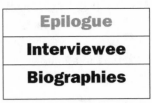

The brief biographies that follow were compiled primarily from interviews recorded on video tape between 2001 and 2005 for a documentary on the Montford Point Marines. The questions asked were designed to explore the subjects' experiences as Marines, not their lives after leaving the Corps, although each interviewee was asked to speak about his postservice career. Some responded in considerable detail; others said practically nothing. Since the project and the interview questions focused on the Montford Pointers' experience as Marines, no further effort was made to persuade the subjects to provide details about their lives after leaving the Corps. Some additional information was obtained by telephone conversations, but contacting all of the interviewees after the initial interview was impossible, as contact information, especially for those interviewed prior to 2004, proved to be no longer reliable. Some of the Montford Point Marines have died since being interviewed. Unfortunately, it is inevitable that others will die before this work is published.

Master Sergeant Fred Ash was born on a Mississippi farm and joined the Marine Corps in 1945. A career Marine, he served with occupation forces in Saipan and Guam; in Korea, where he fought in both the Inchon and Chosin Reservoir campaigns; and in Vietnam. After leaving the Corps, he worked with Mayflower Van Lines and eventually retired to live in Jacksonville, North Carolina, where he died in March 2005.

Master Sergeant Al Banker grew up in New Orleans. After a career in the Marine Corps, he joined the security forces of Grumman Aerospace Corporation, where he became a senior officer, inspecting plants across the United States. Retired, he resides in Bolivia, North Carolina.

Master Sergeant Adner Batts, a native of Edgecombe in rural eastern North Carolina, made the Marine Corps a career. He entered the Corps in 1948, retiring more than twenty years later, after service in Korea and two tours in Vietnam. He resides in Jacksonville, North Carolina.

Master Sergeant Turner Blount was born in Keysville, Georgia, and joined the Corps in 1943. During World War II he participated in the invasions of Tinian, Saipan, and Okinawa. He remained in the Corps at the war's end and served in a motor transport unit stationed at Camp Lejeune and in Japan, where he was at the end of the Korean War. He saw action again in Vietnam. After retiring from the Marines, he settled in Jacksonville, North Carolina, where he worked for Sears. Active in community affairs, he is a four-term member of the Jacksonville City Council.

Gunnery Sergeant Melvin Borden was raised on an Alabama farm and joined the Corps in 1948. Trained as a cook and steward, he worked in officers' clubs and with several generals, serving overseas in Japan, Okinawa, and Korea, as well as other duty stations. He later was a supply instructor at Camp Lejeune, retiring from the Corps in 1968. He then obtained a civil service position at a warehouse on Camp Lejeune, where he worked for twenty-three years before retirement. He resides in Jacksonville, North Carolina.

Sergeant Calvin Brown, a native of Lake Charles, Louisiana, served two enlistments in the Marine Corps, first joining in 1946. He fought in the Chosin Reservoir campaign in Korea. After leaving the Corps, he settled in Baltimore, Maryland, where he worked for the Bethlehem Steel Company for thirty-three years, eventually retiring to New Bern, North Carolina.

Lieutenant Colonel Joseph Carpenter, a native of Washington, D.C., joined the Corps in 1943 after finishing high school. He served stateside as a clerk until 1946, when he was discharged. After receiving a college degree, he reentered the Corps in 1956, obtained a commission, and, working primarily with data processing, rose to the rank of lieutenant colonel. He lives in retirement in Washington, D.C.

Registered Nurse Fannie Coleman, born in Oriental, North Carolina, attended nursing school at Community Hospital in Wilmington. After a career in nursing, she entered local politics in Jacksonville, North Carolina, where she now resides and serves as a member of the City Council.

Corporal Thomas Cork, a Kentucky native, joined the Corps after World War II and served in Korea, fighting at both Inchon and the Chosin Reservoir. Returning to Kentucky, he worked as a postal employee for thirty-one years. Retired, he lives in Louisville, Kentucky.

Corporal Averitte Corley, born in Indianapolis, Indiana, entered the Corps in 1945 and was recalled for a tour of duty during the Korean War, but served at Montford Point. He left the Corps in 1951, completed a bachelor's degree in agriculture at Purdue University and a master's in education at Indiana

University, and went on to a successful career as an educator. He resides in Indianapolis.

First Sergeant Ellis Cunningham was born on a farm near Florence, South Carolina. He joined the Corps in 1944 and saw action at Iwo Jima. A career Marine, he served in Korea and in Vietnam, where he participated in the Tet Offensive campaign. Retiring from the Corps in 1970, he worked with the South Carolina Electric and Gas Company on the Charleston bus system, took a leave of absence to work four years with urban mass transit systems in various cities, and then returned to South Carolina Electric and Gas, from which he retired in 1991. He resides in Charleston, South Carolina.

Corporal Herman Darden Jr., a Washington, D.C. native, joined the Corps in 1943 and was discharged at the end of World War II. He resides in Washington, D.C.

Gunnery Sergeant/Acting Master Sergeant Charles Davenport grew up in Monongahela, Pennsylvania. After graduating from high school in 1942, he joined the Marine Corps. During World War II he served in the Marshall Islands. He also served in Korea. Leaving the Corps in 1957, he received a degree in psychology from Washington and Jefferson College in 1962 and enjoyed a twenty-seven-year career as a psychologist working with delinquent teenagers for the Pennsylvania State Department of Welfare. He resides in Washington, Pennsylvania.

Corporal Lawrence Diggs is originally from the delta country of Mississippi but moved to Chicago as a young man. He joined the Corps in 1943, and went ashore with an ammunition company at Peleliu Island. After the war he returned to Chicago, where he worked for the United States Steel Corporation. He resides in Columbia, Missouri.

Private David Dinkins was born in Trenton, New Jersey, where he finished high school. He joined the Corps in 1945 and, after stateside duty, was discharged the following year. He completed a degree in mathematics at Howard University in 1950 and a law degree from the Brooklyn School of Law in 1956, after which he practiced law in New York City until 1975. Politically active, he became president of the New York City Board of Elections in 1975 and in 1989 was elected mayor of New York City. Defeated by Rudi Guiliani in a 1993 bid for reelection, Dinkins serves as a professor of public affairs at Columbia University and on the boards of numerous organizations. He remains active in politics and continues to reside in New York City.

Sergeant Gene Doughty, born in Stamford, Connecticut, moved to New York City, where he finished high school and entered City College. He joined the

Corps in 1943 and participated in the invasion of Iwo Jima. After his discharge in 1946, he earned a degree in health and physical education from City College. He worked as a social investigator for the New York City Department of Social Services until 1954 and then became a store manager for Vim Electric Company, a position from which he retired in 1969. In retirement, he has served both the Marine Corps Scholarship Foundation and the Montford Point Marines Association in several positions. He resides in the Bronx, New York.

Corporal Lee Douglas Jr., a native of Columbia, South Carolina, joined the Corps in 1943 and participated in the invasion of Peleliu. Discharged from the Corps after World War II, he settled in Baltimore, Maryland. There he worked for the Bethlehem Steel Company for forty years. During the last twenty-five years of his employment with Bethlehem Steel he also worked for the city of Baltimore as the director of an urban services agency, referring clients to needed health, educational, and social services. Retired, he lives in Baltimore.

Master Sergeant Frederick Drake, an Alabama native, completed high school and briefly attended Daniel Payne College, an African Methodist Episcopal school in Birmingham. He joined the Corps in 1948. He served for thirty years, primarily as a cook or chef, with overseas tours in Japan, the Philippines, and Vietnam. He lives in Port Royal, South Carolina.

Corporal Roland Durden, born and raised in Harlem in New York City, completed high school and joined the Marines in 1943. He served in the Pacific, participating in the invasion of Iwo Jima, and was discharged in 1946. Returning to New York City, he held several positions during a career with the New York City Transit Authority, retiring in 1986 as assistant general superintendent. He lives in retirement in Security, Colorado.

Sergeant Hulon Edwards, from a farm near Mendenhall, Mississippi, was drafted into the Army in 1942 and served with the 367th Infantry in North Africa, Italy, France, and Germany. Discharged from the Army, in 1946 he joined the Marines. Retiring after twenty years of service, including tours in both Korea and Vietnam, he resides in Jacksonville, North Carolina.

Corporal James Ferguson, born in Washington, D.C., joined the Marine Corps in 1943. He participated in the battle for Okinawa. Discharged in 1946, he returned to Washington to work with the Federal Power Commission. In 1948 he accepted employment as a mail carrier and worked his way up the ranks within the Post Office to retire as a station manager in 1979. In retirement he enjoys competitive swimming and continues to reside in Washington.

Corporal Johnnie Givian was born on a tenant farm near Selma, Alabama, and moved to Atlanta as a youth. He joined the Marines in 1946. A twenty-year veteran, he served in Korea. After retirement he worked in a plywood factory and as a retail clerk. He has also served as pastor of a church for over thirty years. He resides in Jacksonville, North Carolina.

Sergeant Paul Hagan, from Roopville, Georgia, joined the Corps in 1946 and was assigned to the 8th Ammunition Company, serving in Hawaii until the outbreak of the Korean War. In Korea he worked to supply Marines with ammunition from the Inchon landing to the Chosin Reservoir campaign. Retiring from the Corps in 1967, he obtained a civil service position in transportation management at Camp Lejeune. Like many retired Marines, he lives in Jacksonville, North Carolina.

Corporal Harry Hamilton, from Tutwiler, Mississippi, joined the Corps in 1943 and served until 1950. As a member of the 52nd Defense Battalion he did occupation duty on both Saipan and Guam. After leaving the Marines, he moved to Chicago, where he worked with the Post Office for thirty-seven years. Retired, he resides in Chicago.

Gunnery Sergeant Ruben Hines, born in Chicago, received a grade school education in Alabama, where he moved with his parents as a youth. He joined the Corps in 1942 and became a career Marine. He served in the Pacific with the 52nd Defense Battalion during World War II; in Korea, where he participated in the Chosin Reservoir campaign; and in Vietnam, where he served as a helicopter crew chief. After retiring from the Corps, he attended the University of North Carolina, completing all the requirements for a doctorate in history except for the dissertation. He taught history at Fayetteville State College in Fayetteville, North Carolina, and at Johnson C. Smith University in Charlotte, North Carolina. Retired, he resides in Charlotte.

Corporal Paul Holtsclaw, born in Statesville, North Carolina, joined the Marines in 1943 after two years at North Carolina Agricultural and Technical College in Greensboro and a year of teaching at the Palmer Memorial Institute in Sedalia, North Carolina. He served with an ammunition company in Hawaii and several of the occupied Pacific islands. Discharged in 1946, he worked with the United States Signal Corps and then taught in the Baltimore, Maryland, school system, retiring in 1993. He resides in Owings Mills, Maryland.

Gunnery Sergeant F. M. Hooper, from Brooklyn, New York, joined the Corps in 1948. He served as a military policeman both shipboard and in Korea and Japan. In Vietnam he served in an aviation supply unit and participated in the Tet Offensive campaign. He retired in 1971 and resides in Wilmington, North Carolina.

Sergeant Oliver Lumpkin was born in Richland, Georgia. He joined the Corps in 1946 and served with the 51st Defense Battalion in the Ellice Islands. After leaving the Corps, he attended Fort Valley State College in Fort Valley, Georgia, and taught in Savannah, Georgia. He obtained a master's degree from Tuskegee University and a doctorate from Ohio State University, after which he served on the faculty of Clemson University for fifteen years. He resides in Savannah.

Staff Sergeant Henry McNair, born in Dillon, South Carolina, completed the seventh grade before joining the Marine Corps in 1945. He served with the 52nd Defense Battalion in occupied Saipan and Guam. A career Marine, he saw combat during the Korean War in both the Inchon and Chosin Reservoir campaigns and in Vietnam. Upon retirement, he resided in Jacksonville, North Carolina, until his death in 2006.

Gunnery Sergeant Reuben McNair, a Mississippi native, joined the Corps in 1944. During World War II he participated in the invasion of Peleliu and was stationed on several occupied islands in the Pacific. A career Marine, he participated in the Chosin Reservoir campaign in Korea and served in the Mediterranean. Upon retirement in 1964, he worked for two years as a corrections officer in Washington, D.C., and then became an investigator for the government of the District of Columbia, a position he held for twenty-two years. He remains active in a business he founded fifteen years ago, Laser Art, which supplies printers, copiers, and printing supplies to D.C. area businesses and to the District's government. He resides in the District.

Gunnery Sergeant Leroy Mack of Brooklyn, New York, was a career Marine, joining the Corps in 1948. A broken back, obtained in a football game, kept him out of Korea, but he served in Vietnam. He resides in Albany, Georgia.

Private First Class Walter Maddox, from St. Louis, joined the Corps in 1942. A member of the 51st Defense Battalion, he served in the Marshall Islands and other Pacific locations. Discharged in 1946, he worked briefly with the Post Office in St. Louis and then was employed by the Department of Defense's Aeronautical Defense Mapping, Space Command, where he worked for forty-five years. After retiring, he lived in St. Louis until his death in October 2004.

Corporal Archibald Mosley was born in Carbondale, Illinois, and joined the Corps in 1943. With the 36th Depot Company, he participated in the invasion of Iwo Jima and served in Guam and occupied Japan. Leaving the Corps after World War II, he entered Payne Theological Seminary at Wilberforce University, became a Methodist minister, and enjoyed a long career. Retired, he resides in Pontiac, Michigan.

Private Joseph Myers, from Atlanta, Georgia, joined the Marine Corps in 1942 after completing high school. He participated in the invasion of Iwo Jima and served on Guam and in occupied Japan. He resides in University City, Missouri.

Herman Nathaniel, from Sumter, South Carolina, joined the Marines after finishing high school and served with the 52nd Defense Battalion in the Marshall Islands and Guam during World War II. After the war he worked for the General Dynamics Corporation, first building submarines, then in a California airplane factory installing radar equipment. He later worked in the nuclear power industry. He resides in Norwalk, California.

Corporal Benjamin Patterson, a Baltimore native, joined the Corps after graduating from high school in 1942. He served with the 51st Defense Battalion in the Ellice Islands and left the Corps at the war's end. He returned to Baltimore, where he lived and worked for the remainder of his life. He died in 2005.

Private Norman Payne was born on Chicago's south side and served with the 52nd Defense Battalion in the Marshall Islands during World War II. After the war, he returned to Chicago, where he resides.

Gunnery Sergeant Wilmore Perry was born in Washington, D.C., where he completed high school and a year of business school. Before entering the Corps in 1943, he was employed by the federal government with the Foreign Broadcast Intelligence Agency. He served in Guam and the Mariana Islands and was discharged in 1946, returning to Washington to work for the Foreign Broadcast Intelligence Agency until it was taken over by the Central Intelligence Agency in 1947. He then joined the Post Office, where he worked until he retired in 1978. He lives in Washington.

Gunnery Sergeant Carrol Reavis was reared on a farm near Lawrenceville, Virginia, and joined the Corps in 1943. Placed in an ammunition company, he was stationed in Hawaii during World War II. Mr. Reavis remained in the Corps and saw duty in Korea. Retiring after twenty-one years in the Corps, he went to San Diego, California, where he trained as a barber and completed an associate's degree in real estate at a local community college. He operated a barber shop and sold real estate in his community for thirty-seven years. Now fully retired, he lives in San Diego.

Sergeant Steven Robinson grew up in Pittsburgh, where he graduated from high school. He joined the Marines in 1942 and saw action on Iwo Jima. Discharged at the war's end, he attended the University of Pittsburgh, eventually obtaining a law degree. He practiced law for more than fifty years in Warren, Ohio, where he was active in local and state politics. He is deceased.

Private George Taylor, an Indianapolis native, grew up in Chicago. After being drafted into the Marines, he was assigned to the 51st Defense Battalion and stationed in the Marshall Islands. After the war he returned to Chicago and then settled in Lansing, Michigan, where he was employed by the City of Lansing Convention Center until his retirement.

Master Sergeant Johnnie Thompkins grew up in McCormick, South Carolina, where he completed high school. He attended Winston-Salem State Teachers College before joining the Marines in 1945. A career Marine, Thompkins served in occupied Japan, on Guam, and in Vietnam. Retiring from the Corps, he worked as a butcher in a St. Louis packing house. After retiring, he moved to New Bern, North Carolina, where he resides.

Walter Thompson Jr., a St. Louis native, joined the Corps in 1942 and was assigned to the 52nd Defense Battalion, serving in the Marshall Islands and Guam during World War II. Discharged in 1947, he returned to St. Louis, where he worked for Swift and Company for fifteen years. Later he worked in construction. Retired, he resides in St. Louis.

Sergeant Major William Vann, a native of Wilmington, North Carolina, joined the Corps in 1949. He served for more than thirty years, seeing duty in both Korea and Vietnam. Retired, he resides in San Diego, California.

Gunnery Sergeant LaSalle Vaughn, from Baton Rouge, Louisiana, joined the Marines in 1942 and was assigned to the Stewards Branch, where he became an accomplished baker and chef. During his career as a Marine, he served at Parris Island, in officers' clubs at various bases, and as the chef for several generals. He lives in retirement in Port Royal, South Carolina.

Corporal Joseph Walker, born in Richmond, Virginia, grew up in Durham, North Carolina. He joined the Corps in 1943, was assigned to the 51st Defense Battalion, and saw duty in the occupied islands of the Pacific. Trained as an electrician in the Corps, he returned to Durham after the war and worked for forty-three years in that trade. Retired, he resides in Winston-Salem, North Carolina.

Sergeant Major Johnny Washington grew up on a Mississippi farm, graduated from high school, and joined the Corps in 1946. He made a career of the Marine Corps, seeing action in both Korea and Vietnam. Upon retirement he made his home in Indianapolis, Indiana.

Gunnery Sergeant Glenn White, born in South Carolina, moved to Washington, D.C., where he completed high school and joined the Corps. A thirty year veteran of the Corps, he served in World War II, Korea, and Vietnam. Retiring in 1973, he resides in Jacksonville, North Carolina.

Master Sergeant Andrew Wiggins, born in St. Augustine, Florida, moved as a youth to Jacksonville, Florida, where he was an apprentice bricklayer. He joined the Corps in 1943, served with the 7th Marine Depot Company in the Ellice Islands during World War II, and saw action in Korea. Upon retiring from the Corps, he entered the ministry and has served the same church for forty years. He resides in Albany, Georgia.

Technical Sergeant James Wilson, of Utica, Mississippi, joined the Corps in 1946. A twenty-year veteran, he served at several bases in the United States and in Korea. After retiring from the Corps, he worked with the United States Geological Survey for nineteen years. Upon retiring from that agency, he moved to Wilmington, North Carolina, where he worked part time for the North Carolina Ports Authority until 1997. Now fully retired, he lives in Wilmington, North Carolina.

Further Reading

While the literature on African Americans in the military can hardly be called volu-minous, a substantial, and growing, body of work allows the interested reader to explore the subject in more detail. This essay, although not intended as a compre-hensive bibliography, provides a starting point for readers wishing to learn more about African Americans in the military and the Montford Point Marines.

There are a number of general surveys of African Americans in the military, most of which at least mention Montford Point. One of the most recent and most readable is Gail Buckley's *American Patriots: The Story of Blacks in the Military from the Revolution to Desert Storm* (New York: Random House, 2001), which devotes several pages to the Montford Point story. So do Bernard C. Nalty's *Strength for the Fight: A History of Black Americans in the Military* (New York: Free Press, 1986); Michael Lee Lanning's *The African American Soldier: From Crispus Attucks to Colin Powell* (New York: Birch Lane Press, 1997); and Gerald Astor's *The Right to Fight: A History of African Americans in the Military* (Novato, Calif.: Presidio Press, 1998). Yvonne Latty's oral history, *We Were There: Voices of African American Veterans from World War II to the War in Iraq* (New York: Amistad, 2004) contains an interview with a Montford Point veteran. *Blacks in the United States Armed Forces: Basic Docu-ments* (Wilmington, Del.: Scholarly Resources, 1977), a thirteen-volume collection of documents spanning the period from the Revolution to the Vietnam War, edited by Morris J. MacGregor and Bernard C. Nalty, complements the narrative surveys.

A number of works also chronicle the story of the long, hard struggle of black Americans to gain entry into and then to integrate fully the American military. *Fox-holes and Color Lines*: *Desegregating the U.S. Armed Forces* (Baltimore: The Johns Hopkins University Press, 1998), by Sherie Mershon and Steven Schlossman, gives an excellent recent overview. Leo Bogart's earlier work, *Project Clear, Social Re-search and the Desegregation of the United States Army* (Chicago: Markham Pub-lishing Company, 1969), explores the racial attitudes common in the Army during the early 1950s. Published at approximately the same time, Richard M. Dalfiume's *Desegregation of the U.S. Armed Forces: Fighting on Two Fronts, 1939–1953* (Colum-bia: University of Missouri Press, 1969) provides a narrative supplement to Bogart's sociological study.

The civil rights revolution prompted a flurry of publications on the role of Afri-cans Americans in the military during specific conflicts. Benjamin Quarles's *The Negro in the American Revolution* (Chapel Hill: University of North Carolina Press,

1961) is an excellent example and remains a good work with which to begin to explore the topic.

Not surprisingly, scholars have produced a substantial body of work on African Americans in the Civil War. James M. McPherson's *The Negro's Civil War: How American Negroes Felt and Acted during the War for Union* (Urbana: University of Illinois Press, 1965), like Quarles's work on the Revolution, was published at the height of the modern civil rights movement. McPherson's work enlarged the scope of the more narrowly focused *The Sable Arm: Negro Troops in the Union Army, 1861–1865* (Lawrence: University of Kansas Press, 1956) by Dudley T. Cornish. Noah M. Trudeau's *Like Men of War: Black Troops in the Civil War, 1862–1865* (New York: Little Brown & Company, 1998) provides a more recent narrative account, and *Black Soldiers in Blue: African American Troops in the Civil War Era* (Chapel Hill: University of North Carolina Press, 2003) edited by John David Smith, contains a collection of essays on the subject by leading scholars in the field. Service in the Navy is chronicled in Steven Ramold's *Slaves, Sailors, Citizens: African Americans in the Union Navy* (DeKalb: Northern Illinois University Press, 2002). For documents relating to African Americans in the Civil War, see *Freedom's Soldiers: The Black Military Experience in the Civil War*, edited by Ira Berlin, Joseph P. Reidy, and Leslie S. Rowland (New York: Cambridge University Press, 1998).

A surprising number of works survey the era between the Civil War and World War I. Again, their publication dates reflect the interest in African American history generated by the civil rights movement. Two works combine to provide a narrative history of African American soldiers during the period, William H. Leckie's *The Buffalo Soldiers: A Narrative of the Negro Cavalry in the West* (Norman: University of Oklahoma Press, 1967) and Arlen Fowler's *The Black Infantry in the West, 1869–1991* (Westport, Conn.: Greenwood Publishing Corporation, 1971). *The Black Military Experience in the American West*, edited by John M. Carroll (New York: Liveright, 1971), offers a curious, but entertaining and informative, collection of essays by journalists, military men, and historians, some by writers of the period and some by contemporary writers. Willard B. Gatewood's *"Smoked Yankees" and the Struggle for Empire: Letters from Negro Soldiers, 1898–1902* (Urbana: University of Illinois Press, 1971) is perhaps the best source for the soldier's view.

For a comprehensive overview of the role of African Americans in World War I, see *The Unknown Soldiers: African American Troops in World War I*, by Arthur Barbeau and Florette Henri (Philadelphia: Temple University Press, 1974). Two recent unit studies supplement the survey by Barbeau and Henri, Rod Paschall's *Harlem's Hellfighters: The African American 369th Infantry in World War I* (Dulles, Va.: Potomac Books, 2003) and Frank Roberts's *The American Foreign Legion: Black Soldiers of the 93rd in World War I* (Annapolis, Md.: Naval Institute Press, 2004).

Neil A. Wynn's *The Afro-American in the Second World War* (New York: Holmes and Meier Publishers, 1993) provides an overview of the role of black troops in that conflict. Any number of detailed unit studies supplement Wynn's survey. The Tuskegee Airmen have attracted the attention of scholars and journalists. Among the best works on the subject is Lawrence Womack's *Double V: The Civil Rights Struggle of the Tuskegee Airmen* (East Lansing: Michigan State University Press, 1994). Kareem Abdul-Jabbar and Anthony Walton have written the most recent of several studies of the 761st Tank Battalion, *Brothers in Arms* (New York: Broadway, 2004). The black GI's point of view can be obtained from Phillip McGuire's *Taps for a Jim Crow Army: Letters from Black Soldiers in World War II* (Lexington: University of Kentucky Press, 1983). Service in the Navy is surveyed in Richard Miller's *The Messman Chronicles: African Americans in the U.S. Navy, 1932–1943* (Annapolis, Md.: Naval Institute Press, 2004).

Two works that combine to record the African American experience in the Korean War, although neither provides a comprehensive treatment, are William Bowers, William Hammond, and George MacGarrigle's *Black Soldier, White Army: The 24th Infantry Regiment in Korea* (Washington, D.C.: Center for Military History, U.S. Army, 1996) and Lyle Rishell's *With a Black Platoon in Korea* (College Station: Texas A&M University Press, 1993).

James E. Westheider's *Fighting on Two Fronts: African Americans and the Vietnam War* (New York: New York University Press, 1997) provides a starting point for further exploration of the role of African Americans in that conflict. Westheider's scholarly study is balanced by Wallace Terry's *Bloods: An Oral History of the Vietnam War by Black Americans* (New York: Ballentine Books, 1984).

Unfortunately, there is to date no standard book-length history of the Montford Point Marines. By far the best surveys of the Montford Point experience now available are two pamphlets published by the Marine Corps. *Blacks in the Marine Corps* (Washington, D.C.: History and Museums Division, Headquarters, U.S. Marine Corps, 1976; reprinted, 2002), by Henry I. Shaw and Ralph W. Donnelly, carries the story of blacks in the Marine Corps from World War II through Vietnam. A briefer work, which concentrates on the World War II years, is Bernard C. Nalty's *The Right to Fight: African American Marines in World War II* (Washington, D.C.: Marine Corps Historical Center, 1995). It can be found on the Web at <http://www.nps .gov/wapa/indepth/extContent/usmc/pcn-190-003132-001/sec10.htm>. *Montford Point, Camp Lejeune, New River, North Carolina* (Montford Point, 1943), published by the men of Montford Point as a yearbook, contains some excellent visual material. Jesse J. Johnson's *Roots of Two Black Sergeants Major, Sergeants Major Edgar R. Huff and Gilbert H. "Hashmark" Johnson: Profiles in Courage: A Documented History* (Hampton, Va.: Carver Publishing, 1978) provides details of the lives of

Montford Point's two most celebrated drill instructors, both legends among Montford Point veterans.

Additional details about Montford Point and the men who trained there can be found in several memoirs. Bill Downey's *Uncle Sam Must be Losing the War* (San Francisco: Strawberry Hill Press, 1982) is easily the most readable. Others include Fred De Clouet, *First Black Marines: Vanguard in Legacy* (Nashville: J. C. Winston Publishers, 1995); Brooks Gray and Perry Fischer, *Black and White Together through Hell* (Turlock, Calif.: Millsnow Publishing, 1994); Winston W. De Vergee, *Assignment in Hell* (New York: Vantage Press, 1991); and James H. Ferguson, *The Story of the Ninth Marine Depot Company* (published by the author, 1996). *Montford Point Marines, 1942–1949: Final Roll Call* (Beltsville, Md.: International Graphics, 2004), by Herman Rhett, also falls into this category. Sponsored by the Montford Point Marines Association, it contains a variety of personal recollections by Montford Point veterans. The Montford Point Marines Association Website provides some useful information, but is most valuable for understanding the significance of the veterans of Montford Point to those African Americans who followed them into the Marine Corps. It is located at <http://www.montfordpointmarines.com/index .html>.

Those seeking a fictionalized treatment of the Montford Point experience can find it in Hari Rhodes's somewhat autobiographical novel, *A Chosen Few* (New York: Bantam Books, Inc., 1965).

Index of Interviewees

Vann, William, 116–17, 190
Vaughn, LaSalle, 100, 190

Walker, Joseph, 22, 65–73, 122–23, 190

Washington, Johnny, 73–74, 165, 175–76, 190
White, Glenn, 74–75, 91–92, 166, 190
Wiggins, Andrew, 75–76, 190–91
Wilson, James, 35, 191

INDEX OF INTERVIEWEES

Index

MORRIS AUTOMATED INFORMATION NETWORK

0 1004 0213139 3

DATE DUE

MAR - - 2007

WITHDRAWN